Globalization and State Transformation in China

Globalization has thrown up challenges and opportunities which all countries have to grapple with. In his book, Yongnian Zheng explores how China's leaders have embraced global capitalism and market-oriented modernization. He shows that, with reform measures properly implemented, the nation-state can not only survive globalization, but can actually be revitalized through outside influence. To adapt to the globalized age, Chinese leaders have encouraged individual enterprise and the development of the entrepreneurial class. The state bureaucratic system and other important economic institutions have been restructured to accommodate a globalized market economy. Zheng observes that, in rebuilding the economic system in this way, the Chinese leaders have been open to the importation of Western ideas. By contrast, the same leaders are reluctant to import Western concepts of democracy and the rule of law. The author argues that, ultimately, this selectivity will impede China's progress in becoming a modern nation-state.

Yongnian Zheng is Associate Professor at the East Asian Institute, National University of Singapore. His previous publications include *Discovering Chinese Nationalism* (1999) and *China's Post-Jiang Leadership Succession* (2002).

CAMBRIDGE ASIA–PACIFIC STUDIES

Cambridge Asia–Pacific Studies aims to provide a focus and forum for scholarly work on the Asia–Pacific region as a whole, and its component sub-regions, namely Northeast Asia, Southeast Asia and the Pacific Islands. The series is produced in association with the Research School of Pacific and Asian Studies at the Australian National University and the Australian Institute of International Affairs.

Editor: John Ravenhill

Editorial Board: James Cotton, Donald Denoon, Mark Elvin, Hal Hill, Ron May, Anthony Milner, Tessa Morris-Suzuki, Anthony Low

Published titles in the series are listed at the back of the book.

Globalization and State Transformation in China

Yongnian Zheng
National University of Singapore

CAMBRIDGE
UNIVERSITY PRESS

PUBLISHED BY THE PRESS SYNDICATE OF THE UNIVERSITY OF CAMBRIDGE
The Pitt Building, Trumpington Street, Cambridge, United Kingdom

CAMBRIDGE UNIVERSITY PRESS
The Edinburgh Building, Cambridge CB2 2RU, UK
40 West 20th Street, New York NY 10011–4211, USA
477 Williamstown Road, Port Melbourne, Vic 3207, Australia
Ruiz de Alarcón 13, 28014 Madrid, Spain
Dock House, The Waterfront, Cape Town 8001, South Africa

http://www.cambridge.org

First published 2004

Printed in China through Bookbuilders

Typeface Plantin 10/12 pt.   *System* LaTeX 2ε [TB]

A catalogue record for this book is available from the British Library

National Library of Australia Cataloguing in Publication data
Zheng, Yongnian.
    Globalization and state transformation in China.
    Bibliography.
    Includes index.
    ISBN 0 521 83050 8.
    ISBN 0 521 53750 9 (pbk.).
    1. Globalization.   2. China – Economic conditions – 1976–.
    3. China – Politics and government – 1976–.   I. Title.
    (Series : Cambridge Asia-Pacific studies).
338.951

ISBN 0 521 83050 8 hardback
ISBN 0 521 53750 9 paperback

For Yang Lijun

Contents

Figures

Tables

Abbreviations

ABC	Agricultural Bank of China
ACFTU	All China Federation of Trade Unions
BOC	Bank of China
CBC	Construction Bank of China
CC	Central Committee (of the CCP)
CCP	Chinese Communist Party
CIB	China Investment Bank
CITIC	China International Trust and Investment Corporation
CRS	Contract Responsibility System
ETO	Economic and Trade Office
FDI	Foreign Direct Investment
FIEs	Foreign-Invested Enterprises
FLG	Falun Gong
GATT	General Agreement on Tariffs and Trade
GDP	Gross Domestic Product
GITIC	Guandong International Trust and Investment Corporation
HK	Hong Kong
ICBC	Industrial and Commercial Bank of China
IMF	International Monetary Fund
INGOs	International Non-Government Organizations
IT	Information Technology
KMT	Kuomintang
MITI	Ministry of International Trade and Industry (Japan)
NATO	North Atlantic Treaty Organization
NPC	National People's Congress
OECD	Organization for Economic Co-operation and Development
PBOC	People's Bank of China
PCs	Personal Computers
PLA	People's Liberation Army
SCSTIND	State Commission of Science, Technology and Industry for National Defense
SDPC	State Development Planning Commission
SEC	State Economic Commission

SETC	State Economic and Trade Commission
SEZs	Special Economic Zones
SOEs	State-Owned Enterprises
SPC	State Planning Commission
TICs	Trust and Investment Companies
TNC	Transnational Corporation
TVEs	Township and Village Enterprises
UK	United Kingdom
USA	United States of America
WAP	Wireless Application Protocol
WTO	World Trade Organization

Preface

Globalization in the past few decades has swept every corner of the world. While many countries have benefited from unprecedented global flow of capital, human talent, scientific knowledge and other resources that a country's modernization requires, globalization has also brought about enormous unexpected consequences. In the early 1990s, scholars were optimistic that globalization would herald the onset of a global democratic movement that would bring about greater representation and prosperity to the global community. But the 1997 financial crisis and the political instability that ensued corrected this sanguine view. The world had barely recovered from the consequences caused by rapid and massive capital flows when it was confronted with another scourge – global terrorism. The 9–11 attacks in the United States was the harbinger of terrorist acts in other parts of the world such as Southeast Asia. In essence, globalization has not brought about unmitigated benefits but has a reverse side as well. With globalization, as with physics, every action or new development has its own reaction or consequences.

This study examines the impact of globalization on the Chinese state in the Asian context. For many years, Asian countries have become the foci for scholarly exploration. Major events such as the 1997 Asian financial crisis, Indonesia's turbulent transition to democracy, China's entry into the World Trade Organization (WTO), and the spread of terrorism in many Asian countries, have prompted me to reflect on globalization and its impact on the nation-state in Asian societies. I believe that if it is inevitable for every country to be an integral part of the world community in a globalized age, the nation-state has to make a right choice in order to get the best out of globalization while minimizing its negative consequences. How can a nation-state achieve this goal? Asian states have responded to globalization in different ways. This book is about globalization and the Chinese state.

Despite its communist legacy, China is not particularly different from other nation-states in reacting to globalization. The world has witnessed the rise of Chinese nationalism, and anti-globalization is an important part of this new nationalism. Chinese nationalists have worried that globalization is weakening the power of the national government in managing domestic affairs, and that China is losing its identity as a unique nation-state in world affairs. Indeed, outside of China, there are scholars and journalists who are doubtful whether China will be able to survive globalization. Some have argued that China is suffering a serious crisis of governance, while others have even predicted its impending collapse.

The impact of globalization needs to be examined in greater detail. While scholars have focused on the economic costs and benefits of globalization for China, less attention has been devoted to the political impact of globalization. Although many scholars are of the view that China's political institutions will be greatly affected by globalization, they are not ready to elaborate what such impacts will be and in what manner they will come. This book attempts to examine how the Chinese state has adjusted itself in order to deal with globalization.

Like elsewhere, globalization has posed serious challenges to the Chinese state. Nevertheless, the Chinese leadership has regarded globalization as a unique opportunity to rebuild the Chinese state. Since the reform and open-door policy, the leadership has vigorously promoted globalization. How has the Chinese leadership been motivated to push the country towards globalization? I find that a particular mindset prevails among Chinese leaders. While nationalism is directed at building a strong and wealthy China, Chinese leaders recognized that such a goal could only be realized by integrating the country into the global community. Such a mindset was firmly rooted among Chinese leaders throughout the post-Mao reform era. Despite the often bitter political struggles among top leaders, the process of globalization has never slowed down. A deep ideological commitment to globalization has enabled the leadership to make greater efforts to legitimate capitalism as a means to achieve a prosperous and strong Chinese state. The leadership has also rebuilt the bureaucratic system, economic institutions and other major national institutions. Institutional rebuilding has enabled the Chinese state to cope with globalization. While it is too early to say if the Chinese state will become stronger with greater integration with the global community, it is reasonable to say that so far the Chinese state has benefited from globalization while mitigating its negative impact.

By giving a detailed examination of the impact of globalization on the Chinese state, this book tries to achieve three major goals: to assess the degree of seriousness of the problems resulting from globalization, to examine the ability of the Chinese state to cope with these problems, and to locate the future challenges of globalization. First, I found that globalization generates opportunities rather than crises for a developing country like China. Globalization has produced many problems for the Chinese state, but many of these problems are transitional. In coping with all these problems, the Chinese state is given unprecedented opportunities to reconstruct itself. There is no sound basis to argue that globalization will lead to a collapse of the Chinese state. My second finding is that the Chinese state has displayed remarkable flexibility in adjusting itself at both the ideological and the institutional levels. This is contrary to conventional wisdom on the rigidity of the communist system. The communist system can be reformed, and it can transform itself through continuous adjustment to globalization. Third, I found that the real challenges of globalization lies in the Chinese Communist Party (CCP), not the Chinese state. To a great degree, globalization requires a rule-based state governance. Globalization has enabled the Chinese state to rationalize and institutionalize itself, and in many aspects, the state has been quite successful in doing so. The CCP has also made efforts in accommodating globalization such as changing its ideological stand and recruiting capitalists into the party, but it has been unwilling to subject itself to the rule of law. As a matter of fact, the party has been a major barrier to a full institutionalization of the Chinese state.

In the process of research and writing, I have benefited from many individuals. I would first like to thank my colleagues in the East Asian Institute. Wang Gungwu, Director, has consistently provided me strong intellectual and moral support. His deep historical insights enabled me to go beyond the mere economic calculations of globalization to discern the long-term impact of globalization on the nation-state. John Wong, Research Director and an economist, has shared with me his own views on the impact of globalization on China's economic system. Many other colleagues have also provided different forms of support in different stages. When I presented my initial plan and ideas on the project, they had many valuable comments. Among others, Liu Zhiqiang, He Baogang, Lam Peng Er, Zou Keyuan, Lai Hongyi and Lang Youxin deserve special thanks.

For years, the East Asian Institute has invited many overseas scholars on visiting programs or conferences. Frequent visits by these scholars provide an invaluable link between the institute and the international intellectual community, and I have benefited greatly from these exchanges. I was able to discuss various issues regarding this research project with scholars from different parts of the world. Among others, I would like to thank Peter Katzenstein, Andrew Walder, Lynn White, Gilbert Rozman, Kjeld Eric Brodsgaard, Wu Guoguang, Pei Minxin, Kong Qingjiang, Ignatius Wibowo, Wang Hongying, Chien-min Chao, Chen Weixing, Xiao Gongqing, Zheng Shiping and Zhong Yang. I have also benefited from several workshops on China's state building in the past two years and my thanks go to Wang Shaoguang, Chu Yunhan, Hu Angang, Zhou Jianming, Cui Zhiyuan, Shi Tianjian, Wang Hui, Wang Xi, and Cao

Jingqing. Lye Liang Fook, Sarah Chan and Wong Chee Kong provided valuable research assistance. Many librarians in the East Asian Institute Library sourced information I requested.

I also want to acknowledge the helpful editorial support and guidance provided by Marigold Acland and Amanda Pinches at Cambridge University Press, and by Carla Taines. Acland deserves special thanks, and she worked with this manuscript from the initial review process to the end of its production.

An earlier version of chapter 7 was published as Yongnian Zheng, "State Rebuilding, Popular Protest and Collective Action in China," *Japanese Journal of Political Science* (2002), 3: 45–70 (copyright © 2002 Cambridge University Press, reproduced with permission).

1 Globalization: State decline or state rebuilding?

Globalization has thrown up challenges and opportunities which all countries, especially developing ones, have to grapple with and China is no exception. In fact, China, the most populous country in this world, has globalized rapidly over the past two decades. When Deng Xiaoping opened China's door in the late 1970s, no one expected that China would be integrated into the rest of the world at such a dramatic pace. The country has transformed "from a policy of self-reliance and suspicion to one of openness and integration."[1] With its membership in the World Trade Organization (WTO) and other major world and regional organizations, China has become an integral part of the world community. The significance of a rapidly globalizing China has led scholars, policy consultants and policy-makers alike to pay intensive attention to the impact of China's globalization on world politics.[2]

China's rapid globalization has been driven by capitalistic economic development. Capitalism was "illegally" pursued initially as a way of economic development after the Chinese leadership began to implement the reform and open-door policy in the late 1970s, and was legitimized only after Deng Xiaoping's southern tour in early 1992. Globalization has brought about sea changes to every aspect of economic and social life in China. Nevertheless, the Chinese state appears to have remained in its traditional Leninist form. Many questions have therefore been raised regarding the impact of globalization on the Chinese state such as: How has capitalism driven globalization? Why has the Chinese leadership legitimized capitalism as a way of globalizing the country? How has the Chinese state responded to globalization? Is the Chinese state able to accommodate globalization and its socio-economic consequences? Will economic globalization bring about political democracy to China?

The purpose of this study is to examine the impact of globalization on the Chinese state and the responses of the Chinese state to globalization. I am interested in exploring how globalization has provided developing countries like China an opportunity for state transformation, that is, re-making their state systems.

1

Globalization has weakened the power of the Chinese state in some areas, and the state has responded to its declining power consciously in some cases and unconsciously in others. The Chinese state has not merely played the role of the fire brigade, reacting passively to the negative consequences of economic transformation and globalization. Instead, the state has adopted a proactive approach to re-make the state system. These conscious actions have not only modernized the Chinese state but also strengthened the power of the state in many aspects.

This introduction aims to provide the reader some background for the chapters that follow. It first examines the process and major aspects of China's globalization, and shows how globalization has challenged the Chinese state in some major areas. Then, drawing on a growing body of literature on globalization, it discusses key arguments on how globalization has affected the state; and finally, it provides a tour of the chapters that follow.

Globalizing China

Globalizing the country in an economic sense has been an integral part of China's post-Mao reform. "Reform" (*gaige*) and "opening" (*kaifang*) have been the two sides of the same coin. The aim of reform and opening was to integrate China into the international community. Gradually, international integration or globalization became an important force further pushing the reform and open-door policy.[3] After the reformist leadership legitimized capitalism as a way of promoting economic growth in the early 1990s, the tide of globalization became irreversible. Not only has globalization generated its own dynamics;[4] more importantly, the reformist leadership tends to be highly dependent on globalization for overcoming difficulties associated with domestic reforms.[5]

The first phase of China's reform started with agricultural reform. The reform immediately resulted in a rapid growth in agricultural production and a sharp rise in rural incomes for the peasants. As agricultural productivity increased, greater agricultural surplus was available for non-farm development. This, in turn, led to the mushrooming of township and village enterprises (TVEs), which soon became the driving force for China's economic growth.[6]

Once the agricultural sector had accomplished its initial reform, the leadership moved on to reform the industrial sector in urban areas. Industrial reform has been facilitated by the country's links with the outside world. A revamp of the foreign trade system in the early 1980s ended the monopoly of the state trade corporations over the export-import business, and thousands of Chinese companies were allowed to trade internationally. The setting up of special economic zones (SEZs) and the opening of dozens of coastal cities to foreign businesses immediately led to an influx of foreign capital, which was lured by many preferential policies towards foreign-funded enterprises.[7]

The 1989 crackdown of the pro-democracy movement resulted in unfavorable domestic and international repercussions for China's economic globalization. The central leadership debated the direction of the reforms, and the conservative elements in the party, especially the ideologues, who were on the ascendancy, openly questioned the ideological implications of economic reform. Nevertheless, the Deng Xiaoping leadership was able to re-legitimize the reform course by pointing to the benefits the country had gained from the initial stages of globalization. Deng made a high-profile trip to the south to rally support for his new reform initiatives. The south, with its SEZs and open cities, was already many steps ahead of the north in terms of economic reform and exposure to international capitalism. As the prosperous economy of the south was most threatened by the post-Tiananmen austerity policy, the south was much more inclined to open up the country further to recapture its high economic growth.

Deng's southern tour has become a milestone in modern Chinese history since it ended the longlasting ideological debate on whether China's development should be socialistic or capitalistic.[8] Despite the setting up of the SEZs, the opening of coastal cities and the significant progress in the trading regime, the process of globalization was tightly controlled and managed by the state before Deng's southern tour. Apart from high tariffs and non-tariff barriers, imports were subjected to planning and licensing controls, and had to be handled by specific state trading corporations. Exports were also strictly regulated. More seriously, the foreign exchange regime was rigid, with the widening gaps between the official rate and the parallel rate determined at the "swap centers." Central to Deng's southern tour talks was that China had to learn from capitalism in its transition from a partially reformed planned economy to a market-oriented one. Deng's concept of market economy was incorporated into the official ideology of the Chinese Communist Party in 1992. From then onwards, capitalism was legitimized as a way of globalizing the country and integrating it with the international community.

Deng's southern tour triggered a sustained wave of economic growth and accelerated the country's globalization. As shown in Table 1.1, the Chinese economy grew at 10.5 percent during 1991–99, compared to the pre-southern tour growth of 9 percent during 1978–91. Much of China's economic growth after 1978 was essentially investment driven, with fixed assets investment growing at 20.3 percent for the period 1978–99. But

Table 1.1 Economic growth in China

	1978–99	1978–91	1991–99	1991–96
GDP growth (%)	9.6	9.0	10.5	12.0
Fixed assets investment (%)	20.3*	17.9*	23.7	32.6
Total FDI (US$ billion)	306**	23.3**	28.7	156
FDI growth (%)	30.0***	28.2***	32.3	57.0
Total exports (US$ billion)	1,625	466	1,231	669
Exports growth (%)	15.5	16.6	13.3	16.0

* The starting year is 1980.   ** The starting year is 1979.   *** The starting year is 1983.
Sources: The State Statistical Bureau, *Zhongguo tongji nianjian 1999* (China Statistical Yearbook 1999) (Beijing: Zhongguo tongji chubanshe, 1999). The data from 1999 are from Xinhua News Agency, 6 March 2000.

investment growth was faster after the southern tour: 23.7 percent for 1991–99 as opposed to 17.9 percent for 1978–91.

High economic growth was associated with an increase in degree of economic marketization. The state-owned enterprises' share of gross output value of industry declined from about 80 percent by the end of the 1970s to less than 26.5 percent by the end of the 1990s.[9] According to a research report in 1999 by Unirule (*Tianze*), a non-government research institute in Beijing, the market coordinated more than 85 percent of commodity prices, 65 percent of labor force markets, 66 percent of agriculture, 50 percent of industry and 54 percent of foreign trade.[10] Another report by the State Administration of Industry and Commerce revealed that by mid-1999, the number of private businesses had increased to 1.28 million, employing 17.84 million workers with 817.7 billion yuan of registered capital.[11]

The most convincing economic effect of the southern tour has been the explosive growth of foreign direct investment (FDI) that flowed into China after 1992. China has become the most favored destination of all developing countries for FDI. From 1988 to 2000, actual or utilized FDI increased at an average rate of 23 percent per annum to reach a cumulative total of US$339 billion (see Figure 1.1). FDI had contributed most significantly to China's phenomenal export growth where foreign-invested enterprises (FIEs) had grown to account for almost half of all exports from China. As shown in Figure 1.2, FIEs were responsible for 48 percent of China's total exports in 2000, up from 20 percent in 1992.[12]

China has emerged as a major trading economy in the world. China's exports increased at a hefty annual rate of 17 percent from US$13.7 billion in 1979 to US$249.2 billion in 2000. As a result of the 1997 Asian

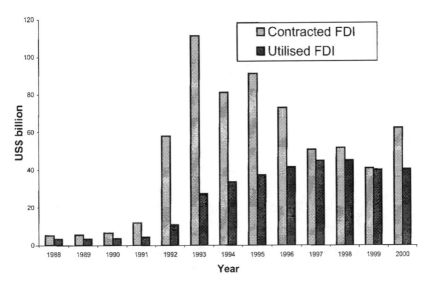

Figure 1.1 Foreign direct investment in China, 1988–2000
Source: Ministry of Foreign Trade and Economic Cooperation, *China Statistical Yearbook*, various issues.

Figure 1.2 FIEs' contribution to China's exports, 1992–2000
Sources: The State Statistical Bureau, *China Statistical Yearbook*, various issues, and *China Customs Statistics* (Monthly Exports and Imports), Dec. 2000.

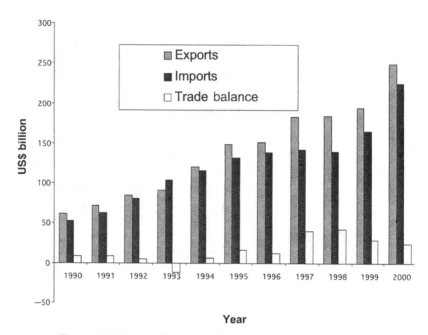

Figure 1.3 Exports, imports and the trade balance, 1990–2000
Sources: The State Statistical Bureau, *China Customs Statistics Yearbook 1999, China Customs Statistics* (Monthly Exports and Imports), Dec. 2000.

financial crisis, most Asian economies saw their export growth plunge into negative territory. China's export growth also stagnated, growing at a mere 0.5 percent in 1998, compared to 21 percent in 1997. However, China's export growth rebounded quickly at 6 percent in 1999 and then shot up to the startling double-digit rate of 28 percent in 2000 (Figure 1.3). By early 2001, China had become the world's 9th largest exporting nation.[13]

With this dramatic increase in foreign trade, the Chinese economy became much more open to the world during the 1990s. China's merchandise trade balance with the world moved towards surplus in 1990 and grew to over US$43 billion in 1998. For six years in a row after 1993, China was second to the US in the world for foreign capital inflow. During the 1990s, China sucked in about half of all foreign direct investment that went to the developing economies. On top of that, China has built up one of the world's largest foreign exchange reserves. In 1999, its forex reserve surpassed US$150 billion.[14]

The rise of information society

China's globalization is driven not only by foreign investment and trade, but also by the rapid development of an information society. The Chinese government began to focus on building an information society in the mid-1980s to spur economic growth.

The build-up of telecom infrastructure in China since the mid-1990s is staggering. Switchboard capacity reached 100 million in 1997, from 50 million in 1994. The number of fixed-line phone subscribers reached 10 million in 1992, shot up to 50 million in 1996, and reached 100 million in 1999 – increasing tenfold within seven years (Table 1.2).

By 2000, China had become the world's second biggest telecom market, in terms of network capacity and number of subscribers. The country had installed 179 million lines, with 144 million fixed-line phone subscribers (Table 1.3). Penetration rate (total number of fixed-line and mobile telephones per 100 persons) stood at about 18 percent, while teledensity (number of main telephone lines per 100 residents) had reached 12 percent (Table 1.4).

China's telecom growth has also been driven by the expansion of mobile telephony. The number of mobile phone subscribers was only 1 million in 1994; it increased to 5 million in 1996, passed the 20 million mark in 1998 and surpassed 80 million in 2000 (Table 1.5), an eighty-fold increase over six years. In late 2000, China, with more mobile phone users than Japan, became the world's second biggest mobile phone market after the United States. About 30 percent of China's users accessed the Internet via their mobile phones, through wireless application protocol (WAP).[15] Such an increase amplified the code capacity from 50 million to about 500 million, which should meet the country's demand by 2010.[16]

The rapid growth of the telecom industry laid a foundation for the formation of the Internet society. Table 1.6 shows the rapid expansion of China's Internet sector, with telecom service providers such as China Mobile and China Unicom offering Internet services such as the WAP networks.

The rise of Internet society and information technology (IT) has also led to the emergence of China's new economy. By the beginning of the twenty-first century, China was already very much caught up in the relentless global process of the IT revolution. Since the beginning of the Chinese government's drive for reform and liberalization, China's IT industry has grown rapidly, at about 30 percent annually.[17] In 1999 alone, total IT sales increased by 16.2 percent to reach 172 billion yuan (US$20.8 billion).[18] By the middle of 2000, the number of

Table 1.2 Number of fixed-line phone subscribers in China, 1978–2000

| Year | Fixed-line phone subscribers | |
	No. of subscribers (million)	% Change
1978	1.925	
1979	2.033	5.61
1980	2.141	5.31
1981	2.221	3.74
1982	2.343	5.49
1983	2.508	7.04
1984	2.775	10.65
1985	3.120	12.43
1986	3.504	12.31
1987	3.907	11.50
1988	4.727	20.99
1989	5.680	20.16
1990	6.850	20.60
1991	8.451	23.37
1992	11.469	35.71
1993	17.332	51.12
1994	27.295	57.48
1995	40.706	49.13
1996	54.947	34.99
1997	70.310	27.96
1998	87.421	24.34
1999	108.716	24.36
2000	144.000	32.46

Sources: The State Statistical Bureau, *China Statistical Yearbook* and *Yearbook of China Transportation and Communications*, various issues. For the 2000 figure, see Ministry of Information Industry website, http://www.mii.gov.cn/.

registered Internet users hit 16.9 million, of which 14 percent had tried e-commerce.[19]

The rapid development of IT infrastructure in China laid a solid foundation for the emergence of its new economy. In 1999, a total of 4.9 million personal computers (PCs) were sold in China. Domestic computer hardware sales registered a 13 percent rise over 1998 to reach 130 billion yuan, while sales of software and information services products amounted to 41.5 billion yuan, a 27.5 percent increase. At the same time, sales of telecommunications products reached about 100 billion yuan in 1999, while total telecommunications business turnover grew 24 percent to hit 240 billion yuan in the same year.[20]

Table 1.3 Local switchboard capacity in
China, 1985–2000

Year	Local switchboard capacity	
	Million lines	% Change
1985	6.134	
1986	6.724	9.62
1987	7.739	15.10
1988	8.872	14.64
1989	10.347	16.63
1990	12.318	19.05
1991	14.922	21.14
1992	19.151	28.34
1993	30.408	58.78
1994	49.262	62.00
1995	72.036	46.23
1996	92.912	28.98
1997	112.692	21.29
1998	138.237	22.67
1999	153.461	11.01
2000	179.000	16.64

Sources: The State Statisical Bureau, *China Statistical Yearbook* and *Yearbook of China Transportation and Communications*, various issues. For the 2000 figure, see Ministry of Information Industry website, http://www.mii.gov.cn/.

The weakening of the Chinese state

While globalization has brought about enormous economic benefits to the country, the Chinese state has suffered from both expected and unexpected social and political consequences. China's firms, in both the state sector and the non-state sector, are facing increasingly high pressure from the domestic industrial transformation and economic globalization. Among other problems, unemployment has worsened. The deepening of economic reforms and improvement in economic efficiency have already caused massive layoffs in state enterprises, not to mention the millions of excess labor in the rural areas. As China strives to meet the WTO challenges, the army of unemployed is expected to grow.

Rapid economic transformation and globalization are leading to what Shaoguang Wang called "distributive conflicts."[21] Social groups and regions have benefited from globalization very unevenly. Distributive

Table 1.4 Penetration rate and teledensity in
China, 1985–2000

Year	Penetration rate	Teledensity
1985	0.60	–
1986	0.67	–
1987	0.75	–
1988	0.86	–
1989	0.98	–
1990	1.11	–
1991	1.29	–
1992	1.61	–
1993	2.20	–
1994	3.20	–
1995	4.66	3.36
1996	6.33	4.49
1997	8.11	5.68
1998	10.53	7.00
1999	13.00	8.64
2000	18.00	12.00

Sources: The State Statistical Bureau, *China Statistical Yearbook* and *Yearbook of China Transportation and Communications*, various issues. The 2000 figure for penetration rate is calculated based on the number of fixed line and mobile phone subscribers per 100 persons in China's total population. For teledensity in 2000, see "China Telecom IPO faces crucial test", *South China Morning Post* (9 April 2001).

conflicts are politically significant since they have contributed to the rise of social protests in both rural areas and urban cities (see Chapter 7).

Economic transformation has also weakened the ethics of the state, resulting in a waning of the people's confidence in the government. While the Chinese state has played an extremely important role in pushing the process of economic transformation and globalization, it has also inadvertently created serious problems. The close links between the government and businesses have led to widespread corruption among party cadres and government officials.[22] Many forms of official corruption are clearly associated with globalization. Smuggling is an example. Towards the end of the 1990s, smuggling became very prevalent and beyond the control of the central government (see Table 1.7). Smuggling had damaged China's economy and reduced central revenue. The smuggled goods included drugs, weapons and counterfeits, raw industrial materials (e.g., cement, steel, petroleum, etc.), consumer goods and articles

Table 1.5 Number of mobile phone subscribers in
China, 1988–2000

	Mobile phone subscribers	
Year	No. of subscribers (million)	% Change
1988	0.0032	
1989	0.0098	206.25
1990	0.0183	86.73
1991	0.0475	159.56
1992	0.177	272.63
1993	0.639	261.01
1994	1.568	145.38
1995	3.629	131.44
1996	6.853	88.84
1997	13.233	93.10
1998	23.863	80.33
1999	43.300	81.45
2000	85.260	96.91

Sources: The State Statistical Bureau, *China Statistical Yearbook* and
Yearbook of China Transportation and Communications, various issues;
for the 2000 figure, see Ministry of Information Industry website,
http://www.mii.gov.cn/.

Table 1.6 Number of Internet subscribers in China,
1995–2000

	Internet subscribers	
Year	No. of subscribers (million)	% Change
1995	0.0072	
1996	0.0357	349.27
1997	0.1602	349.22
1998	0.6768	322.58
1999	3.0145	345.44
2000	9.1300	202.87

Sources: The State Statistical Bureau, *China Statistical Yearbook* and
Yearbook of China Transportation and Communications, various issues;
for the 2000 figure, see Ministry of Information Industry website,
http://www.mii.gov.cn/.

Table 1.7 The development of smuggling in China, 1979–98

	Smuggling cases seized by customs	Value of smuggled goods seized (10 million yuan)	Average value of each smuggling case (10 million yuan)
1979	13,422	0.07	0.05
1980	36,616	0.51	0.14
1981	34,870	1.06	0.30
1982	32,507	1.02	0.31
1983	33,220	0.59	0.17
1984	27,162	1.36	0.50
1985	23,545	7.09	3.00
1986	18,453	6.11	3.31
1987	13,018	1.67	1.28
1988	10,206	2.34	2.29
1989	11,960	5.58	4.67
1990	11,676	6.01	5.15
1991	13,321	7.13	5.35
1992	9,954	13.18	13.24
1993	6,962	23.00	33.93
1994	6,614	22.88	34.59
1995	5,832	44.30	75.96
1996	6,130	92.89	151.33
1997	7,285	67.35	92.70
1998	8,361	154.00	183.75

Source: Jingji ribao (Economic Daily), 26 January 1999.

for daily use (see Table 1.8). The availability of smuggled goods brought down the prices of commodities for which custom duties were paid. Smuggling benefited consumers but reduced government revenues and harmed the development of domestic industries normally protected by tariffs. Moreover, smuggling tended to be corporatized, with business enterprises directly involved in smuggling, or commissioning the activity, or fiddling the paperwork. Smugglers were organized professionals. Methods used included false customs declarations, fake certificates of approval or seals. Even if the smugglers were caught, they managed to obtain authentic documents, or intimidated or obstructed investigations.[23]

The seriousness of smuggling eventually led to a nationwide crackdown by the central government on smuggling in the coastal provinces such as Guangdong and Fujian in 1998.[24] Chinese Premier Zhu Rongji even warned then that anti-smuggling was an issue of life and death. According to Zhu,

Table 1.8 Major smuggled goods seized by customs in 1998

Goods smuggled	Smuggling cases	Value (10 million yuan)	Volume	% of the total value
Mobile communications equipment	28	394,013	2,497 (pieces)	37.4
Chemical industrial raw materials	368	170,954	914,489 (tons)	16.23
Edible oil	41	96,994	147,842 (tons)	9.21
Chemical fibers	182	92,153	737,107 (tons)	8.75
Computers	11	70,792	43,163	6.72
Finished petroleum	151	53,198	318,029 (tons)	5.05
Cigarettes	57	52,416	23,662 (boxes)	4.98
Automobiles	169	45,601	3,887	4.33
Wool	32	38,432	9,272 (tons)	3.65
Steel	59	38,248	165,094 (tons)	3.63
Total	1098	1,052,801		100.0

Source: *Jingji ribao* (Economic Daily), 26 January 1999.

If smuggling cannot be stopped, it will not only have an impact on the reform and open-door policy, but also undermine our economy, our political regime and our party. Therefore, anti-smuggling is not only an important economic struggle, but also a serious political struggle.[25]

Economic transformation and globalization have also resulted in decentralization with attendant significant political consequences. Decentralization means that the Chinese state has given powers back to society. New social organizations have emerged all over China and at various levels. Towards the end of the 1990s, there were 160,000 government-registered civil associations at the national and provincial levels, excluding non-profit organizations, religious associations and all local social organizations.[26] The emergence of civil associations represents the re-making of civil society in China. A nascent spontaneous social order has imposed a serious political challenge to the existing political order. While economic globalization and the IT revolution have contributed directly to China's economic transformation, they have also provided an important medium for a new form of associational activity to rise. The Internet has been used as a forum for civil discussions. There are plenty of Chinese websites, chat rooms, and informal e-mail exchanges and lists where people hold civil discussions on contemporary political and social affairs. Citizens are now able to express their own political views, regardless of whether the government sanctions it or not. In other words, the IT revolution has created a new tool for political participation. More importantly, as will be discussed later, globalization and the IT revolution have provided tools and resources for social movements, especially religious movements as exemplified by the Falun Gong (FLG) (Chapter 7).

The list of challenges associated with globalization grows ever longer. Overall, globalization in China, as elsewhere, has unleashed many forces that are often beyond the control of the state. The question naturally arises: What will be the fate of the Chinese state? While this study is organized around this question, it is helpful to set this question in the scholarly context of how globalization has affected states.

Globalization and the state

Over the last decade, rapid globalization has refocused scholarly attention on the role of the state. "What future for the state?" has become a pertinent question.[27] Scholars disagree with one another about the impact of globalization on the state, but the dominant view is that globalization weakens the power of the state, and even leads to the death of the state.

Among others, neo-Marxist and neo-liberal scholars are the major source of this argument. What Peter Evans called "the discourse of eclipse of the state" has become prevalent among these scholars,[28] especially among scholars in Western Europe where the argument for the epitaph of the nation-state has gained most political support. Advanced capitalist states, especially in Western Europe, have offered the most empirical evidence for the students of globalization.[29]

Neo-Marxism, especially its world-system theory, regarded globalization as the expansion of the capitalist system around the globe. Capitalism knows no bounds, as Marx noted more than a century ago.[30] Marx expected the European economy to become a truly global system, and in many ways it had.[31] Immanuel Wallerstein has given us a contemporary version of Marxist theory of the linkages between capitalism and globalization in his world-system theory.[32] While states play a supporting role in the world-system analysis, more contemporary authors focus on the diminishing role of the state in the age of globalization. According to Kenichi Ohmae, capital can establish plants wherever they want to, for either cost or market reasons; government actions, regarding either tax or regulation, are constrained by the desire not to "scare away the global economy."[33] Consequently, "traditional nation-states have become unnatural, even impossible business units in a global economy."[34] Mathew Horsman and Andrew Marshall even argue for the end of the nation-state, "[The state] has become marginalized by the autonomy of companies operating in the transnational economy."[35] Susan Strange puts it more directly, "state authority has leaked away, upwards, sideways, and downwards," and in some matters "just evaporated."[36]

The eclipse of the state results from the interaction between the market and the state in both international and domestic zones. Economic globalization is bringing about a "de-nationalization" of economies through the establishment of transnational networks of production, trade and finance.[37] This de-nationalization occurs because economic globalization has been accompanied by the formation of an international financial market, rapid growth of foreign investment, and a dramatic increase in foreign trade.[38]

With the formation of a global financial market, capital is now so mobile that markets will ensure that holders of financial assets receive roughly the same, risk adjusted, real return everywhere. Any country that offers significantly lower returns will experience capital outflow and a rapidly depreciating exchange rate. It is virtually impossible now to go back to exchange controls as an economic regulator.[39] Another negative effect of financial and corporate globalization is the government's loss of corporate taxes, as global corporations learn how to avoid taxes.

The rapid growth of FDI through transnational corporations (TNCs) imposes constraints on the economic sovereignty of the nation-state. The sense of identity associated with "national" companies and the loyalties flowing from that identity are disappearing. The dominance of TNCs in trade flows has changed the meaning of "exports" and "imports." The mobility of capital and the importance of FDI have subtly changed the nature of national economic policy.

Changes in the trade field of a qualitative kind are also having a serious effect on economic sovereignty. A substantial segment of trade is now intra-industry rather than inter-industry, often due to specialization within TNCs. In large parts of the economy it is no longer possible to disentangle "national" exports and "foreign" imports for trade policy purposes. Tradable services can mould cultural values and provide information through news, entertainment, and advertising, besides cutting to the heart of the nation's sense of identity. As economic systems become more deeply integrated through trade as well as investment, the traditional, explicit barriers to trade disappear.

When wealth and power are increasingly generated by private transactions that take place across the borders of states, it becomes harder to sustain the old image of states as the pre-eminent actors at the global level.[40] When transnational economic activities become essential to domestic development, the state has to relinquish power to these global actors. The OECD PUMA research group concludes that there remain few purely "domestic" issues.[41]

Globalization not only affects the relations between the state and transnational actors; more importantly, as Strange noted, it also affects the relations between the state and other domestic actors. The asymmetries of state authority have increased. The state may suffer some loss of authority, yet that loss has been to markets, not to other states. Furthermore, some authority over less politically sensitive issues has shifted from national states to international authorities of various kinds, both interstate institutions and private and commercial organizations (upward and sideward). In many states, authority has shifted "downwards," from central authority to local and regional authority. As a result mainly of the integration of the world economy, there are some important responsibilities of political authority that no one in a system of territorially defined states is in a position to discharge fully.[42]

Neo-liberal scholars focus on the nature of interdependence among nation-states and thus the impact of globalization on state behavior in world politics. According to Robert Keohane and Joseph Nye, globalization has produced a more complex system of interdependent states in which transnational rules and organizations have gained influence.[43] James Rosenau contends that radical globalization has forced governments and societies across the globe to adjust to a world in which a clear distinction between international and domestic, external and internal affairs no longer exists.[44] While states still retain the ultimate legal claim to effective supremacy over what occurs within their own territories, this is juxtaposed, to varying degrees, with the expanding jurisdiction of institutions of international governance and the constraints of, as well as the obligations derived from, international law.[45] Neo-liberals believe that with radical economic globalization, a liberal global regime, which is above all nation-states, has been established. This global regime is based on a set of formal and informal institutions, rules, norms, and shared assumptions. Though it originated in the West, reflected Anglo-American ideological prescriptions, and was expanded by Western powers, once established, it can function by itself. This is largely because of economic globalization. Without such a regime, it will be very difficult to coordinate international economic and financial activities, since selfish national states may bring about economic disasters on other countries.

For neo-liberals, the liberal international regime, manifested in the General Agreement on Tariffs and Trade (GATT) and now the WTO, becomes extremely important in shaping the role of individual nation-states in both domestic and international arenas. The regime has widely accepted formal rules of the game, to which individual states have to commit themselves or risk becoming economic pariahs. Thanks to such a regime, economic gains can be pursued independently of national sovereignty. Consequently, as Evans points out, "becoming more actively engaged in trying to improve local economic conditions risks the opprobrium, not just of powerful private actors, but also of the global hegemony," and any state intervention thus becomes "a very risky proposition."[46] The functioning of this global regime is still dependent on national states, but state authorities have to behave in accordance with the rules and norms of this global regime. The global ideological consensus, which is sometimes labeled the "Washington consensus," has further reinforced the perception that the less individual states behave as economic actors, the better off the world will be.[47]

The weakening of the power of the nation-state can also be understood by looking at the impact of globalization on domestic politics, especially state–society relations. According to Dani Rodrik, globalization has created three sources of tension between the global market and domestic social stability.[48] First, it has reduced barriers to trade and investment and accentuated the asymmetry between groups that can cross international borders and those that cannot, and thus fundamentally transforms the employment relationship. Second, globalization has engendered conflicts within and between nations over domestic norms and the social institutions that embody them. As the technology for manufactured goods becomes standardized and diffused internationally, nations with very different sets of values, norms, institutions, and collective preferences begin to compete head on in markets for similar goods. Third, globalization has made it exceedingly difficult for governments to provide social insurance – one of their central functions and one that has helped maintain social cohesion and domestic political support for continuing liberalization throughout the postwar period. All these tendencies might lead to a loss of authority of those who govern in the name of the nation-state. The state cannot protect its citizens in ways they have come to expect, and the state can no longer rely on the loyalty of its citizens.

More importantly, globalization has led to the decline of state power over domestic social forces. Globalization has made it difficult for the national state to control civil society, just as economic globalization has made it almost impossible for state power to control private economic activities. This power is especially vulnerable in authoritarian states. Authoritarian states often exercise tight political control over domestic economic transactions, thus controlling their population who are engaged in these economic transactions. However, globalization has created an economic sector which is beyond state control, and this sector-related population is undoubtedly beyond state control. Moreover, globalization has also created international civil societies such as international non-governmental organizations (INGOs), which are not confined to national boundaries and are beyond the reach of national power.[49] For neo-liberals, the rise of (domestic and international) civil society is of significance for the nation-state. It could possibly become "a solution to the social and political side of public well-being, one that could make the state politically obsolete, just as global markets made the state economically obsolete."[50]

The argument

Will the Chinese state come to end, as some neo-Marxist and neo-liberal scholars would argue? This study shows a different direction of development for the Chinese state. Economic transformation and globalization have undoubtedly challenged state power; nevertheless, the Chinese state has been an integral part of China's globalization process, and it has played an important role in pushing globalization and economic transformation. Rather than sitting idle and awaiting its demise, the Chinese state has responded to globalization and its consequences very forcefully. While the power of the state in some traditional areas was weakened, it was strengthened or consolidated in some other new areas. The responses of the state to globalization are leading to a drastic transformation of the Chinese state system.

This study does not attempt to do a cost–benefit analysis of globalization on state power. Globalization can strengthen state power in some cases, and weaken it in other cases, depending on how the state responds to globalization. This study is interested in how globalization has affected state transformation. Globalization has created opportunities for the Chinese leadership to re-make the state system. I argue that the Chinese state, as the most important political institution, has consciously responded to globalization and its consequences. With reform measures properly thought out and implemented, the state can not only survive globalization, but can also borrow external pressure to transform itself. Globalization therefore creates an impetus for the state to become more modern.

One important caveat has to be added here. This study focuses more on the Chinese state than the Chinese Communist Party (CCP) for a number of reasons. First, although the state and the CCP are interwoven, and scholars have traditionally reviewed the Chinese state as a party-state, for the sake of analysis here, the state and the party can be regarded as two distinguishable political entities.[51] Second, as will be seen later, while globalization has also had an impact on the CCP, it is the Chinese state that has been affected most seriously. The CCP has played a role in adjusting party ideology to accommodate global capitalism, but most responses have come from the Chinese state. Third, since the early 1990s, the leadership has emphasized the reform of the Chinese state rather than of the CCP itself. In the 1980s, Deng Xiaoping defined the goal of China's political reform as *dang zheng fen kai* (separation of the party from the government). The *dang zheng fen kai* reform led to a period of political liberalization until the 1989 pro-democracy movement. Since the government's crackdown on the pro-democracy movement, the CCP leadership has never addressed the issue of *dang zheng fen kai*. The Jiang Zemin leadership perceived that the CCP, as the ultimate power source of the government, should serve as the final guarantor of political stability, should mistakes be made during the process of China's globalization.[52] So, virtually all the measures introduced are directed at reforming the state, and no serious party reform has been implemented.

Nevertheless, this does not imply in any sense that globalization does not pose any challenges to the CCP. The party is actually facing enormous difficulties in transforming itself and thus increasingly appears to be a main barrier for the building of a rule-based governance in China. The issues surrounding the party shall be addressed at the end of this book. To a great degree, focusing on the Chinese state will enable the reader to see that while the CCP has played an important role in the process of state transformation, the lack of party transformation has in turn made it difficult for the Chinese state to become fully modernized.

The organization

This study consists of nine chapters. Following this introduction, Chapter 2 will provide the theoretical framework of this study, i.e., a state-centered approach to globalization. Globalization is defined as a process of selective importation of Western state products, i.e., ideas on state-building.[53] It is the state that has selected these Western products to rebuild the state and make it more modern. The leadership, as the agent of the state, plays the most important role in this process. I shall discuss some important issues relating to globalization, the state and the leadership.

Chapter 3 highlights the connection between globalism and nationalism. I argue that one major factor that pushed the Chinese leadership to rebuild the state while accepting globalization is its ideological commitment. Apparently, the post-Mao era has witnessed the rise of Chinese nationalism, which somehow stands opposed to globalism. Many facets of Chinese nationalism seem anathema to globalization. This chapter discusses how nationalism has become compatible with globalism in the development of modern China, and how the leadership has justified globalization by playing up Chinese nationalism. This justification is important; without it, globalization would have lost its legitimacy. On the other hand, nationalism also serves as a serious constraint on the leadership's choice when they "select" Western state products.

Chapter 4 describes how the leadership has made great efforts to establish a new political order in accordance with changing socio-economic circumstances. Capitalist development has given rise to an interest-based social order, which is incompatible with the old Maoist political order. When this growing interest-based social order began to intrude into the political realm, the leadership, despite opposition from within, was quite determined to change the old state framework to accommodate new social forces.

Chapter 5 examines how the leadership has reconstructed China's bureaucratic system not only to accommodate the market but also to lead the country's economic development. The four waves of reform (one with Zhao Ziyang, two with Li Peng, and one with Zhu Rongji) are compared to show how the bureaucratic system was rationalized. Emphasis is given to Zhu Rongji's 1998 reform since this reform was directly aimed at promoting China's market development. The restructuring allowed the bureaucratic system to accommodate the market, and, more importantly, it strengthened the power of the state in leading the market.

Chapter 6 discusses the process of building a modern economic state. While the Chinese state has promoted market development, it has also attempted to build a framework in which the market can function. Three cases are examined, i.e., the taxation reform, the financial system reform, and the enterprise system reform. Among other goals, the aim of building such a modern economic state is to strengthen the power of the state in coping with economic globalization.

Chapters 7 and 8 shift the focus away from the state to society. Globalization has affected not only the Chinese state, but also society. Though the autonomy of the Chinese state is quite strong, it does not mean that the leadership can rebuild the state at will. Instead, different social forces have attempted to participate in the process of state-building in different ways. The leadership somehow has to take these social voices into consideration.

Chapter 7 discusses social protests by Chinese peasants and urban workers. It shows how globalization and state rebuilding have affected peasants and urban citizens, and how they have responded to the state. Chapter 8 examines how Chinese intellectuals have tried to have their "say" over state-building. Globalization and socio-economic transformation have led Chinese intellectuals to split into different schools. Among others, new liberalism and a new left have stood out as two main intellectual streams. The two schools of scholars have struggled for ascendancy over each other on the discourse regarding state-building.

In concluding, Chapter 9 addresses an important question: Will globalization enable the Chinese leadership to build a rule-based system of state governance? In the Chinese discourse, globalization means that China should follow international rules and norms (*jiegui*). In other words, globalization is a process of the universalization of institutions, rules and norms among nation-states. This chapter shows that the monopoly of power by the CCP has presented real challenges for the Chinese state to build a rule-based governance structure.

2   The state, leadership and globalization

Most scholars have propounded the rather pessimistic view that globalization weakens the power of nation-states, with some even predicting their demise. Nevertheless, if we look at how the Chinese state has responded to globalization, a different conclusion may arise. Whether globalization weakens or strengthens the power of the state depends on how the state responds to it.

This chapter first presents the scholarly context of the connections between the state and globalization. The state here is treated as an independent variable. I attempt to show that the state *per se* has been a part of globalization, and a major driving force behind the process. For developing countries like China, globalization means not only capitalist development; more importantly, it means the spread of the modern state from the West to the rest of the world. After the review of the scholarly context, this chapter then sets up a theoretical framework for this study.

The scholarly context: the state and globalization

Both neo-Marxists and neo-liberals have linked the decline of the power of the state to economic globalization, but their argument is not without criticisms. According to Michael Mann, they are vulnerable to criticism since they have downplayed political power relations. Mann points out, "With little sense of history, they exaggerate the former strength of nation-states; with little sense of global variety, they exaggerate their current decline; with little sense of their plurality, they downplay inter-national relations."[1]

Mann has observed that globalization and capitalist transformation seem to be somewhat weakening the most advanced nation-states of the North, yet successful economic development strengthens nation-states elsewhere. The decline of militarism and "hard geopolitics" in the North weakens its traditional nation-state core, yet identity politics may actually strengthen nation-states. These patterns are too varied and contradictory, and the future too murky to permit us to argue simply that the nation-state and the nation-state system are strengthening or weakening.[2]

Evans has also argued that the processes of globalization have contributed to the perceived evaporation of state authority, but the situation is more complicated than many scholars perceive. The state is not eclipsed by the simple fact of its becoming more dependent on transnational trade. Instead, a look at the nations that have been economically successful suggests that high stateness may even be a competitive advantage in a globalized economy. This is especially true in East Asia, where the state has played a central role to effect dramatic changes in the country's position in the international division of labor. According to Evans,

East Asia successes force us to re-examine the idea that effective participation in a globalized economy is best achieved by restricting state involvement in economic affairs. They suggest that successful participation in global markets may be best achieved through more intense state involvement. . . . East Asia demonstrates the possibility of a positive connection between high stateness and success in a globalizing economy.[3]

More importantly, the state will not allow its power to decline. As the most important political institution in modern society, the state will struggle for its own survival. Eclipse is not a likely occurrence. Evans argues,

The danger is not that states will end up as marginal institutions but that meaner, more repressive ways of organizing the state's role will be accepted as the only way of avoiding the collapse of public institutions. Preoccupation with eclipse cripples consideration of positive possibilities for working to increase states' capacity so that they can more effectively meet the new demands that confront them.[4]

Vicent Cable also points out that there are no direct connections between globalization and the decline of the nation-state.[5] Domestic policy-making and politics have been internationalized and foreign policies have been subjected to growing domestic pressures. The state has "lost" sovereignty to regional and global institutions and to markets on one hand, and has acquired new areas of control in order to promote national competitiveness on the other. While technological change may have pushed in one direction, social and political forces may have pulled in another.

More critical scholars have cast doubts on globalization *per se*. For them, globalization is a myth.[6] In comparison with the age of world empire, the international economy has become considerably less global in its geographical embrace. According to Linda Weiss, a realistic assessment of globalization should not lead to the conclusion that globalization has led to the decline of the power of the nation-state.[7] Weiss has argued that the impact on the autonomy and power of national governments has been less than claimed by many commentaries. In reality, governments have adapted to changing patterns of trade and investment, and in some cases, countries such as Japan, Taiwan, and Korea have promoted internationalization.

Robert Wade has reached a similar conclusion that the death of the nation-state has been exaggerated. According to Wade, a high proportion of production in most countries is for domestic consumption. Those countries that have very high levels of imports and exports relative to national production have high volumes of trade in goods that are imported and re-exported. There are few genuinely international corporations; rather, there are companies based in one state with production and distribution facilities in other countries. When governments make policy to attract inward investment, they often use special export-processing zones or special economic zones, where there are different levels of taxes, regulations, and labor rights.[8]

For realists, globalization does not lead to a less state-centric world order. Governments are not the passive victims of internationalization but its primary architects. Robert Gilpin considers internationalization a by-product of the US-initiated multilateral economic order which, in the aftermath of the Second World War, created the impetus for the liberalization of national economies.[9] While neo-liberals see that economic globalization and interdependence are leading to a peaceful world order, realists see an opposite trend. According to realists, economic activity is undergoing significant regionalization as the world economy evolves in the direction of three major financial and trading blocs, that is, Europe, Asia-Pacific and North America.[10] Moreover, internationalization has not been accompanied by an erosion of North–South inequalities but, on the contrary, by the growing economic marginalization of many "Third World" states as trade and investment flows within the rich North intensify to the exclusion of much of the rest of the globe.[11]

Such inequality contributes to the advance of both fundamentalism and aggressive nationalism rather than the emergence of a global civilization, and the world is fragmenting into civilizational blocs and cultural and ethnic enclaves.[12] The notion of cultural homogenization and a global culture are thus further myths. The deepening of global inequalities, the realpolitik of international relations and the "clash of civilizations" expose the illusory nature of global governance. Realists thus reject the popular myth that global governance is undermining the power of national governments or state sovereignty today.[13]

Globalization and the re-making of the state

The state is undoubtedly under pressure from within and without. As the most important institution in modern society, the state is unlikely to disappear even with radical globalization. Central to its survival will be the ability to carve out a role that is compatible with both the forces of global economic integration and the internal strains created by the politics of identity. In other words, what is important is to see how the state transforms itself to accommodate globalization and its consequences. Before examining this issue, it is worthwhile outlining how modern (Western) states have transformed themselves and spread to the rest of the world in different historical periods.

Modern (Western) states

When the modern state is discussed, it usually refers to the state that originated in the West and then spread to the rest of world. It is almost impossible to talk about the state in developing countries without referring to the modern Western state. As French scholar Bertrand Badie argued, globalization is a process of the Westernization of the political order – "the establishment of an international system tending towards unification of its rules, values, and objectives, while claiming to integrate within its center the whole humanity."[14] Therefore, before we discuss how globalization has affected the Chinese state, it is important to discuss what the modern state is and how it has spread to the rest of the world.

Max Weber provided us with an ideal-type definition of the modern state: an organization, composed of numerous agencies led and coordinated by the state's leadership (executive authority), that has the ability or authority to make and implement the binding rules for all the people as well as the parameters of rule making for other social organizations in a given territory, using force if necessary to have its way.[15] In other words, modern states distinguish themselves from all previous forms of political organizations by claiming a proper symmetry and correspondence between sovereignty, territory, legitimacy, and democracy. The concept of sovereignty lodges a distinctive claim to the rightful exercise of political power over a circumscribed realm.[16] It specifies the political authority within a community which has the right to determine the framework of rules, regulations and policies within a given territory and to govern accordingly.

More concretely, according to David Held et al., modern states have the following unique features. First of all, while all states have made claims on territories, it is only with the modern nation-state system that exact borders have been gradually fixed. Second, the claim to hold a monopoly on force and the means of coercion became possible only with the "pacification" of people, the breaking down of rival centers of power and authority within the nation-state. Third, the modern state is an impersonal and sovereign political order – that is, a legally circumscribed structure of power – with supreme jurisdiction over a territory. Fourth, the modern state obtains the loyalty of citizens and claims to be legitimate because it reflected and represented the needs, wishes, and interests of its citizens.[17] Modern nation-states especially in Europe and North America have acquired a particular political form, i.e., liberal democracy. Liberal democracy means that decisions affecting a community are taken by a subgroup of representatives who have been chosen through the electoral process to govern within the framework of the rule of law. In the arena of national politics, liberal democracy is distinguished by the presence of a cluster of rules and institutions all of which are necessary to its successful functioning.[18]

The formation and development of the modern state has been a long drawn-out process. In essence, modern nation-states are the products of Western political developments and they have undergone drastic transformations over different historical periods. Before the dawn of modern states, multi-ethnic empires and different forms of localized political organizations such as tribes, city-states, and feudal entities prevailed in different territories. The modern state was a political innovation that solved the dilemma faced by all these predominant forms of political organizations.

The modern state was first attributed to the rise of absolutism, which involved the development of a form of state based on a number of elements: the absorption of smaller and weaker political units into larger and stronger political structures; a strengthened ability to rule over a unified territorial area; a tightened system of law and order enforced throughout a territory; the application of a more unitary, centralized and calculable rule by a single, sovereign head; and the emergence of a relatively small number of states engaged in an "open-ended, competitive, and risk-laden power struggle."[19] These changes marked a substantial increase in public authority from above.

The transformation of the absolutist state to modern democracy is a complicated process. A simplified outline of the process is presented here. There were two major transformations: the absolutist state nurtured a bourgeoisie class; but the rising business classes in turn successfully tamed the monarchical state. They successfully challenged the aristocratic claim of government as a prerogative of birth and slowly replaced it with the principle that government is a natural domain of wealthy commoners. Then, as Marx argued, the bourgeois state created a working class. Ultimately, under pressure from organized working class, legitimacy in Western democracies came to rest on the notion that governmental representatives have to be elected by a legally equal citizenry.[20]

The state and the globalization of the state

To see how globalization has affected the state, we have to see how the state has taken part in the process of globalization. While globalization is not a recent phenomenon, its pace has accelerated in recent decades. Indeed, modern states have been the key agent of globalization since the very beginning of the process.[21] Before the formation of modern states, expansionist states and empires had been active in creating regional and global links and they were important elements of the changing historical forms of globalization. Different types of pre-modern states had created distinctive forms of territorial space from loose frontiers to tightly organized boundaries, which had shaped and mediated patterns of regional and global relations, networks and flows. Nevertheless, modern states profoundly altered the nature, form and prospects of globalization. With the development of the modern nation-state, the focal point of rule became national governments and their claims to sovereignty, autonomy and distinctive forms of accountability within a bounded territory.

Scholars have pointed to the important role of European absolutism in the formation of the modern political world.[22] Absolutism helped initiate a process of state-making which began to reduce the social, economic and cultural differences within states and expand the differences among them, that is, it helped to forge political communities with a clearer and growing sense of identity – national identity.[23] Further, the development of state sovereignty was central to the process of mutual recognition whereby states granted each other rights of jurisdiction in their respective territories and communities. The principle of sovereignty implied that all states had equal rights to self-determination which became paramount in the formal conduct of states towards one another.[24]

The world system was mainly shaped by the expansion of European states. The expansion of Europe led to the dismantling of older, non-European types of interstate connections. European features of the modern state system, i.e., the centralization of political power, the expansion of state administration, territorial rule, the diplomatic system, the emergence of regular, standing armies, became prevalent features of the global order. The main vehicle for this was the European states' capacity for overseas operations by means of military and naval forces capable of long-range navigation.

Modern states promoted the process of globalization. Globalization in turn has had a major impact on the state. Does globalization lead to national convergence or national divergence? This has been a perennial question among scholars of globalization. With rapid globalization in recent decades, the question has again been raised.[25] Many have argued that globalization can homogenize modern states. Without doubt, nation-states are now structurally similar in many unexpected dimensions and change in unexpectedly similar ways. The homogenization of modern states seems inevitable. As John Meyer and his colleagues argued, nation-states are theorized or imagined communities drawing on models that are lodged at the world level.[26] According to Meyer and his colleagues, many features of the contemporary nation-state are derived from worldwide models constructed and propagated through global cultural and associational processes. These models and the purposes they reflect are highly rationalized, articulated, and often surprisingly consensual. Worldwide models define and legitimate agendas for local action, shaping the structures and policies of nation-states and other national and local actors in virtually all of the domains of rationalized social life – business, politics, education, medicine, science, even the family and religion.[27]

Empirical evidence seems to confirm the thesis of national convergence. According to Samuel Huntington, there were three waves of democratic development.[28] The first wave occurred from the early nineteenth century to the mid-1920s; the second from the Second World War to the early 1960s; and the third from 1974 onwards. The third wave has secured liberal democracy, a dominant form of nation-states, in the world. In 1974, at least 68 percent of all countries could reasonably be called authoritarian; by the end of 1995, nearly 75 percent of all countries had established procedures for competitive elections and adopted some formal guarantees of political and civil rights.[29]

A more optimistic version of the argument says that there is no alternative to what happens in the West, which is defined as liberal democracy. Francis Fukuyama has argued that the collapse of the communist regimes in Eastern Europe means that the whole world will converge by establishing liberal democratic systems and such political systems are the natural consequence of capitalism.[30] Fukuyama has also argued that central planning is inadequate to generate growth and that growth is good for democracy. According to him, the enormous prosperity created by technology-driven capitalism serves as an incubator for a liberal regime of universal and equal rights. The world's advanced economies have no alternative model of political and economic organization other than democratic capitalism.[31]

Will modern liberal democracy become the final form of the state? Will all nation-states be westernized? There is no certain answer. Huntington observed that underneath the third wave of democratization was the trend towards fragmentation of the world into civilizational blocs and cultural and ethnic enclaves. He has even argued that the West is unique, not universal.[32] Fukuyama has also conceded that the Asian states are unlikely to develop towards either a European or a North American model of democracy. The various deep-rooted features of all the societies will most likely lead them to develop along their own trajectories.[33]

Will globalization lead to international convergence of national economic systems? There are arguments for international convergence of economic systems. In the 1950s and 1960s, scholars argued that technological progress would cause national differences to disappear.[34] For contemporary neo-Marxists and neo-liberals, such convergence is not because of technological progress, but because of the impact of international competition, globalization, regional integration and the deregulation of domestic economies on national structures.[35]

National convergence is especially apparent in areas where globalization is resulting in common ways of producing and organizing economic life. Why is national convergence necessary? According to those who argue for convergence, this is because:

competition, imitation, diffusion of best practice, trade and capital mobility naturally operate to produce convergence across nations in the structures of production and in the relations among economy, society, and the state. Variations may be found from country to country, because of different historical legacies. But such distinctions fade over time, giving way to common economic structures whose efficiency and universality produce superior strength in the market.[36]

Globalization is also leading to national economic convergence in late developing countries. A country has to accept common market rules and structures developed first in advanced industrial nations, and indeed, they will be left out of the process of globalization and remain backward by rejecting these rules and structures. As a matter of fact, developing countries are facing increasing political and economic difficulty in maintaining economic systems that are different from the Anglo-American market pattern. This became especially apparent during the 1997 Asian financial crisis. When Korea, Indonesia, and Thailand got help from the IMF, they had to agree to a list of actions on economic policy, governance issues, and public spending that fit in with the IMF's ideas about how their countries should be run. Other countries also came under pressure from lenders and investors to change accounting and disclosure procedures and to make entry and exit to markets easier for foreigners.

Already the free flow of funds and goods around the world had placed countries under universal pressures.

On the other hand, many scholars do not believe that globalization will make national differences disappear, and they have argued for national divergence.[37] While rising levels of trade, capital flows, new communication technologies, and deregulations do reduce national diversities, they do not make these diversities disappear. National models of economic activities are still quite resilient in the face of globalization. National cultures and institutions are still important factors in shaping national economic systems both in advanced countries and in late developing countries.

Moreover, globalization has encountered national resistance and thus the future of globalization is uncertain. In many countries, globalization has generated a backlash of reaction and resistance in national politics, and new political battles have broken out over whether domestic institutions and practices in one's own society or in someone else's ought to be restructured to conform to institutions and patterns elsewhere. Therefore, "the future of convergence is likely to be shaped by growing political opposition to changes that are perceived to be the response to external pressures."[38]

Globalization and state transformation in China

As elsewhere, globalization has exerted increasing pressure on the Chinese state. In order to cope with globalization and its consequences, the Chinese state has to accommodate market forces and accept the internationally negotiated set of rules and institutions. The Chinese leadership has introduced great changes into its state system. These changes are undoubtedly pushing the Chinese state to become more modernized. In this sense, the Chinese state is becoming more Western. Nevertheless, it is debatable whether all these changes are westernizing the Chinese state. Besides importing Western state products to modernize the state, the leadership has also frequently borrowed from their own country's tradition to serve its goals. Traditional factors such as Confucian values and communist legacy have been built into modern institutions, and the functioning of modern institutions often takes traditional forms. As a result, great divergences between the Chinese state and modern Western states exist, and convergence and divergence co-exist in China.

An important question is: Why does the Chinese leadership want to converge the state to a more Western form while maintaining its Chinese characteristics or Chineseness? This study argues that national convergence and divergence in China are not only the results of national cultures and institutions. More importantly, they are the products of conscious actions by the Chinese leadership in response to globalization and its consequences. National cultures and institutions are important in shaping the form of the Chinese state, but the leadership plays an even more important role in this process. While the modernizing of the state system has become inevitable, the choice of the leadership in reshaping the form of the state is a reflection of new nationalism, the politics of cultural identity, regime survival, and the monopoly of power by the CCP. Consequently, while globalization becomes an irreversible trend, the Chinese state has also displayed its Chineseness.

For the past two centuries, political thought, institutions, and practices, as well as legal codes and economic theories, have migrated from the shores of Europe or North America to the rest of the world. Western colonization and conquest have served as vectors for the spread of the Western states. Nevertheless, as Badie argued, modern "political models are not necessarily exported consciously, nor is such an exportation part of a plot or, even less, a Western stratagem."[39] In other words, Western political models spread and become globalized because they are imported. Political leaders in developing countries like China have a great motivation to "import" the Western forms of the state. Globalization was initiated in and pushed by the West. Without participating in this process, developing countries will be further peripheralized and marginalized. To "import" the Western state is not only an act to be modern, but also an attempt to "centralize" the state in the world system. To a great degree, the modern Western state has been the model for China since the modern Western state is normally associated with strength, wealth, rationality, and efficiency.

Assuming that both national convergence and divergence are conscious choices of the Chinese leadership, this study attempts to explore the relations between the actor, i.e., the Chinese leadership, and the product, i.e., the new form of the Chinese state. By doing so, this study shows how Chinese leaders have been motivated to respond to globalization, and what constraints they have faced. It also suggests how the Chinese national context affects the consequences of globalization.

The Chinese state as an agent of globalization

In thinking about the impact of globalization on the state, most scholars have focused on advanced capitalist countries, especially in Western Europe and North America. While such studies show the reader how globalization has gained momentum, and how it has had a significant impact on the state in the advanced West, they have not paid enough attention to how states in developing countries have been affected by globalization and their response to globalization. This study attempts to explore the latter, i.e., how globalization has created an opportunity for developing countries like China to restructure their state systems.

Globalization has led to the transformation of the Chinese state. Like elsewhere, globalization in China can be understood as a process of the internationalization of Western states. To a great degree, globalization leads to international convergence of the Chinese state since the leadership has to import Western state products to cope with globalization driven by Western capitalism and states. In doing so, the Chinese state has also deliberately increased its divergence in order to accommodate and survive globalization and its consequences. Globalization has made the Chinese society more complicated and more difficult to govern and frequently leads to the rise of nationalism. Facing these challenges and enormous practical difficulties, the leadership cannot westernize the state at will; instead, it has to appeal to traditional means to cope with the negative impact of globalization. Consequently, globalization is making the Chinese state more modern while maintaining its Chineseness.

This study takes a state-centered approach to state transformation in China. It argues that the state still matters. Globalization and its attendant external forces have made the state more important than before. While market forces and transnational corporations do exert new pressures that erode some powers formerly held by the states, they have also deepened and strengthened practices that enhance state capacity. States have shown a remarkable resilience and even relatively weak states have managed to stay intact.[40]

How does the state make decisions to promote and accommodate socio-economic changes? Among various responses to this question, two theories have stood out and become the most popular ones in explaining the behavior of the state, that is, the society-centered and state-centered theories.

According to the society-centered approach, the state and the leadership are reactive. There are societal inputs to the state, and the policy choice is a dependent variable. Demand from society creates the supply of policy. The society-centered forces include the inputs from classes whether in Marxist, neo-Marxist, or dependency theory; the interest groups of pluralist theory, and public choice theory; and political parties and voters.[41] On the other hand, the state-centered approach views the state as having its own objectives. The state is autonomous, and the policy elites are active players. State-centered forces include the technocrat's approach of a benevolent government devoted to increasing national welfare, bureaucratic politics, and forces on the policy-maker on behalf of state interests. This approach as rediscovered by Theda Skocpol et al. emphasizes the autonomy of the state. According to them, the state is neither a passive agent of society at large and its various interest groups contending "horizontally," as in liberal pluralist theory, nor an "executive committee of the ruling class," as in vulgar Marxism, but rather, a dynamic independent force.[42]

Implicit in both the society-centered and state-centered approaches is a notional separation between state and society. Such a separation is theoretically useful and probably unavoidable if scholars are to attempt any kind of coherent theoretical generalization about states and societies. Nevertheless, it also raises many interrelated questions.[43] The state is autonomous from society and particular interests to a greater or lesser degree, and therefore is able to formulate and impose policy upon them. But how does this happen? What mechanisms are used to implement policy? On what basis are the policies formed, and by whom? And how does a state so separate, so autonomous, from society, obtain adequate information and get society to conform to its policies?

Such reflections have led Joel Migdal et al. to propose a "state in society" approach, which recognizes that states are embedded in societies and interact with them constantly in a process of mutual transformation.[44] Evans further argued that state structures themselves are social organizations, which need to be disaggregated and analyzed at different levels.[45] Additionally, we can also make a further argument that the state is more than an abstract entity; it is simultaneously the people who do whatever it is that the state does; there are agents of the state – individual policy-makers, bureaucrats, and administrators who are placed in authority over others.[46]

Logically, policy-makers or state agents play a most crucial rule in the formulation and implementation of policies. State agents make and implement policies in the context of state–society relations. Societal pressures and constraints and historical, cultural, and international contexts are essential variables in policy initiatives not only because they shape the perceptions, options, and actions of those who make authoritative decisions but also because they affect the consequences of those decisions. But to say that decision-making is affected by social forces is not to say that the options available to policy elites are not fully determined by the interests of social classes, organized groups, international actors, or international economic conditions, or by the hold of history or culture on policy choices. As Merilee Grindle and John Thomas argued, though these factors determine the outer boundaries of choice, decision-makers have room for maneuver and capacity to influence the content, timing, and sequence of policy initiatives.[47] Therefore, in examining the formulation and implementation of policies, one needs to look at both the perceptions and the behavior of policy elites and the constraints they encounter. Policy initiatives can only be fully understood by giving due attention to the perceptions, motivations, values, skills, and opportunities of the decision-makers and to the impact that characteristics of the decision-making process have on the choices that are made.[48]

How can the Chinese state be defined? While the Chinese state has been perceived from different perspectives,[49] this study focuses on the leadership side of the state. Since this study focuses on the role of the leadership in leading the transformation of the Chinese state, it defines the Chinese state as a technocratic state, which, to simplify matters, implies that technocrats filled leading positions at the top of China's political system.[50]

The Chinese state under Mao was often regarded as the Leviathan state, bureaucratic state, or factional state. While the Leviathan or bureaucratic state was often believed to be a predatory one, preying on its citizens for the economic benefit of an autocracy, policy elite, or bureaucracy, the factional state only responded to the interests of political factions within the state. I argue that the technocratic state has departed from such a Leviathan or factional state to a great degree. In the technocratic state, technically-trained political leaders rule by virtue of their specialized knowledge and position in dominant political and economic institutions.

China's technocratic state came into being after Deng Xiaoping came to power in the late 1970s. The so-called technocratic movement has occurred in government and CCP organizations at different levels and has introduced drastic changes into the composition of the Chinese leadership. In 1982, the CCP held its first post-Mao congress, symbolizing the establishment of the Deng leadership. During this congress, many technocrats were recruited into the Central Committee (CC). Since then, major leaders have risen and fallen owing to bitter power politics, but the momentum of the technocratic movement remains. Over the years, technocrats gradually replaced revolutionary cadres at different levels of party organizations and government units. By the Fifteenth Party Congress (1997), the movement had reached its peak. At that congress, all 7 members of the Standing Committee of the CC's Political Bureau and 18 of the 24 Political Bureau members were technocrats. The new leadership was thus called a "full-fledged technocratic leadership."[51]

The technocratic state in China, as elsewhere, has engendered a political system of "a group of specialists sharing a common social background, a common education, and a common ideology."[52] Such a state has an important impact on policy changes since it tends to deny the importance of political interest groups and claim that technically-trained experts should stand above other social and political groups to make decisions for China.

The rise of the technocratic state is a reaction to the Maoist elite recruitment policy. One major theme in Maoist China was the conflict between "red" and "expert." Mao initiated waves of campaigns against intellectuals and professionals in the first three decades of the People's Republic, particularly during the Cultural Revolution. This elite recruitment policy was reversed after Deng Xiaoping came to power because the previous policy had brought disasters to the country. The leadership began to appreciate the role of the "expert" and downplayed that of the "red." To promote the country's economic development, the "expert" had to be placed at the center of the whole system.

Moreover, the rise of the technocratic state is also the outcome of depoliticization. Political chaos during the pre-reform period resulted from Mao's political campaigns and mass mobilization. Mobilization in turn led to the politicization of social life. In contrast, recruiting technocrats into the party and government helped depoliticize the decision-making process since unlike politicians who pursue power and interests, technocrats are more concerned with rational thinking, task orientation, and problem-solving.[53] Therefore, the technocratic state helps reduce the role of ideology in policy-making. With generational changes in the leadership, the basis of authority needed to be redefined. The old revolutionaries could appeal to their charisma, revolutionary credentials and ideology for mass mobilization, but new leaders did not have such power resources and had to turn to more secular and pragmatic forms of political authority. For technocrats, ideology cannot be taken as a dogma that provides specific and infallible solutions to immediate political as well as economic issues. Even though it is hard to reduce politics to technical solutions, technocrats do have a pragmatic attitude towards reality.

Because of this pragmatism, technocrats are able to overcome difficulties to reach a consensus.[54] They can:

> evaluate even political decisions in terms of actual outcome rather than ideological value. In developing a range of policy options, each of which carries only different costs, benefits, and feasibility, this way of thinking inclines the bureaucratic technocrats toward compromise and bargaining.[55]

In discussing policy incentives, the conventional view often begins with an assumption of narrowly defined self-interest as the basis of all political action. By conceptualizing policy-makers as "rent-seekers," who are motivated only by the desire to remain in power, such an assumption often leads to pessimistic conclusions about the potential ability of policy elites to conceptualize and act upon some broader vision of the public interest. Instead, this study defines China's top technocratic leaders as having "encompassing interest" in contrast to narrow group interests.[56] While the state everywhere remains an essential variable in economic growth and modernization, as Mancur Olson argued,[57] it is particularly true in China. To use Olson's analogy, the Chinese state resembles the "stationary bandit" as opposed to the "roving bandit." Without legitimate opposition forces and democracy, the Leninist state is solely responsible for socio-economic development and modernization. Although the state often grabs economic wealth ("grabbing hand"), its encompassing interest enables it to provide a helping hand to globalization and modernization. As I will show, though the self-interests of top leaders are important, the leaders are capable of reaching a consensus on the nation's long-term interests.

Globalization: Importation and innovation

To respond to increasing pressure from globalization, the Chinese technocratic leadership does not have much choice but to "import" the form of the state from without. The leadership has to "borrow" the form of Western states, even while loudly condemning such a practice and facing strong resistance from the conservatives and society. The leadership has learned much from the West in its efforts to rebuild the state system economically and politically. The question is not whether the leadership is "importing" the Western form of the state, but why the leadership has "imported" Western products (different building blocks of the Western state) selectively, and how these "imported" parts have been strategically sought after and integrated into the existing state system.

To answer the question, we need to look at how China's technocratic leaders made their choices and understand their incentives and rewards, hopes and expectations, and constraints as well. In other words, their choice is the result of conscious decisions. As will be shown later, not only can the leadership profit from the process of "importing" the state, but more importantly, by doing so, the leadership will also be able to realize the form of the state that they perceive to be the basis of China's power and wealth. In addition, selective importation of Western state products also helps regime consolidation.

To choose Western products or to "import" the Western forms of the state is not an easy task. The Chinese leadership is torn between the logic of adaptation and the logic of innovation. The importation of Western products must be selective and its process gradual. This does not mean that the Chinese political leadership is "wrong." Importation must be accompanied by innovation which is in the interests of the leadership and society as well. In other words, in "importing" the state, China leaders have to meet various goals simultaneously, namely, coping with pressures resulting from globalization, meeting the interests of society, satisfying the interests of ruling elites, and ultimately transforming the state system.

How can these goals be achieved? Successful importation of the state depends on the strategies of the leaders, and their choice of the strategies in turn depends on their perceptions of globalization, the politics of identity, the political context of power relations among the elite, the political alignment between reformist leaders and pro-Western state social forces, and the way the existing state has been developed. While the process of how the Chinese leadership has "imported" and "innovated" the state will be described and analyzed later, some general points can be made regarding the actors and products in the process of importing and innovating the modern state.

First of all, while "importing" the state is in response to globalization and its consequences, the Chinese leadership has to avoid letting a revolution be triggered off by globalization. A revolution can bring totally new sources of political legitimacy, as shown by the 1911 republican revolution and the 1949 communist revolution. A revolution can destroy the traditional political order and thus provide a prerequisite for the leadership to build a new strong state. Nevertheless, a revolution is not what the Chinese leadership desires. To "import" the state is not to replace the existing state, but to reform it. It is a means of introducing change to the old political order and creating tensions within it, and ultimately providing institutional space for a new state.

Second, there are promoters behind the importation of the state. The process of importation produces an importing class and a new generation of westernized elites, who draw their basic values from their educational experiences and perceptions of the Western states. Globalization thus generates its own dynamics. The new class and the westernized elites serve as an important support to the reformist leadership in the process of importing the state. Nevertheless, the reformist leadership has to be cautious in soliciting political support from them. In borrowing Western ideas of modernity, rationality and efficiency, the new class and westernized elites also seek their own power. While globalization brings enormous benefits for this new class and elite groups, it also puts other social and political groups in a disadvantageous position. Therefore, any state policies which are in favor of this new class and elite can generate political tensions between these two classes and other groups and thus create social instability.

Third, the process of importation invites protest since it is a process of power reallocation. Protesters can come from within the regime, i.e., those whose power positions are undermined by globalization, and from beyond the regime, i.e., those social groups or members whose interests are threatened by globalization. Protesters have their own legitimate sources for protests. They can appeal to the politics of identity against "importing" the state. This is especially true for nationalistic intellectuals who claim to be the carrier of traditional culture and values and create discourse against the "westernization" of the state (Chapter 8).

The contradictory forces resulting from globalization require that the reformist leadership adopt a conservative globalization strategy. The leadership has to minimize political risks by claiming to be able to represent different interests. On the one hand, the leadership has to adapt the state system to the new conditions in order to tap additional resources and increase political legitimacy. On the other hand, it has to present modernity as a neutral and universal category, which is hence adaptable to any culture. By doing so, the leadership expects that social and political resistance can be overcome, and that their version of the modern state can be built.

While the leadership plays an important role in "importing" the state, the importation is realized in the context of the interplay between different social and political forces. Also, while the importation makes the Chinese state more modern (Western), the political process of importation also preserves the Chineseness of the Chinese state. Indeed, the selective importation of Western products highlights and strengthens the Chineseness of the state in many aspects.

3 Globalism, nationalism and selective importation

Understanding the perceptions of the Chinese decision-makers is paramount if we are to understand the decision to import Western state products and to integrate the country into the world system. This chapter tries to answer the question: Why does the Chinese leadership want to import Western state products selectively? I will examine how China's leaders formed their globalist worldview over the course of the country's development, and then look at why the post-Mao leadership wants to select economic rather than political products of Western states in its efforts to transform the state.

To actively promote the process of globalization the Chinese leadership had to overcome strong social resistance. Without strong and decisive political initiatives from the top leadership, China would not have signed the trade accord with the United States that paved the way for China to join the WTO. Why did the Chinese state play such a leading role in pushing for globalization? What rationale is behind the leadership's choice to do so? I argue that behind the Chinese leaders' decision to "import" the products of Western states is a mindset or mentality, i.e., globalism. China leaders seem to have no major difficulty in reaching basic consensus on what to "import" to rebuild the state system. This chapter focuses on how this new mindset among Chinese leaders has evolved since the 1990s though it will also touch on the evolution of such a mentality in the previous eras.

Globalism as a mindset

In discussing globalization in China, scholars often refer to either economic integration or institutional integration, that is, how China has been integrated into the world economy, or how China has made great efforts to join or has been pushed to join various types of international organizations.[1] Economic integration is often measured by China's foreign investment and trade, and institutional integration by China's acceptance of existing international rules and norms.[2] While these perspectives help us understand China's relations with the outside world, especially with the West, they can hardly tell us how China's globalization and its integration into the world system have affected the state system. In other words, any examination of how foreign investment and trade affect China's economy, and how institutional integration influences China's foreign behavior, do not reveal much on the actual change of China's state system. Globalization creates mounting pressure on the Chinese leadership to introduce changes into the state system, but it does not automatically affect the state system. How the state system should be changed is an enterprise for the leadership.

In order to respond to globalization, the Chinese leadership has to introduce various reforms to change the state system. Which reforms should be undertaken are determined not only by the leaders' perceptions about globalization, but also by their considerations about power, i.e., whether the specific reform measure will undermine or strengthen the power of the ruling party. Therefore, instead of defining globalization in terms of economic and institutional integration, this study goes further, and explores how globalization affects the Chinese leadership's choice of products to import from Western states.

Before political leaders can "import," they must have the willingness to do so, and then they have to consider how they can justify the importation to both themselves and the public. This is the political background behind globalism. The term "globalism" has been defined in different ways. For example, according to Robert Keohane and Joseph Nye, "globalism is a state of the world involving networks of interdependence at multicontinental distance."[3] There are different dimensions of globalism, including economic globalism, military globalism, environmental globalism, and social and cultural globalism.[4] Since this chapter focuses on perceptions of globalization, I view globalism as a state of mind regarding globalization among Chinese leaders, a mindset which not only enables them to accept the fact of globalization, but also encourages them to reform the state system by selectively importing the products of Western states.

Globalism as a mindset is dynamic as it varies in accordance to changes over generations of political leadership. There are also continuities and discontinuities between different mindsets, depending on how the political leaders perceive the impact of globalization on the Chinese state, their power considerations, and the needs for regime legitimacy.

Globalism as selective importation

Rapid globalization in China has seriously challenged the power of the state. But interestingly, the Chinese leadership did not appeal to nationalism and mobilize popular sentiments against globalization, as leaders in other developing countries did. Instead, the leadership has actively but selectively "imported" Western state products. While successful importation of economic institutional building has taken place, in the political arena, China's leaders since Deng Xiaoping have been reluctant to "import" democratic products of the Western states.

Globalism thus does not mean a wholesale importation of Western state products. Also, in dealing with imported Western products, the leadership has been cautious in their applicability to China. Innovation is imperative if a given imported product is to work effectively. This leads us to ask: What affects the choice of the Chinese leadership in deciding which Western state products to import? Why has the leadership been active in importing economic products while rejecting democratic products? How is innovation carried out on imported products? To answer these questions, globalism as a mindset has to be analyzed.

Nationalism and globalism: Historical legacy

Politically, the decision of the Chinese leaders on which Western state products to import and how to innovate imported products is based on ideological and power considerations. An immediate question arises: How can nationalism become an ideological tool to motivate the leadership to accept and encourage globalization? In other words, how did China's leaders reconcile the two seemingly contradictory 'isms' of nationalism and globalism? It is useful to look to modern history to see how the two forces interacted to form such a mindset.

Political mobilization and identity building

Nationalism and globalism are undoubtedly in tension. Nationalism is often defined as a state of mind in which the individual feels that everyone owes his supreme secular loyalty to the nation-state.[5] On the other hand, globalism, as defined above, means the leadership's willingness to import Western state products to replace the old Chinese ones or to reconstruct the Chinese state.

Since the early 1990s, Chinese nationalism has become a hot research topic among China scholars.[6] Scholars disagree with one another on the definition of Chinese nationalism, but, among others, two major themes of Chinese nationalism can be gleaned. First, nationalism has been used by the Chinese Communist Party as a response to the decline in Maoist faith, and nationalism is ready to become another vision of the CCP ideology. Second, anti-foreignism is an important facet of China's new nationalism. The rise of different but strong voices saying "No" to the West, and emotional and violent reaction to the bombing by the US-led NATO forces of the Chinese Embassy in Belgrade, Yugoslavia, seem to have confirmed this characteristic of Chinese nationalism. Regardless of what China's new nationalism is, all these scholars point to the fact that Chinese nationalism serves as a strong force resisting globalization, especially globalization in terms of westernization.

It is hard to deny the xenophobic nature of Chinese nationalism. Ever since the late Qing dynasty, a common goal among all schools of Chinese nationalists was to restore national pride, power and prosperity above everything else. To achieve this goal, anti-foreignism becomes important, among other attitudes. Dr. Sun Yat-sen, who has been regarded as the founder of the Republic of China, described Chinese nationalism succinctly when he said nationalism was to "advance China's prosperity and preserve national prestige," and "drive out the Tartar Barbarians, restore China and establish a united government."[7] Anti-foreignism has undoubtedly been a theme of Chinese nationalism in the modern era. Indeed, nationalism served as an important factor facilitating China's modernization, and it was mobilized frequently by both the Kuomintang (KMT; Chinese Nationalist Party) and the CCP in their fight with foreign powers, and their struggle for power with each other. It was also mobilized during Mao's time to promote domestic economic reconstruction and rebuild a modern nation-state. Only after Deng Xiaoping came to power and the country began its reform and open-door policy in the late 1970s was nationalism demobilized.[8]

Nevertheless, after a decade of silence in the 1980s, nationalism seems to have made a come-back since the early 1990s. What does this wave of nationalism mean for China's globalization? Wang Gungwu has argued that this new nationalism has many facets. Among others,

the most common face concerns questions of polity and stresses the recovery of sovereignty, the unification of divided territory, and national self-respect. Another is the civilization face. This emphasizes moral order and the preservation, or a rediscovery, of traditional values. [And], there is also a reactionary face, which yearns to assert superiority and dominates other peoples, and hankers for the glorious past of a great empire.[9]

I define nationalism as containing two important elements, i.e., as an identity, and as an institution. Nationalism is about nations and how the notion of 'nation' is crystallized in their institutions. It is an identity, namely, a people's awareness of its nationality and affection for it. Nevertheless, nationalism ultimately has to be expressed by institutions, that is, the nation-state. Nationalism becomes important only when it is organized as a nation-state.[10] Since the goal of China's new nationalism is to rebuild its national identity and nation-state, it is understandable that "restoration" and globalism go together, and nation-building comes with restoration nationalism. Nationalism is inextricably tied to globalism; otherwise, a national identity and a nation-state can hardly be built. While nationalism seeks to create a sense of national identity and foster national unity, globalism aims to import Western state products to augment the institutional base for nationalism.

Many factors have facilitated this restoration of national identity in modern China. First of all, modern Chinese nationalism was formed and developed as a reaction to external threats by foreign powers. National identity means national self-consciousness, which requires differentiation from other national communities. External threats have sharpened an us/them dualism.

Nationalism acts to restore China's sovereignty, prosperity and power. As long as this restoration appears to be impeded by external powers, nationalism is easy to provoke. Throughout the modern era, China's nationalists and political leaders have found that nationalism was imperative for them to build a new nation-state, and even for national survival. This sentiment existed not only among conservatives and extreme nationalists who did not see the importance of China's learning from the West and argued that China's restoration depended on rediscovering great Chinese traditions, but also among the reformers from the early self-strengtheners to the current political leadership who strongly argued that China had to learn from the West in order to be great again. Debates between the two schools were often heated and political conflicts between them intense. Nevertheless, both perceived that foreign threats were real and that nationalism was necessary to defend China.

Among earlier scholars, Liang Qichao was one of the few who contended that the Chinese did not have a sense of national identity. Liang noted that although the traditional Chinese imperial system was highly centralized, it did not play the role of a modern state. The Chinese people were patriotic, they were not nationalistic and the national identity was very weak. According to Liang, in order to build a strong modern state, a strong national identity had to be created first.[11]

It was Dr. Sun Yat-sen who spelt out how a new national identity could be constructed by showing the people how China had been threatened by foreign powers. Sun argued that China's weakness arose from its being a victim of the power competition between imperialistic states that was taking place within China. War was a conflict of imperialism between states, and the only way to fight imperialism was to revive China's lost nationalism and "to use the strength of our four hundred millions to fight for mankind against injustice; this is our divine mission."[12] Sun predicted rather solemnly that if the Chinese could not find some means to recover their lost nationalism, then China would not only perish as a nation but also perhaps as a race.[13]

How can this lost nationalism be revived? According to Sun Yat-sen, there are a few paths to that goal. First, the four hundred million Chinese people had to be awakened to realize the danger China faced from political and economic oppression by the great powers and the rapid growth of population among the foreign powers. According to him, a nation without foreign foes and outside dangers would always be ruined, and one that faced many adversities would be revived. In other words, if a nation thought that it had no outside dangers, that it was perfectly secure, that it was the strongest country in the world and foreigners would not dare to invade it, and that defense was therefore unnecessary, such a nation will crumble. So, "when we are driven to no place of escape, then we have to raise our energies to a life and death struggle with our enemies."[14]

The second approach to reviving nationalism was unity. According to Sun, the Chinese people never had national unity. If the Chinese could cooperate to achieve unity, it should be easy for them to revive their nationalism. He argued, "If the whole body of citizens can realize a great national unity upon the basis of our clan groups, no matter what pressure foreign nations bring upon us, we will not fear."[15]

Sun and his followers struggled to recover China's sovereignty by driving out foreign powers and reconstructing a new Chinese nation-state. These became the goals of the KMT. The 1923 Manifesto of the KMT stated,

In accordance with the Principle of Nationalism our Party will continue to work for the removal of all inequalities of status between our nation and foreign powers and we shall continue to work also for the integration of all the people of our country as a single Chinese nation.[16]

In 1924, the Manifesto of the First National Congress of the KMT stated,

All unequal treaties such as those providing for leased territories, extraterritorial privileges, foreign control of the customs tariff, and exercise of political authority on Chinese territories which impair the sovereignty of the Chinese nation, should be abolished, and new treaties should be concluded on the basis of absolute equality and mutual respect for sovereign rights.[17]

This was also the goal of the Northern Expedition from 1926 to 1928. In its Northern Expedition Manifesto, the KMT declared that though the Expedition was to fight against militarism and to achieve national unity, its ultimate goal was to drive imperial powers out of China.[18]

Although Mao Zedong and Sun Yat-sen were at different places on the ideological spectrum, Mao accepted Sun's view of imperialism. In 1939,

Mao argued that through wars and unequal treaties, the imperialist powers had controlled all the important trading ports, acquired extraterritoriality, operated industries, and monopolized China's banking and finance. The imperialist powers had supplied the warlords with large quantities of ammunitions and a host of military advisers to keep them fighting among themselves. Through missionary work and the establishment of hospitals, schools, and the publication of newspapers, the imperialists had conducted a policy of cultural aggression.[19]

Nevertheless, in attributing China's weakness to imperialism, Mao also saw its domestic roots, that is, Chinese feudalism. Mao pointed out, "Under the twofold oppression of imperialism and feudalism, . . . the Chinese people and particularly the peasants, have become more and more impoverished, living in hunger and cold and without any political rights."[20] According to Mao, the contradiction between imperialism and the Chinese state, and between feudalism and the Chinese people, were the sources of the Chinese revolution.

While nationalists disagreed with each other on how a new Chinese nation-state could be built, it is not difficult to see why they were ready to adopt a more radical approach in dealing with foreign imperialism, partly because they accepted different ideologies imported from the West, and partly because by claiming they were more nationalistic and thus more anti-imperialist than other groups, they were more attractive to their followers. This was especially true of the competition between the KMT and the CCP. As Wang pointed out,

Each set of leaders had to be more virulently nationalistic than their rivals. Indeed, Chiang Kai-shek squandered his many advantages over the Communists by being seen as soft on the Japanese, and the Communist forces did well to portray themselves, despite their obviously foreign ideology, as true nationalists dedicated to restore China to greatness.[21]

Importation of Western state products

Despite strong nationalistic emotions among the Chinese leaders against imperialism, they exhibited an equally strong willingness to learn from the West by importing Western state products. Enormous controversies revolved around the concept of "national essence," and different concepts of nationalism led to varying degrees of contradiction between nationalism and westernization.[22] Some people rejected the West completely, others tried to draw on Chinese traditions to be like the West, and still others attempted to draw selectively. Despite all these scholarly disagreements, political leaders like Sun Yat-sen managed to conflate nationalism and westernization and tried to show there was no essential contradiction between them. In his letter to Herbert A. Giles in 1896, Sun summarized the theme of his restoration nationalism,

To drive out the bandit remnants and reconstruct China in order to restore the order of the Ancients and follow the ways of the West, and thus cause myriads of people to be revived and all things to flourish, this is a task that fulfils Heaven's way and meets the wishes of Man.[23]

"Restoration of the ancient order" by "following the ways of the West" gradually became a mainstream sentiment among Chinese reformist officials in modern China. They, however, disagreed with each other on what and how to learn from the West. Wang observed,

For most of the 20th century, there was virtually no resistance to the idea that China had to modernize. Calls for modern schools and colleges, all using textbooks modeled on Europe, the US and Japan, were heard all over the century.[24]

Even Mao Zedong argued that the Chinese communists had to be internationalists in seeking ways to build a strong nation-state. Mao was known for his uncompromising attitude towards Western imperialism, but he also knew that China had no alternative but to "import" Western state products and then to "innovate" them. Needless to say, Mao's vision of Western products was through Marxism-Leninism. Like Sun Yat-sen, Mao managed to conflate nationalism (or what he called patriotism) and internationalism, and he genuinely believed that a communist who was an internationalist could be a patriot at the same time. According to Mao:

Communists are internationalists, but we put Marxism into practice only when it is integrated with the specific characteristics of our country and it acquires a definite national form . . . For the Chinese Communist Party, it is a matter of learning to apply the theory of Marxism-Leninism to the specific circumstances of China . . . To separate internationalist content from national form is the practice of those who do not understand the first thing about internationalism.[25]

How could nationalism and globalism become compatible in the minds of the Chinese elites? To illustrate, we can look at how political elites of a traditional Chinese Confucian perspective view imported nationalism. Confucianism is often regarded as a form of universalism. In pre-modern China, Confucian high culture and ideology were principally forms of cultural consciousness – an identification with the moral goals and values of a universalizing civilization. Without regard to national boundaries, Confucianism, which represents a universal ethic, considers a "civilized" way of life accessible to any population through education, virtue, and good government. On the other hand, modern nationalism sees the nation-state as the ultimate goal of the community. But interestingly, when nationalism was imported from the West, the Confucian elites were ready to accept this concept.

In his study of the relationship between nationalism and Confucianism in China, Wang distinguished four historical periods and found that the two "isms" were not necessarily contradictory to one another. In the first period from the 1890s to 1925, many Confucians prepared themselves to accept the new forces of nationalism, with the young nationalists being also well-schooled in the Confucian classics, and they genuinely believed that the two would support each other effectively to revive Chinese power against the external enemy, the expansionist empires of the West and Japan. During the second period from 1925 to the middle 1950s, Confucianism was marginalized by the rapid acceptance of modern Western ideas, not only science and technology but also political ideologies and economic modernization. While both the KMT and CCP accepted nationalism, they fought with each other over whether China should seek transformation and renewal through national capitalism (KMT) or revolutionary socialism (CCP). In the third period from the middle 1950s to the end of the Cultural Revolution in 1976, Confucianism was seriously attacked. In the fourth period, since Deng Xiaoping returned to power, Marxist-Leninist doctrines have been continuously revised and Confucianism gradually revived.[26] While Confucianism does not necessarily conflict with nationalism, Chinese nationalists showed no great difficulty in accepting globalism. For Confucian elites and nationalists as well, both nationalism and globalism served as means to build a strong Chinese state capable of standing up to the West.

This is especially true on the issue of importing Western state products. For a long historical period, nationalism and westernization became almost synonymous to the Chinese elites. In order to build a strong Chinese state, they had to import Western state products. Many early reformers such as Feng Guifen and Zhang Zhidong focused on balancing the Chinese traditional political order with that of the modern West. But the fact that the Qing dynasty was not able to resist foreign powers destroyed the confidence among intellectuals and officials that Chinese and Western values were on par with each other. After the fall of the Qing dynasty, the discourse of learning from the West was radicalized, and replaced by a discourse of westernization. By 1919, with the May Fourth Movement, the "restoration of the finer points of 'national essence' was challenged and more or less abandoned by all those who opposed the Nationalist government."[27]

The May Fourth Movement created a high tide of discussion on the virtue of learning from the West. On the one hand, Chinese intellectuals and officials saw how learning from the West could make China strong, but on the other hand, the intrusion of Western powers was accompanied by successive Chinese military defeats and consequent humiliation and unequal status in the world system. Since the mainstream Western model was widely perceived among Chinese leaders as an exploitative system that was impoverishing China, they began to search for an alternative. They looked to the West for an ideology that was more appealing than orthodox capitalism and liberal democracy, something that would help China stand up against the West itself. These alternatives included almost popular "isms" in the West then, such as fascism, national socialism, anarchism, federalism, socialism and communism. Yet none of these "isms" was able to provide the leadership with a feasible way to restore China's wealth and power. Only a nascent and imported nationalism, which was accepted by both the KMT and CCP, survived and played the single most important role in restoring China's greatness. It is worth noting that while nationalism became the foundation of China's nation-state building, it was heavily influenced by other "isms" which would enable China to build a strong state. For most Chinese intellectuals and government officials, facing a world of social Darwinism, China had no choice but to build a strong state.[28]

In China, the modern concept of nationalism and thus the nation-state was "imported" from the West. The spread of nationalism in China was a process of westernization of the Chinese nation-state. The Chinese imported nationalism partly because the nation-states of the European model defeated the traditional Chinese state, and partly because European nationalism in its original meanings was similar to Confucianism. In other words, some valued nationalism because of its ability to strengthen the nation-state, while others valued it because of its scientific spirit, commercial enterprise, political thought and activity. European nationalism, especially its French version, stressed popular sovereignty and the general cooperation of all people in forming the national will, as well as rational faith in common humanity and liberal progress. The French nationalists regarded "liberty, equality, and fraternity" and the Declaration of the Rights of Man and of the Citizen as valid not only for the French people but for all peoples. Chinese nationalists had no great difficulty in accepting all these values. Nonetheless, for them, the question was how a nation-state as strong as the European states could be built in order to express and support these values.

Throughout the modern era, the issue at hand for Chinese nationalists was not whether China should learn from the West, but what and how to learn. China was defeated by the Western powers, and not learning from them could endanger China as a race. What was there to learn? There was no alternative but to import Western state products. Among reformist leaders, there was virtually no question about importing

Western state products. But questions revolved around first, what to import and then, how to import them. This involved a difficult and complicated political process.

In the late nineteenth century, when Chinese leaders began to import Western state products, they found that they had to import Western military products first. This requirement stemmed from the fact that the international system then was characterized by "an age of imperialism." Among European powers and the United States, a nation's power was measured almost invariably in terms of its ability to wage war successfully.[29] Naturally, Chinese leaders saw the mighty nations of the West primarily as military powers with strong arms. Such a perception made Chinese leaders realize that if China was to gain respect abroad and to protect itself, it had to strengthen its armed forces. Military modernization was hence given the highest priority.

Despite great efforts to build itself into a modern military power, China was defeated in the Sino-Japanese war of 1894–95. China learned from the war that without a highly centralized modern state, military modernization alone would not save China. This led Chinese leaders to import other western state products.[30] Modern enterprises and business organizations were established in order to develop the domestic economy, and the government itself engaged in different forms of economic activities. However, what Chinese political leaders were most interested in was the Western political systems, especially the party system.

In his early political career, Sun Yat-sen saw the value of importing the Western democratic state. The Western European and North American multiparty system was among a few most important Western state products that had aroused Sun's interest. He truly believed that this modern system would help China realize popular sovereignty by providing Chinese people with a channel for political participation. He once claimed that he "has always insisted on governing the state through the party."[31] But soon he found that such a notion was too idealistic and would not be realized in the Chinese political context. The 1911 Republic Revolution did not help China build a strong democratic state. The new democratic political arrangements "failed to bring unity and order, not to mention legitimacy. Representative government degenerated rapidly into an autocracy hostile to popular participation and ineffective in foreign policy."[32]

After the failure of the Republic, Sun argued that the process of building a democratic state had to be divided into several stages. In his view, China could not build a democratic state out of thin air. It was also too early to declare the possibility of governing the state through the party since a state did not exist in China. Rather, in Sun's opinion, Chinese revolutionaries had to first confront China's political reality which was characterized by political chaos and social backwardness. Sun claimed that "we do not have a state to be governed. The only thing we can say is 'to build a state through the party.' After a state is built, we can then turn to govern it."[33]

The success of the Communist Party in Russia in building a new state led Sun Yat-sen to shift his attention from Western Europe and North America to Russia. From the Russian experience, Sun formed his state-building strategy, that is, "state-building through party organization."[34] The fact that Russians placed the party above the state led Sun to believe that the Russian model was more appropriate to China's state-building than European or American models. Based on Sun's strategy, the KMT was reformed and became highly organized and centralized in 1924. Sun's successor, Chiang Kai-shek, kept to the course outlined by Sun and used the party to restore unity and order, end foreign humiliation, abolish unequal treaties, regain lost territory, and ultimately restore China's lost grandeur.

Without a doubt, many of Chiang Kai-shek's state-building projects such as the Blue Shirts and the New Life Movement were quasi-fascist.[35] Nevertheless, the KMT lost the Civil War against the CCP following the Anti-Japanese War. This result was partly because the CCP claimed that it was more nationalistic than the KMT in resisting the Japanese, and partly because the CCP was more capable than the KMT in spreading its vision of the nation-state to the population. In the process of state-building, the KMT put much emphasis on the control of urban areas, and did not realize that "in a predominantly rural society, the sphere of influence of cities was much more circumscribed than in the West where such a strategy might well have proved successful."[36] Local elites, on whom the KMT heavily relied, were not able to succeed in fundamentally transforming the lives of the peasant. The KMT regime's urban-centered state-building strategy left rural areas untouched.

On the other hand, by sending its cadres and officials to rural areas, the CCP successfully transmitted its nation-state ideas to Chinese peasants. The rise of peasant nationalism finally led to the downfall of the KMT government and pushed the CCP into power.[37] Nevertheless, like the KMT, the CCP also inherited Sun Yat-sen's legacy and accepted a Leninist party-state political structure. The only difference was that the CCP abandoned Sun Yat-sen's strategy of economic construction and went one step further by eliminating capitalistic elements and establishing a planned economic system, just as its counterpart in Russia did.

Reforms, legitimacy and selective importation

From the above historical review, we can conclude that Chinese political elites have tried to build a strong modern state by importing foreign state products. They always tried too hard and too impatiently to find short cuts to restore China to the self-respect and dignity they believed only a strong modern state could bring.[38] It is also certain that the elites' perceptions about a modern state have not changed much over time, that is, a modern state should be able to pursue wealth and power in the most efficient way, and to serve the needs of the people.

These are still the main tenets of nationalism in the post-Mao era. "To build a modern state by learning from the West" continues to be the aim of reformist Chinese leaders. The present revival of nationalism, however, has not been caused by conventional threats of foreign intervention. In the past, nationalism arose from China's defeats in wars and was used by Chinese leaders to build a new national identity and new nation-state. Yet China, especially since the reform and open-door policies began in the late 1970s, has not encountered serious external threats. Why then has there been a revival of nationalism? How have nationalism and globalization come to be reconciled on the contemporary political agenda?

While the present revival of nationalism has not been caused by conventional threats of foreign intervention, it does have an external dimension: it has been provoked by the opening up of China to international relationships at all levels. While China was forced to open to the outside world in the modern era, the opening up in the post-Mao era was done deliberately so China could join the world. There has been a continuous effort to build a modern nation-state. Nevertheless, the primary push behind such effort has been all along different. In the modern era, Chinese leaders faced the danger of China being eliminated as a race by foreign imperialism. In the post-Mao era, the search for political legitimacy has replaced the foreign threat and has become the primary factor underpinning the revival of Chinese nationalism. In other words, the main sources for nationalism in the post-Mao era are domestic rather than external. This difference has led the Chinese leaders to alter their priorities when determining which Western state products to import.

Developmentalism as political legitimacy

Searching for a new base of political legitimacy has been the major theme of China's reform over the past two decades. While various reform measures have been implemented in accordance with changing economic, social and political circumstances, one major theme has stood out and remained unchanged, that is, all reforms have to enable the regime to enhance or strengthen its political legitimacy. When Deng came to power, he and his followers identified three major sources of political legitimacy: economic development, stability, and national unity. Deng viewed economic reform and development as the single most important means to cope with growing internal and external pressures, which would in turn help strengthen the political legitimacy of the CCP.

Furthermore, stability was a prerequisite for reform and development. In order to achieve stability domestically, the leadership has to maintain social and political stability and prevent any sort of chaos from occurring, and internationally, it has to adopt a "right" international strategy to solicit a peaceful environment.

Amidst its multifarious concerns, the CCP's highest priority was national unity, and the leadership was prepared to fight for national integrity at any cost. However, for Deng Xiaoping, domestic development and national unity were inextricably linked. The issue of national unity could be resolved through domestic development. National unity depended on whether rapid development could be achieved.

The failure of political reform in the 1980s

While Deng called the post-Mao reform and opening up a second revolution, he did not intend to undermine the Leninist old regime, let alone overthrow it. Instead, he meant that the old system needed to be reformed and a new economic and political order established so that China would be able to pursue economic development inside and international influence outside.[39] When Deng took over power, he inherited a Leninist state from Mao Zedong. This state was virtually rendered ineffective by waves of political movements during Mao's time, especially the Cultural Revolution. Politically, it was no longer able to provide a stable political order for Chinese society, while economically it failed to deliver economic goods to the people. Not only social members, but also party cadres and government officials lost confidence in the state, and a crisis of state identity was prevalent in Chinese society. Deng and other senior political leaders believed that such an identity crisis was rooted in China's non-development and backwardness. As is well known, the leadership therefore adopted a hardline stance against the destabilizing pro-democratic movements, while implementing a preferential policy to encourage action-oriented reform movements in both rural and urban areas.

A huge gap in the perception of political reform existed between the leadership and various social groups that had demanded radical political reform. For these social groups, especially Chinese intellectuals, political reform meant that China should follow the Western way of democracy such as political participation from below, multiparty system and freedom of expression.[40] But for the leadership, especially Deng himself, political reform only meant reforming the party and state leadership. In his well-known speech on political reform, Deng attributed the great sufferings that the party caused to the country to China's political system.[41]

In the mid-1980s, Deng began to put much emphasis on political reform. On several occasions he discussed why political reform was important for China's ongoing economic reform. According to Deng, political reform was necessary because, first of all, all economic achievements that had resulted from the reform movement had to be protected by political reform, and second, all barriers that had stood in the way of economic reform had to be removed by political reform. He indicated that political reform had to be democratization-oriented by arguing "without democracy, without socialism."[42]

It is hard to doubt the leadership's sincerity on the necessity of political reform. During the Thirteenth Congress of the CCP in 1987, political reform was a major topic on the agenda for the leadership. In the following years, political leaders, especially Zhao Ziyang, devoted themselves to vigorous debates on what types of political reforms China should engage in and how they could be implemented.[43]

Regardless of how the leadership perceived political reform, one thing was certain: political reform was to be initiated from the top and managed by the leadership. The leadership did encourage social groups to engage in heated debates about political reform, but it did not allow social discourse on political reform to become public discourse, let alone to affect the leadership's decision-making. Whenever it was deemed necessary to maintain social and political order, the leadership initiated waves of so-called anti-bourgeois campaigns, and it even cracked down on the pro-democracy movement in 1989.[44]

Growth-based legitimacy in the 1990s

In the 1990s when the Deng-centered second generation leadership was passing from the political scene, the search for new sources of legitimacy became even more important for the new leadership. While the second generation leadership could base its political legitimacy on the charisma and revolutionary credentials of individual leaders, the Jiang Zemin-centered third generation leadership did not have such qualifications. Nevertheless, the third generation leadership did not go beyond the developmentalist framework set by Deng.

The Chinese leadership perceived the 1989 pro-democratic movement as a consequence of the loosening of political control after the Thirteenth Party Congress in 1987. This perception led the leadership to tighten political control. The crackdown on the pro-democratic movement represented a huge setback both for the nascent democratic forces and for democratic-oriented reform. Henceforth, the leadership became even more cautious about initiating any new political reform.

The collapse of communism in the former Soviet Union and East Europe in the early 1990s reinforced this perception among Chinese leaders. The radical democratization in the Soviet Union and East Europe led to the collapse of communism and the breakup of the Soviet Union. The impact of what happened in the Soviet Union on the Chinese leadership should not be underestimated. Since then, no one, either conservative or liberal, has undertaken initiatives to reform the country's political system.

Regime survival became the leadership's highest priority in the early 1990s. Deng was pragmatic enough to conclude that the rise of people's power in the Soviet Union and East Europe was due to the failure of economic reform and to the unbridled opening up of political space. The former led the populace to lose confidence in the communist regimes and led the regime to lose the source of its political legitimacy, while the latter provided the people a legitimate channel to first criticize and then overthrow the party and government.

To avoid the fate of regime collapse, the Chinese leadership had to meet two basic conditions. First, it had to initiate radical economic reform, which would enable the government to provide people continuously with economic goods, and thus expand the sources of political legitimacy. Second, it initiated no political reforms, thus depriving social forces of the opportunity to participate in the political process or express their political demands. What happened inside and outside China was a somber reminder to the Chinese leadership that economic changes would lead to the rise of social forces. More often than not, it was the leadership that provided social forces with opportunities to become politically powerful. This did not mean that the leadership could afford to do nothing politically. Instead, the leadership needed to adjust the political system in accordance with the changing social and economic situation. Nevertheless, such adjustments were made independently, without input from any social forces.

How could radical economic reforms be initiated? In 1992, Deng made a high-profile tour of southern China. During the tour, Deng gave a series of talks on the reform and open-door policy. Deng's unprecedented initiative had a nationwide impact. During the Fourteenth Party Congress in 1992, the leadership revised the Party Constitution so Deng's theory became its core. The Fourteenth Party Congress ended the official debate on socialism and capitalism. The Fifteenth Party Congress in 1997 further legitimized the market economy as the country's goal in restructuring its economic system (see Chapter 4 for detail). What happened in the early 1990s led to the formation of China's model of reform, that is, "economic reform without political reform."[45] This model, despite enormous criticism against it, provided the regime with a strong base for its legitimacy.

First of all, the leadership emphasized that its reform policies had brought about rapid economic development and had provided enormous benefits to the majority of the population. As discussed in Chapter 1, the Chinese economy had experienced unprecedented growth since the reform and open-door policy, and economic performance was even more spectacular after Deng's southern tour. Impressive economic performance provided the leadership with a solid base of political legitimacy. Rapid development not only raised the living standards of the Chinese, but also propelled China into the ranks of the major economic powers in the world. Though the country is still experiencing serious income disparities among different social groups and regions, the majority of the population has benefited greatly from various reform policies. Also, people are increasingly proud of their country's economic success. The reforms and the consequent rapid development have provided the country with opportunities to recover its old glory in world affairs. It is no exaggeration to say that rapid development has led many people to feel proud, for the first time since the twentieth century, of being a Chinese. A comparison of national sentiments of the 1980s, represented by the TV series "River Elegy," with those of the 1990s, represented by bestsellers such as *The China that Says No*, shows this dramatic change.[46] The CCP and the government have shown a strong willingness to use such popular sentiments to strengthen their political legitimacy.

Second, Jiang Zemin and his colleagues have maneuvered the issue of socio-political stability to reinforce the regime's political legitimacy. The leadership has emphasized two functions of stability: stability as a prerequisite for economic growth, and stability as a justification for the regime's authoritarian rule. The utility of "stability" has changed over time. In the 1980s, party leaders had great difficulty justifying the use of stability as a prerequisite of economic reform. They attempted to use the East Asian model of development to defend the measures they had introduced to maintain socio-political stability, since they believed that it was stability that had helped East Asian countries achieve rapid and continuous economic growth. But many social groups were skeptical. They believed that by emphasizing stability, the CCP government was only trying to maintain its authoritarian rule. Throughout the 1980s, while the government consistently stressed the importance of stability, nascent social forces called for political reform to open up the political process to popular participation. These forces gradually grew into something close to a social movement by the late 1980s, as shown in the 1989 pro-democracy movement.

Without the demise of the Soviet Union in the early 1990s, the CCP would have encountered increasing pressure for political reform. The collapse of Eastern European communism and the breakup of the Soviet

Union as a nation-state radically changed the socio-political environment within China. The necessity of political stability seemed to have been "naturally" justified by what happened outside China. The notion that radical political reform would push China irrevocably along the path of the ex-Soviet Union was not far-fetched, and authoritarian rule became more acceptable as a price to pay for continuing economic improvement. The leadership certainly welcomed the changed popular perceptions on stability, and it took every opportunity to show that only the CCP was able to provide the country with stability and to guarantee continuous economic growth. In fact, the leadership believed that as long as the regime is capable of providing people with economic goods, authoritarian rule seems to be acceptable for the majority.

Third, the issue of national unity has also been used to enhance the regime's political legitimacy. It was under Deng's leadership that the country reached agreements with Britain and Portugal on the return of Hong Kong and Macao, respectively, to China. But it was Jiang Zemin who enjoyed the fruits of national unification. The new leadership has reiterated its efforts to bring together different parts of China. National unification has been a most sensitive issue which can easily arouse patriotic sentiments.[47] Therefore, the beneficial impact of Hong Kong's and Macao's return to China on strengthening the political legitimacy of Jiang's leadership cannot be underestimated.

Nationalism, selective importation and innovation

Successful economic initiatives led to a wave of importation of Western state products. Though China's economic development still has its uniqueness, it is increasingly clear that what has supported economic activities are Western forms of economic institutions.

As briefly described in Chapter 2, economic reform was not without its unique set of challenges. The implementation of the reform and open-door policy has been accompanied by an apparent weakening of central power over finance, revenues and key areas of decision-making. To a large extent, the more successful the economic reforms, the greater the threats to the present political system. Capitalistic reform measures have challenged the CCP to cleanse itself of rigidity and inefficiency, to move from the "dead hand" of centralized planning to a new combination of the visible hand and the invisible hand. The loosening of central controls has released more energy than expected. Growth has been uneven, with the favored coastal areas developing much faster than the relatively neglected interior. Many divisions of government have failed to cope with the speed of change. Further, rapid development benefited the enterprising and the bold, but unfortunately also the greedy and the corrupt. Thus the mood among the majority of ordinary people is for a stronger sense of direction, for greater checks on growth, and even nostalgia for the days when things were more certain and predictable. These desires undoubtedly pose serious challenges to the leadership.

How can the various challenges arising from capitalistic development be dealt with? We have seen different discourses regarding China's future path. Heated debates have arisen among social groups, especially intellectuals, despite tight control from the government (Chapter 8). These debates are not markedly different from those taking place almost a century ago when China faced challenges from foreign imperialism. There are not many alternative views, and some of them are more realistic than others.

Among Chinese leaders, some have argued that the country needs to be saved from the immoral and the wicked by a return to better planning and tighter controls, and powers need to be more centralized to enable the national government to correct the growing imbalance between the interior and the coastal regions. Some even have called for a return to traditional values to combat the rapid spread of Western ideas.

The more realistic and reformist leaders are less attracted to appeal to moral values and ideologies. What is of importance is to build sound political institutions to support capitalist economic activities and social transformation. In a globalized world, the Chinese leadership does not have much choice. Maoist institutional building is no longer very useful since all the elements have changed beneath an unchanged political system. Radical political reform was out of the question. A more viable alternative was a return, according to the suggestion made before by Li Hongzhang, Sun Yat-sen and others, to a willingness to follow the ways of the West selectively as a means of modernizing and making Chinese civilization great again.

Importation had to be selective, and innovation of imported products was imperative. Several factors stood out as contributing to this position. First, for the leadership, importation need not undermine the leadership and the rule of the CCP. Importation of Western state products strengthens, not weakens, the Chinese state. What the leadership desires is to change the institutional base of its political legitimacy, but not to change the ruler.

Second, radical importation has become less desirable nowadays because there are no serious external threats. Globalism is taking place in an age largely devoid of foreign imperialism. Chinese nationalism has witnessed a great transformation from pursuing power and wealth to expressing power and wealth.[48] Throughout the modern era, Chinese leaders never stopped importing Western state products as a way first to save the nation, and then to build a strong nation-state. Nevertheless, the process always occurred in the face of serious external threats. As a consequence, the emotional side of nationalism became important and anti-foreignism was a theme in different periods of nation-state building. While China was still pursuing power and wealth in the 1990s, nationalism took on a new connotation, i.e., expressing its power and wealth in world politics. Capitalist development had brought the country great wealth and power along with enormous problems. Certainly, the leadership had become more confident in selecting which Western state products to import. Importation was used not only to solve the problems the country was facing but also to build an institutional framework for newly rising economic activities and social transformation. More importantly, it was also to build an institution for China to express its power and wealth.

Understandably, for the Chinese leadership, importing Western state products is not westernizing the Chinese state, but restoring China's greatness. Wang observed that:

among the People's Republic of China leaders and intellectuals, residual hopes survived that the Chinese economic experiments today are not merely for regime-maintenance in China alone, but could be a model for other developing countries in the region, if not in the world.[49]

Historically, China has been a model for its neighbors for many centuries. With China's growing power and wealth, "it was therefore natural for the Chinese to expect their country to become a model for other countries again."[50]

The aim of becoming a model certainly has discouraged the Chinese leadership from importing Western state products without innovation. While capitalistic means have been used to develop a market economy, the leadership has been reluctant to legitimize the concept of capitalist market economy. Instead, they have insisted on using the term "socialist market economy." This was not because the Chinese leaders wanted to hide their embarrassment that capitalism was now rampant in the country, nor because they did not understand modern economics and used the term incorrectly. Instead, the concept was deliberately crafted to serve the regime's nationalistic goal. By considering divergent economic solutions to address basic problems of livelihood, Chinese leaders attempted to develop a way to position China to play its rightful role in global affairs.[51]

Deng insisted that there was no inherent contradiction between capitalism and socialism as long as both were understood as means to pursue wealth and power. Similarly, for the post-Deng Chinese leadership, there are no inherent contradictions between nationalism and globalism, or between importation and innovation. To import Western state products selectively is not to westernize China's political order, but to provide an institutional base for changing social and economic contents. To paraphrase an old Chinese saying, "Chinese learning as the base, and Western learning for application" (*zhongxue wei ti, xixue wei yong*). This has been a century-long practice in China's dealing with the outside world, and it remains relevant in explaining how post-Mao globalization is unfolding in China.

4 Power, interests and the justification of capitalism: Constructing an interest-based political order

In the *Manifesto of the Communist Party*, Marx and Engels argued:

The bourgeoisie has through its exploitation of the world-market given a cosmopolitan character to production and consumption in every country. . . . All old-established national industries have been destroyed or are daily being destroyed. . . . In place of the old wants, satisfied by the productions of the country, we find new wants, requiring for their satisfaction the products of distant lands and climes. In place of the old local and national seclusion and self-sufficiency, we have intercourse in every direction, universal interdependence of nations. And as in material, so also in intellectual product. The intellectual creations of individual nations become common property. National one-sidedness and narrowmindedness become more and more impossible, and from the numerous national and local literatures, there arises a world literature.[1]

Marx and Engels are cited here not only because this was among the earliest and best statements about globalization; more importantly, it is because this statement has been frequently quoted by Chinese government-scholars to justify globalization in China and the integration of the country into the capitalistic world system.[2] According to Gu Yuanyang, the Director of World Economy and Politics at the Chinese Academy of Social Sciences, while globalization since Marx has been associated with capitalism and the bourgeoisie, it cannot be viewed as solely belonging to the bourgeoisie as socialists are also globalists.[3] This is what Deng Xiaoping meant when he argued during his southern tour in 1992 that "the planned economy cannot be equated to socialism since capitalism also has plans; the market economy cannot be equated to capitalism since socialism also has markets; both plans and markets are economic instruments."[4]

With globalization's close association with capitalism, Chinese leaders' justification of globalization is also tied to their justification of capitalism. Without Deng's justification of capitalism, the leadership would not have promoted the country's globalization in such a radical way, and imported Western state products, albeit selectively, to rebuild China's state system.

While no consensus has been reached between the leadership and people on whether China should be globalized in a capitalistic way, the leadership has been determined in pushing China's globalization, and has made enormous efforts to facilitate the process.

Chapter 3 discussed why, and how, nationalism and globalism have become compatible in China, and how the importance of political legitimacy has pushed the leadership to selectively import Western state products. The CCP did not give up its goal of eliminating capitalism until Deng initiated the reform and open-door policy. The party has now not only justified capitalism and globalization, but also pursued capitalistic development and international integration. This transition is somewhat radical, and needs to be explained by looking beyond China's leaders' ideological justification and considerations for political legitimacy.

This chapter focuses on how politics has played an important role in pushing China's leadership to legitimize capitalism as a way of pursuing China's wealth and power. My argument is that while both nationalism and globalism justify the importation of Western state products, it is politics that has motivated the leadership to justify capitalism politically. Underpinning the Chinese leaders' ideological justification was their motivation to stay in power and establish a new socio-political order.

Passions for an interest-based social order

Deng's southern tour began China's transition from an ideologically constructed social order to an interest-based one, from a political society to an economic one. In the aftermath of the 1989 movement, the government had to provide social members with an economic "exit" in order to direct popular passions away from political interests to economic interests. While the crackdown of the 1989 movement showed social members the high cost of pursuing political interests, the opening of an economic "exit" led them to realize that the shift from political interests to economic interests would be beneficial. In Albert Hirschman's term, this is a strategy to transform people's "public action" (demands for political reform) to "private interest" (economic activities).[5] The political significance of such an economic "exit" motivated the leadership to de-ideologize capitalism as a means of economic expansion. This strategy resulted in almost a decade of rapid development and socio-political stability.

Interest has been the fundamental force that motivates or should motivate the action of the actor.[6] While "interest" motivates action, actors
define "interest" differently: interest can include honor, glory, self-
respect, an afterlife, economic advantage, etc.[7] Regardless of the various
possible definitions of "interest," this study understands "interest" as
"methodical pursuit and accumulation of private wealth."[8] An interest-
propelled action is characterized by *self-centeredness*, that is, "predominant
attention of the actor to the consequences of any contemplated action for
himself," and *rational calculation*, that is, "a systematic attempt at evalu-
ating prospective costs, benefits, satisfactions, and the like."[9]

There are political benefits in the creation of an interest-based social
order. First of all, an interest-based social order is more governable
than one based on other non-interest-based factors such as various
forms of passion because interest-guided individual behavior is more
predictable than a passion-guided act. As Hirschman noted, "A world
where people methodically pursue their private interests was . . . far
more predictable, and hence *more governable*, than one where the citizens are vying with each other for honor and glory" (emphasis in
original).[10] Second, in an interest-based social order, individual behavior
is expected to be stable and continuous. When individuals pursue "single-
mindedly material interests," their behavior will not exhibit turbulent
change.

Third, the combination of economic expansion and the onset of
an interest-based social order can make individual behavior increasingly peaceful. In what Hirschman called the French thesis of the *doux
commerce*, "commerce was often regarded as a powerful civilizing agent
diffusing prudence, probity, and similar virtues within and among trading
societies."[11] This theme was expressed by Montesquieu in the *Spirit of
Laws* when he declared, "it is almost a general rule that wherever manners
are gentle there is commerce; and wherever there is commerce, manners
are gentle. [C]ommerce . . . polishes and softens barbaric ways as we can
see every day."[12]

Fourth and even more significantly, the principle of *doux commerce* is
applicable not only to democracy, but also to other types of regime such
as monarchy and despotism. Economic expansion can soften a regime's
resolve to resort to coercion. It can even lead to regime changes by eliminating arbitrary and authoritarian decision-making by the sovereign. For
Montesquieu, with the rise of specific new economic institutions resulting from economic expansion, the state will be largely deprived of its
traditional power such as the power "to seize property and to debase the
currency at will." Furthermore, economic expansion can also empower
the people. The advance of commerce and manufacturing gives rise to a
general diffusion of the spirit of liberty, because it enhances the ability of

certain social groups to resort to collective action against oppression and mismanagement.[13]

Finally, many scholars have argued that the economic benefits from economic expansion will make the state soften its rule over economic activities and respect people's basic economic freedom. Adam Smith once argued that economic expansion and individuals' pursuit of wealth and interest could lead to a spontaneous social order. According to him, market exchange can produce a "natural progress of things toward improvement" because it induces individuals to consume and produce in rational ways. Free market exchange thus can ensure that the consumer is "led by an invisible hand to promote an end which was no part of his intention."[14] In other words, the market generates a "public interest" that encompasses national wealth, a non-coercive society, and the freedom to choose and cooperate that emerges when individuals have the option and incentive to make rational choices.[15]

Surely, it is all these advantages of an interest-based social order that have led the Chinese leadership to justify capitalism. The leadership has been quite successful in organizing an interest-based social order and drawing benefits from such an order in the 1990s. But rapid capitalistic development soon generated enormous contradictions between the existing political order and the emerging social order, which in turn created pressure for building a new political order in accordance with such an interest-based social order.

Economic expansion and political interests

In the pre-reform era, China can be regarded as a politically constructed society. It was organized in accordance to major political leaders' perceptions of what a society should be and realized by forceful organizational weapons. As Franz Schurmann correctly pointed out in the 1960s, "Communist China is like a vast building made of different kinds of brick and stone. However it was put together, it stands. What holds it together is ideology and organization."[16]

The leadership under Mao Zedong initiated various political experiments, especially during the Cultural Revolution from 1966 to 1976, to reorganize China, basically according to Mao's own utopian ideals of society. Whatever Mao did, his aim was to eliminate all possible private space and politicize the Chinese society. Totalitarian state power penetrated every corner of society and coercive institutional mechanisms were used to snuff out private space and manage public space.[17] Various organizational measures such as the household registration (*hukuo*) system, the work unit (*danwei*) system and other enormous mass organizations made China resemble "a conscription society."[18]

A highly organized and politicized society, together with a planned economy, enabled the party-state to mobilize numerous social groups into the political arena, and thus created new power resources within the Chinese society to implement profound tasks of social engineering such as land reform, collectivization, and nationalization of business and commerce. Nevertheless, over time, the reach of the party-state was shortened. As Vivienne Shue has pointed out, the highly organized and efficacious party-state gradually degenerated into a regime obsessed with ideology and lacking almost any genuine social base beyond its party-state apparatus; and eventually it becomes increasingly difficult to govern either legitimately or effectively.[19]

In the late 1970s, the Deng leadership began to shift its emphasis to economics as a way of reorganizing the country.[20] In the 1980s, China achieved high rates of economic growth by expanding its market space.[21] But it was only after Deng's southern tour in 1992 that the Chinese leadership legitimized capitalism as a way of promoting economic expansion.

Why was the CCP not able to legitimize capitalism in the 1980s? After the bitter and uncertain thirty years of experimentation following 1949, many leaders realized that learning from capitalism conforms to historical necessity, and capitalism is a stage that cannot be skipped on the way to socialism. Although the party had an idea of the nineteenth-century capitalism that Marx drew inspiration from, the reform and open-door policy enabled party cadres and government officials to see what had happened to capitalism in China's neighbors, especially the four little dragons (Hong Kong, Taiwan, Singapore, and South Korea), besides Japan and the United States. The leadership saw how capitalism had helped raise the standard of living of the vast majority of the people in these economies, and had enhanced their status in international arenas, goals that the CCP had fought for since its establishment.[22] The leaders realized that if China wanted to achieve rapid economic growth, its economic system had to be overhauled. This was the motivation behind the decision of the leadership to implement economic reforms. Many social groups, especially young intellectuals, advocated publicly for capitalism, genuinely believing that capitalism could pave the way for China to grow into a strong and affluent nation. Spurring the country on was the capitalist West, which was quite friendly to China in the 1980s, as they believed China's market-oriented economic reform and open-door policy would eventually lead to two transformations, that is, from a planned economy to a free market system, and from political authoritarianism to democracy.

However, in that decade, the Chinese revolutionary leaders had quite different perceptions of the market economy and capitalism.[23] While at the practical level, they did not oppose carrying out different forms of capitalistic experiment, ideologically, they were unwilling to legitimize capitalism.[24] It was only after they saw that market economy did not harm the socialist system which they had fought hard for that they became willing to recognize its legitimacy. This can be seen from changes in the official definition of China's economic system. At the CCP's Twelfth Congress in 1982, the leadership defined the country's economic system as one in which the "planned economy is the main pillar and market economy a supplementary element." The market economy did not have even theoretical legitimacy then. Five years later in 1987, at the Thirteenth Congress, the leadership defined the economic system as one "combining planned and market economies;" here the market economy acquired a status equal to that of the planned economy in party ideology. However, in the aftermath of the 1989 pro-democracy movement, capitalism came under serious attack. Conservative leaders regarded the development of the pro-democracy movement as the result of the spread of capitalism as an idea and as a practice.[25]

Why then did a sudden change take place after Deng's southern tour? Besides the imperative for regime survival and political legitimacy as discussed in the previous chapter, Deng's determination to develop a market economy undoubtedly played an important role in leading to such a drastic change. Deng was known for his pragmatism throughout his entire political career. He was not particularly against capitalism as a way to promote economic growth. While Mao Zedong emphasized "morality" or "virtue" as a way of motivating people's behavior, Deng seemed to favor "interests." While Mao tended to use a political approach to organize society, Deng favored an economic one. Although Deng set xiao-kang (a comfortable standard of living) as the country's target of economic development in the late 1970s, it was not until the 1990s, after more than a decade's search, that he realized that capitalism was the only way to achieve that goal.[26]

This, however, does not fully explain why Deng worked so hard to persuade the leadership to legitimize capitalism and why the party accepted capitalism, which it had strongly opposed in the previous decades. Two important and subtle issues are involved here. First, the political interests of the regime were restructured after Deng's southern tour, the need for reconstruction first being perceived by Deng himself, and later accepted by the new leadership. Second, the reconstruction of political interests created an ideological rationale for capitalism as a way to reorganize society. In other words, Deng believed that it was possible for the party to

Table 4.1 Gross industrial output in China, 1980–98

Year	State-owned enterprises %	Collective-owned enterprises %	Individually owned enterprises %	Other types of enterprises %	Total%
1980	76.0	23.5	0	0.5	100
1985	64.9	32.1	1.9	1.2	100
1990	54.6	35.6	5.4	4.4	100
1991	56.2	33.0	4.8	6.0	100
1992	51.5	35.1	5.8	7.6	100
1993	47.0	34.0	8.0	11.1	100
1994	37.3	37.7	10.1	14.8	100
1995	34.0	36.6	12.9	16.6	100
1996	33.7	36.5	14.4	15.4	100
1997	29.8	35.9	16.9	17.4	100
1998	26.5	36.0	16.0	21.5	100

Source: calculated from the State Statistical Bureau, Zhongguo tongji nianjian 1999 (China Statistical Yearbook 1999) (Beijing: Zhongguo tongji chubanshe, 1999), p. 423.

make use of capitalism to strengthen its political legitimacy, while fending off any negative political consequences associated with capitalism.[27]

The rise of an interest-based social order

An interest-based social order is not the natural result of economic expansion, but a conscious pursuit by the party and its leadership. What the leadership pursued was not only economic expansion *per se*, but also beneficial political consequences from rapid economic expansion. What motivated the leadership's conscious pursuit was a crisis of political legitimacy resulting from drastic changes in China's internal and external environments in the late 1980s and early 1990s. Without such a crisis, capitalism would not have been justified as a means of economic expansion, and an interest-based social order would not have been legitimized in party ideology. Without the leadership's conscious pursuit, an interest-based social order would not have been developed at such a fast pace; and without an interest-based social order, a decade of relative peace and stability would not have been possible.

Economic expansion has generated enormous political benefits, not only because it increased the regime's political legitimacy; more importantly, it has changed the structure of space in the country. The conscious pursuit of economic expansion has led to the emergence of an

Table 4.2 The development of the private sector in China, 1989–97

	Private enterprises*				Individually owned and operated enterprises*			
	Number	Change %	Employees (million)	Change %	Number (million)	Change %	Employees (10,000)	Change %
1989	90,581		1.6		12.5		19.4	
1990	98,141	8.3	1.7	3.7	13.3	6.5	20.9	7.8
1991	107,843	9.9	1.8	8.2	14.2	6.7	22.6	7.9
1992	139,633	29.5	2.3	26.1	15.3	8.3	24.7	9.3
1993	237,919	70.4	3.7	60.8	17.7	15.2	29.4	19.1
1994	432,240	81.7	6.5	73.3	21.9	23.8	37.8	28.5
1995	654,531	51.4	9.6	47.5	25.3	15.6	46.2	22.2
1996	819,252	25.2	11.7	22.2	27.1	7.0	50.2	8.7
1997	960,726	17.3	13.5	15.2	28.5	5.4	54.4	8.5
1998	1,200,978	25.0	17.09	26.7	n.a	n.a	n.a	n.a
1999	1,508,857	25.6	20.22	18.1				

* According to the definition given by the Chinese government, "private enterprises" refer to those with more than eight employees and "individually owned and operated enterprises" refer to those with less than eight employees. Annual percentage change in number of employees may not be exact due to rounding off of figures of number of employees.

Sources: Adapted from Zhang Houyi and Ming Zhili (eds.), Zhongguo siying qiye fazhan baogao 1978–1998 (A Report on the Development of Private Enterprises in China, 1978–1998) (Beijing: Shehui kexue wenxuan chubanshe, 1999), pp. 60, 66; The State Statistical Bureau, Zhongguo siying jingji nianjian (The Yearbook of Private Businesses in China, 2000) (Beijing: Zhongguo tongji chubanshe, 2000), p. 402.

interest-based social order,[28] which in turn has resulted in the creation and expansion of a private arena.[29]

The rapid expansion of the private space is reflected in the decline of the state sector and the development of the non-state sector, as shown in Tables 4.1 and 4.2. From Table 4.1, we can see that the gross industrial output by the state-owned enterprises declined from 55 percent in 1990 to 27 percent in 1998, while that by individually owned enterprises increased from 5 percent to 16 percent during the same period. The non-state sector, comprising individually owned enterprises, collective-owned enterprises and other enterprises, has outstripped the state sector.

The private sector has become economically significant. For example, it consumed 4 percent of the total retail sales in 1996, and the figure increased to 13.5 percent in 1999. During the same period, the industrial and commercial taxes paid by the private sector increased from 1 percent to 2.6 percent of the national total.[30] The private sector has become even more important in its contribution to revenue streams at local

Table 4.3 Contribution to revenue by private enterprises and
individually owned enterprises, 1986–98*

	Tax revenue (billion yuan)	% of the total budgetary revenue	% of the total GDP	% of the total industrial output
1986	4.93	2.32	0.48	2.76
1990	14.57	4.96	0.79	5.39
1991	17.42	5.53	0.81	4.83
1992	20.33	5.84	0.76	5.80
1993	29.34	6.75	0.85	7.98
1994	37.03	7.10	0.79	10.09
1995	42.96	6.88	0.73	12.86
1996	46.96	6.34	0.69	15.48
1997	56.79	6.56	0.76	17.92
1998	70.00	7.09	0.89	17.11

* "Private enterprise" and "individually owned enterprise" are two different concepts in China, the former refers to enterprises which have more than eight employees, while the latter refers to those enterprise which have fewer than eight employees.
Source: Hu Angang (ed.), *Zhongguo tiaozhan fubai* (China: Fighting Against Corruption) (Hanzhou: Zhejiang renmin chubanshe, 2001), p. 50.

levels. According to a calculation, as of the middle 1990s, the private sector had contributed about 10 percent of the total tax revenue at the provincial level, 20 percent at the prefectural level, and 30 percent at the county level.[31] For instance, in 1996, the private sector in Zhejiang contributed 4.4 billion yuan in industrial and commercial taxes, equivalent to 13.4 percent of the total industrial and commercial taxes in that province. In some rich areas, the private sector contributes as much as 60 percent of township revenue.[32]

While the private sector has become increasingly important, its motivation to pay tax revenue to the state is low. For example, in 1999, the private sector consumed 13.5 percent of retail sales of consumer goods, but paid only 2.6 percent of total industrial and commercial taxes. The low incentive to contribute revenue is also reflected in Table 4.3. From 1986 to 1992, revenue contribution by the private sector was largely in accordance to its share of the total national industrial output. After 1992, the gap between the two has increased dramatically. For instance, in 1998, while the private sector contributed only 7 percent of the total national budgetary revenue, its share of total industrial output was more than 17 percent.[33]

The rapid expansion of private space has undermined the old ideologically constructed social order. The household registration system has been eroded since the emergence of a market economy in the 1980s.

With basic daily necessities available through the market, the state was no longer able to effectively control population movement from rural to urban areas, from interior to coastal areas, and from small to large cities. The system was further undermined by intensive economic competition among regions. To attract talented people, many cities have substantially relaxed the registration requirements for the employment of non-local residents.[34]

In Russia and some other East European communist states, the collapse of the ideologically constructed social order resulted in socio-economic chaos. But this was not the case in China. The creation and expansion of a private arena explains the key difference in outcomes. Although the rise in private space is confined to the non-political arena, it has significant political implications. First of all, it provides societal members with an "exit" from the public arena. Without such a private exit, societal members have to struggle for what they want in a highly politicized public arena. When societal members fight hard to win, sometimes at any cost, in the public arena, political conflict among individuals intensifies. The expansion of a private arena reduces greatly the intensity of political conflicts, and thus the political burden on the party and the government.

Second, the existence of a private arena makes it possible for citizens to remain apolitical, if they do not need to be involved in politics. In an ideologically constructed society, political indifference is possible, but politically risky. Since all economic benefits are distributed through political means, societal members ignore politics at their own peril. In contrast, an interest-based social order not only allows people the option to stay out of politics, but also encourages them to devote themselves to economic activities. In other words, political indifference is no longer risky, and politically indifferent citizens can obtain their basic necessities through the market.

Third, with the creation of an interest-based social order, China's economic development has been elevated to a more stable and predictable footing. In an ideologically constructed social order, political change would inevitably affect economic activities. In the worst case scenario, economic activities would be held hostage to the dictates of politics. But in an interest-based social order, economic activities are less affected by political changes and have a momentum of their own. An interest-based social order has an inherent capability to resist the impact of political changes. This does not necessarily mean that the government is less interventionist in regulating economic activities, but it is the case that any decision undertaken by the government in the economic realm is increasingly based on economic considerations or in favor of an interest-based social order. This will further enhance the legitimacy of the government.

Table 4.4 Background of owners of private enterprises in China (1) (percentage)

Original position	Business established before 1988	Business established between 1989 and 1992	Business established in 1992	Total
Professionals	1.9	4.3	4.9	4.6
Party cadres	19.8	16.0	25.5	25.5
Workers	13.2	8.6	10.8	10.7
Peasants	20.8	17.9	15.8	16.7
Household-business owners	35.8	46.3	36.9	38.2
Others	8.5	6.8	6.1	6.5
Total	100	100	100	100

Source: Zhang and Ming (eds.), Zhongguo siying qiye fazhan baogao 1978–1998, p. 153.

How political order was affected

The rise of an interest-based social order was beneficial in enhancing the legitimacy of the party-state in an early stage. Nonetheless, a continuously expanding interest-based social order has generated its own dynamics with consequences beyond the intention of Chinese leaders. In particular, an interest-based social order has gradually undermined the existing political order and created pressure for political reform of the leadership.

With rapid economic expansion, the private arena has become more profitable than the public arena. The nascent interest-based social order has thus attracted not only societal members, but also party cadres and government officials. This is especially true in the period after Deng's southern tour. Party cadres and government officials were allowed, even encouraged, by the reformist leadership to turn to business. This soon resulted in a nationwide wave of *xiahai* (literally "plunging into the sea").[35] As shown in Table 4.4, in 1992, party cadres and government officials were the second largest group (25.5 percent) to establish private businesses, after household business owners (36.9 percent). By the middle 1990s, as shown in Table 4.5, they had become the largest group in private enterprises.

In allowing such development, the reformist leadership sought to reduce their perceived political resistance to radical economic reforms. To a great degree, the goal was realized. But it was achieved at a high cost.

Table 4.5 Background of owners of private enterprises in China (2)
(percentage)

	1993 survey			1995 survey		
	Urban areas	Rural areas	Total	Urban areas	Rural areas	Total
Professionals	3.9	1.6	3.3	4.1	2.3	3.3
Cadres in urban state & collective sectors	43.2	16.6	36.3	33.2	11.8	24.0
Rural cadres	4.1	16.9	7.5	3.5	11.2	6.8
Cadres in the non-state sectors	11.2	17.9	13.0	11.0	17.9	14.0
Peasants	4.4	16.3	7.5	6.3	17.3	11.0
Workers	22.9	11.4	19.7	21.7	17.5	19.9
Small-scale individual business owners	8.8	18.2	11.2	15.8	18.1	16.8
No occupation	1.5	1.0	1.4	4.5	3.8	4.2

Source: Lau Siu-kai, et al. (eds.), *Shichang, jieji yu zhengzhi* (Market, Class and Politics) (Hong Kong: Hong Kong Institute of Asian-Pacific Studies, The Chinese University of Hong Kong, 2000), p. 328.

First of all, many talented people moved from the state to the private arena, especially those who had promoted China's market reform. Since they had been involved in new forms of economic activities, they were more knowledgeable than others on how to make profits in an emerging market. Such an "exit" indeed weakened the ranks in leadership. Second, party cadres and government officials were given opportunities to utilize their public power to gain private economic benefits. For example, party cadres and government officials attempted to build up their connections (*guanxi*) with the private sector. In a survey conducted in 1993, when asked to name their closest friends, private entrepreneurs noted the following: professionals (16.6 percent), cadres in the government sector (24.4 percent); cadres in SOEs (18 percent), workers (1.3 percent), farmers (3.7 percent), specialized artisans (6.4 percent), staff in the service sector (9.5 percent), small enterprise owners (8.9), and others (2.9).[36] According to the study, in building their connections with the private sector, party cadres and government officials aimed to: 1) gain economic benefits for themselves and their family members; 2) search for opportunities to *xiahai*, i.e., to leave the government sector and turn to business; and 3) seek political support from the private sector due to its increasing political importance.[37]

When public power is used for economic benefit, corruption becomes inevitable and increasingly serious. While in the old days political loyalty was the most important standard used to evaluate the political achievements of party cadres and government officials, "money" has now replaced political loyalty. Corruption has undermined not only the effectiveness of the government, but also popular confidence in the government. The question of political legitimacy has once again loomed large for the party and the government.

The rise of an interest-based social order has also rendered ideological decline irreversible. An interest-based social order accords official ideology a much less prominent role in regulating the daily life of party cadres and government officials, let alone societal members. Indeed, in order to promote rapid economic development, the leadership downplayed the role of ideology. The official ideology has shifted from an offensive position to a defensive one, i.e., from being a means to control party cadres, government officials and to guide decision-making, to providing justification for party and government policies. There is nothing wrong with this transformation. Both the leadership and the country have benefited greatly from it. However, it has given rise to some unexpected consequences.

The most serious threat is that the party is facing increasing pressure to incorporate rising social forces into its political order. The CCP made a conscious effort to establish an interest-based social order, with the aim of encouraging people to be distracted from political interests and turn to economic interests. This strategy was rather successful. After the party legitimized capitalism in the early 1990s, societal members focused their energies on money-making, and their political passions subsided. So did the political pressure on the party and the government. To a great extent, the government has gained legitimacy from this interest-based social order. But an increase in legitimacy has been achieved at the expense of political indifference. Although political indifference has reduced the political burden on the government, it has correspondingly made the existing political order increasingly irrelevant to an interest-based social order. In other words, the emerging social order has yet to be integrated into the existing political order, and therein lies the greatest danger. This social order is largely based on economic interests. This does not mean, however, that the interests of this social order will not change. Once this social order begins to demand its own share of political space, there would be great political pressure on the regime.

The nascent social order has a great incentive to demand its own share of political space since government policies have an impact on its rise and fall. Table 4.6 sets out the results of nationwide surveys of businesspeople conducted in 1995 and 1997. Taxation policy, credit policy,

Table 4.6 Key political factors affecting private businesses

	1995	1997
Legal protection of property rights	5.1	4.1
Government propaganda	5.0	6.0
Taxation policy	18.8	n.a.
Credit policy	31.8	27.2
Government macro-economic adjustment	23.6	17.9
Industrial and commercial management	2.6	31.9
Household system	0.6	5.2
Ownership	5.0	0.4
Others	7.5	7.2
Total	100	100

Source: Zhang and Ming (eds.), *Zhongguo siying qiye fazhan baogao 1978–1998*, p. 150.

Table 4.7 Social problems with the most serious negative impacts on private businesses

	1995 (%)	1997 (%)
Unjust income distribution	5.1	9.9
Exchange between power and money	37.3	37.6
Worsening public order	20.6	41.1
Arbitrary fees, arbitrary fines, and arbitrary levies	31.4	6.3
Business involvement of government and military in businesses	2.6	3.9
Others	8.1	1.3
Total	100	100

Source: Zhang and Ming (eds.), *Zhongguo siying qiye fazhan baogao 1978–1998*, p. 148.

government macro-economic adjustment, and industrial and commercial management, among others, were seen as the most important political factors affecting their business activities. More and more, private businesspersons expect to participate in policy-making or at least to have some input into policy-making. Moreover, the private sector has been affected not only by relevant government policies, but also by various forms of social and political practices prevalent in China. As shown in Table 4.7, "exchange between power and money," "worsening public order" and "arbitrary collection of fees, fines and levies" have been regarded as having had the most serious impact on private businesses. To change

Table 4.8 Representatives from the private sector in political
organizations

Year	Representatives in the People's Congress at the county level and above	Representatives in the CPPCC at the county level and above*	Representatives in mass organizations**
1990	5,114	7,238	4,603
1994	7,296	11,721	7,671
Change	42%	62%	67%

*CPPCC: The Chinese People's Political Consultative Conference
**Such as the Communist Youth League, and the Women's Federation
Source: Zhonghua gongshang shibao (China Industrial and Commercial Daily),
April 29, 1996.

such social and political practices is no easy task and would require the
political participation of private businesspersons.

Indeed, private entrepreneurs have been making great efforts to participate in the political process, especially in local politics. No systematic
national statistics are available to show the degree of political participation
by private businesspersons. But as shown in Table 4.8, a rapid expansion
of their involvement in local politics took place in the early 1990s. According to a survey conducted in 1993, on average, each private entrepreneur
had membership in 2.75 organizations such as private enterprise associations, guilds, different democratic parties, Youth League, and even the
Chinese Communist Party. Almost 84 percent of private entrepreneurs
believed it imperative to establish their own organizations.[38] Joining the
CCP is another way for private entrepreneurs to influence China's political process. According to various surveys, more and more private entrepreneurs have joined the party. In 1993, among private entrepreneurs,
13 percent were CCP members, 17 percent in 1995, and 16.6 percent in
1997. In 2000, this figure increased to almost 20 percent, far higher than
for other social groups such as workers and farmers.[39]

Political participation by private entrepreneurs is still extremely limited at the national level. For example, only 46 out of more than 2,000
representatives of the Ninth Chinese People's Political Consultative
Conference in 1998 were private businesspersons.[40] A low degree of political participation has caused dissatisfaction among this group. As shown
in Table 4.9, while self-evaluation by private businesspersons about their
economic and social status has been consistent, that of their political
status has deteriorated. It is worth noting that their self-evaluation for
political status was lowest in 1997, the year the private sector was formally legalized by China's Constitution.[41]

Table 4.9 Self-evaluation by private businesspersons
of their economic, social and political status

	Economic status	Social status	Political status
1993	4.5	4.0	4.6
1995	4.5	4.2	5.1
1997	4.7	4.6	5.7

The highest score: 1.0   The lowest score: 10.0
Source: Zhang and Ming (eds.), *Zhongguo siying qiye fazhan baogao
1978–1998*, p. 163.

Against an interest-based political order

Strong demands for political participation from private entrepreneurs
and their actual penetration into China's political process, especially at
local levels, have worried China leftists such as Deng Liqun and other
old style ideologues. Before the party's Fifteenth Congress in 1997, the
leftists mounted a major "ideological" campaign, warning of the political
threat from the rising entrepreneur class. They were afraid that such a
development would change the socialist nature of the regime, with the
bourgeoisie and its representatives taking over political power. As a widely
circulated *Wan Yan Shu* (literally 10,000-word letter) stated,

An economy of state ownership is the pillar of the Chinese state. State enterprises
are where China's industrial workers are located and are sources of national revenues. The shrinking of state enterprises will necessarily lead to the weakening
of the party's leading position and the decline of central power and its capacity
to cope with various problems, thus posing a serious threat to the CCP regime.
[Moreover], a rising private sector is increasingly becoming the underlying force
behind the newly emerging bourgeoisie and their political demands. Historically,
during their rise to prominence, the European bourgeoisie won their struggle for
political power on the basis of the principle of "without representatives, without taxes." Representatives of the Chinese bourgeoisie have also begun to "buy,"
through the "taxation mechanism," "public goods" from the government such as
the rule of law, order, national defense, and even democracy.[42]

Despite the controversies and political resistance from the left, the party
congress in 1997 further legitimized the private sector, and a constitutional amendment the following year formally provided constitutional
protection for private ownership. Once the private ownership was legitimized and given constitutional protection, the next logical question was:

should private entrepreneurs join the party and share political power with other traditional ruling classes such as workers and farmers? In 2001, a year before the party's Sixteenth Congress, the leftists again mounted a campaign to oppose the admission of private entrepreneurs into the party. Among other vocal opponents, Lin Yanzhi, Deputy Secretary of the Jilin Provincial Committee of the CCP, published a long paper in *Zhenli de zhuiqiu*, a Beijing-based leftist journal.[43]

Like other leftists, Lin argued that a new bourgeoisie had formed in China and posed a serious political challenge to the power of the CCP. The formation of this new class, according to Lin, can be measured not only by statistical data, but also by its organization. According to statistics, the size of this new class already outnumbered the old bourgeoisie class. For instance, in 2000, China had 1,760,000 privately owned enterprises, ten times the number in 1956; and they employed more than 2 million workers, 7 times as many as in 1956; and their total assets reached 1,330.7 billion yuan, 30 to 40 times the value in 1956.[44] Furthermore, this new class has various forms of organizations at both national and local levels, their own ideological representatives such as pro-privatization economists, and propaganda machines such as liberal-oriented journals and newspapers.[45]

According to Lin, although the new bourgeoisie had grown out of China's communist system, the exploitative nature of this new class had not changed. Many new capitalists were former CCP cadres and government officials, who had lost their party (CCP) identity after they entered the business world. The new class is as exploitative as its predecessors in old China and in the world Marx described.[46] Worst, it is undermining the very foundation of the socialist system. In the old days, the bourgeoisie tended to support the socialist system since Chinese capitalists then were also exploited by foreign capitalists. This allowed the CCP to form an alliance with this class in its struggle for a socialist system. But nowadays, the newly rising bourgeoisie class does not have any experience of being exploited by foreign capitalists. Many of them indeed view the socialist system as the barrier to their further development, and they attempt to lead China towards capitalism. Therefore, it is imperative for the CCP to "lead and control" (*lingdao he jiayu*) this new class.

How can the CCP lead and control this rising new class? The key lies in making the new bourgeoisie "voluntarily accept the CCP's leadership."[47] According to Lin,

The key to control socialist market economy is to control bourgeoisie and its capitalist component; the key to control the bourgeoisie is that there is no capitalist within the party; and the key to no-existence of capitalists in the party is to see clearly their true colors [emphasis in original].[48]

Specifically, two main measures should be taken to enable the party to "lead and control" the bourgeoisie. First, the party must consolidate "the dominant position of the state economy, and enable the state sector to lead and control the whole national economy. *The bottom line is that the private economy cannot be larger that the state economy*" (emphasis in original).[49] Second, the party must maintain its purity. Lin argued that:

the CCP cannot recruit capitalists, and there cannot be any representatives of the bourgeoisie within the party. Only organizational purity will enable the party to recognize [the bourgeoisie] thoroughly, to unify its guiding principle, to empower its cohesiveness and fighting capacity, and to lead socialist market economy [emphasis in original].[50]

According to Lin, the recruitment of capitalists in the party will generate enormous negative consequences for the party, and the party's survival will be threatened. The party will face three main threats. First, the recruitment of capitalists will lead to pluralism within the party. Lin contended,

The pluralization (*duoyuanhua*) of classes within the party means to provide an organizational foundation for political pluralism and thought pluralism. *A pluralist party will inevitably lead to dissensions.* [And] only a unified CCP will be capable of leading pluralist economies and pluralist classes in China [emphasis in original].[51]

Second, the recruitment of capitalists implies that the CCP supports the exploitative system. Lin believed that the CCP aimed to eliminate the exploitative system; but once such a system becomes legitimized, the CCP has to change itself completely. According to him, "*once these capitalists enter the party, they will first devote all their energy to struggle for leadership of and change the nature of the party. And, such changes are irreversible*" (emphasis in original).[52] And, third, the party will become alienated from the workers and peasants. These two traditionally leading classes have been the very foundation of the CCP leadership. Given the capitalists' strong economic power, once they enter the party, worker and peasant party members will become subordinate to the capitalists. Consequently, the CCP will have no choice but to give up its leadership.[53]

Similarly, Zhang Dejiang, Party Secretary of Zhejiang Provincial Committee of the CCP, strongly argued that private entrepreneurs should not be allowed to join the CCP.[54] Zhejiang was among the few provinces where the private sector had made rapid inroads and had played an increasingly important role in the local economy and even politics. Zhang's strong opposition clearly suggested that there was no consensus within the party leadership on the political role of the private sector. Indeed, such arguments were representative of and were popular among old style leftists.

The admission of private entrepreneurs into the party has been a very controversial issue within the party. The private sector played an important role in the pro-democracy movement in 1989, and many private entrepreneurs not only contributed financial resources to the movement, but also played a leadership role.[55] In the aftermath of the 1989 crackdown, the Central Committee of the CCP issued a regulation on August 28, 1989, entitled "A Notice on Strengthening Party Building" (Document no. 9, 1989), stating, "Our party is the vanguard of the working class. Since an exploitative relationship exists between private entrepreneurs and workers, private entrepreneurs cannot be recruited into the party."[56] Jiang Zemin, who had then been summoned to Beijing to replace Zhao Ziyang as Party Secretary of the CCP, was among the major proponents of this regulation. At a national party conference on August 21, 1989, Jiang argued that:

I completely agreed with the regulation that private entrepreneurs cannot join our party. Our party is the vanguard of the working class. If we allow those who do not want to give up exploitation and those who live on exploitation to join the party, what kind of party are we going to build?[57]

After Deng's southern tour, the private sector developed rapidly. More importantly, the *xiahai* movement pushed many party cadres and government officials to turn to businesses and become capitalists. More and more private entrepreneurs joined the Party throughout the 1990s. Liberals within the party proposed that the party should allow private entrepreneurs to join so as to expand the party's social base. For example, Guo Shichang, vice governor of Hebei province, argued in a conference on economic reforms that "the dynamics of economic development in our province lies in the private economy in the future. All departments concerned must provide support and protection to the development of the private economy."[58] Li Junru, a well-known theorist of the CCP, argued that the party should legitimize private entrepreneurs' party membership.[59] Such liberal arguments triggered strong reactions from the leftist side.

Constructing a new political order

The new leadership has made great efforts not only to legitimize and institutionalize this interest-based social order, but also to search for a political order which will be compatible with this emerging social order. While the party-state has attempted, with some success, to incorporate selective social groups into the regime, it will not tolerate any direct democratic challenge to its authority. This uncompromising stand is well illustrated by the reaction of the authorities to attempts by Chinese pro-democracy activists to organize an opposition party towards the end of the 1990s. Within a short span of a few months in 1998, the preparatory committees of China's Democracy Party were established in twenty-three out of China's thirty-one provinces and major cities. Applications to register the new party were made in fourteen provinces and cities.[60] Given the democratic movement's potential to mount a serious political challenge, the authorities swiftly crushed it. As long as the party-state "refuses" to face the democratic challenges directly, it will remain irrelevant to these newly emerging forces.

The tough action undertaken by the authorities does not mean that it has rejected accommodation of the newly rising social forces. In fact, since the late 1990s, the party leadership has made greater efforts to adjust China's political system to the changing socio-economic dynamics in the country. This responsiveness can be illustrated by outlining the changes made to the country's Constitution.

Constitutional change in China can occur in two ways: a complete change in the Constitution itself (1954–82), or an amendment to the existing Constitution (1982–99). When political situation changes, the old Constitution is likely to be replaced by a new one. Thus the 1975 Constitution is called the "Cultural Revolution Constitution," the 1978 Constitution the "Four-Modernization Constitution," and the 1982 Constitution the "Reform and Open-Door Constitution." Each revision of the Constitution was prompted by political considerations including the desire of the leadership to adjust the political system to the changing economic and social situation. It is worth briefly examining the Constitutional changes made in regards to the private sector.

According to the 1954 Constitution, the first in the history of the People's Republic, China's political system was led by the working class as its leading class and the worker–peasant alliance as its foundation (Article 1). Regarding the economic system, the Constitution stipulated that the state would aim to eliminate the exploitative system and build a socialist system. While the state sector should dominate, other sectors such as collective cooperatives, individually owned enterprises, private capitalist economy, and state capitalism were allowed to coexist (Articles 5 and 10). Furthermore, the Constitution protected citizens' ownership of legal incomes, savings, properties and other forms of productive materials (Article 11), and the right of inheritance of private properties (Article 12). The state, however, had the right to collect and even confiscate land and other forms of productive materials in accordance with laws and regulations in order to meet the needs of public interests (Article 13), and everyone was prohibited to utilize his/her private properties to undermine public interests (Article 14). The Constitution also declared that public properties were sacred and inviolable, and it was every citizen's duty to protect public properties (Article 101).

Many waves of political movements such as the Anti-Rightist Movement and the Cultural Revolution rendered void much of the 1954 Constitution. In 1975, the party leadership under the "Gang of Four" drafted a new Constitution. The 1975 Constitution formally nullified many articles regarding citizens' rights that had existed in the 1954 Constitution, and added articles to meet contemporary political needs. Citizens were granted the right to support the party, and also to rebel. The revised Constitution was reduced to 30 articles from the original 106.

After the death of Mao Zedong and the smashing of the Gang of Four in 1976, the CCP leadership under Hua Guofeng revised the Constitution again in 1978. Though the Constitution was expanded to 60 articles by restoring some articles of the 1954 Constitution, it was based on the 1975 Constitution. In accordance with the political climate then, the use of material incentive to promote the four-modernizations was legalized.

After Deng Xiaoping came back to power, the CCP leadership passed a new constitution, the 1982 Constitution. This constitution restored almost all articles in the 1954 Constitution, and additional articles were added (from 106 articles in 1954 to 138) to meet new political and economic needs. Though the 1982 Constitution still emphasized that the state sector had to be dominant in China's economy, it recognized that economic activities by individuals in both rural and urban areas were complementary to the state sector (Article 11). What were later to be called the "private enterprises," which employed more than eight workers, were not legalized.

In 1988, the first alteration to the 1982 Constitution was made. Two significant changes were made regarding China's economic system. First, an additional paragraph was inserted under Article 11:

The state allows the private economy to exist and develop within the legal boundary. The private economy is a complement to the socialist public economy. The state protects legal rights and interests of the private economy, provides it with leadership, supervision and management. (Article 11, para. 3)

Second, paragraph 4 of Article 10 was revised: the state recognized that "land use right can be transferred in accordance with legal regulations."

This change was significant since it meant that the state legalized employment, capital accumulation, land commercialization and other newly rising economic activities. Five years later, in 1993, the second constitutional amendment was made. The 1993 amendment relinquished the planned economic system, and formally declared that a socialist market economy was to be established.

The official confirmation of the market economy sparked off serious criticisms against capitalistic development by the leftists, both old and new, in the mid-1990s. Despite controversies, the leadership decided to press on. The Fifteenth Party Congress in 1997 declared a program of partial privatization of state-owned enterprises (see Chapter 6 for detail). Based on the 1993 amendment, the Second Session of the Ninth National People's Congress (NPC) in 1999 passed a constitutional amendment, which, for the first time since the establishment of the People's Republic, provides constitutional protection for the private economy.[61]

While it will take a long time for the CCP to establish an interest-based political order, the constitutional changes of the 1990s show that the party leadership has made considerable effort to adjust China's political system not only to promote further economic development, but also to accommodate capitalist economic institutions.

After capitalism was justified constitutionally, the party leadership began to initiate practical steps to accommodate capitalists. In February 2000, Jiang Zemin raised a new concept of *san ge dai biao* (literally "three represents"). According to this concept, the CCP represents the "most advanced mode of productive force, the most advanced culture, and the interests of the majority of the population."[62] In his speech celebrating the party's eightieth anniversary on 2 July 2001, Jiang further declared that the party would recruit members from people working in the non-state sector such as professionals in the foreign-owned enterprises and joint ventures, private entrepreneurs, and other sectors. According to Jiang, changes in the make-up of classes had become a reality in China, and only by recruiting elites from these social groups could the party be revived further.[63] Traditionally, the CCP had claimed that it represented the interests of five major groups: workers, peasants, intellectuals, military, and cadres. The majority of its members were also recruited from these groups. By allowing capitalists to join the party, the leadership sought to expand the social base of the CCP and to establish or at least accommodate an interest-based political order. At its Sixteenth Congress in 2002, the party leadership revised the party constitution, and the "three represents" theory was established as the guideline for the party. This revision formally legitimized the admission of capitalists into the party.[64]

Conclusion

Building an interest-based political order has been a gradual process. This chapter has attempted to spell out the domestic political consequences of the economic expansion that followed Deng's southern tour of China. After the crackdown on the 1989 pro-democracy movement, the leadership deliberately constructed an interest-based social order. This order brought a decade of domestic stability and rapid development. With the establishment of an interest-based social order, societal members turned their attention mainly to the private economic arena. They did so not only because the private arena had become profitable but also because of the high costs involved in the public political arena, as the crackdown against the 1989 pro-democracy movement had shown. When political passions were transformed into economic ones, the result was political indifference. With such a development, the regime's political burden was greatly reduced. Also, the focus on the private economic arena generated its own dynamics for rapid economic expansion, which enhanced the regime's legitimacy.

Nevertheless, an interest-based social order has, over time, generated some unexpected political consequences for the regime. The leadership's aim in consciously leading people towards an interest-oriented society was to replace political passions with economic ones. It succeeded, to a great degree. But then, the existing political order becomes increasingly irrelevant to the interest-based social order. The danger is that once people's economic passions are met, they will demand a political role for themselves. While the regime had enjoyed political benefits arising from economic expansion, it came face to face with the political fallout of such an expansion.

It is now impossible for the regime to go back to an ideologically constructed social order. Once capitalism, together with rapid globalization, became a means for regime survival, the leadership all but lost its ability to reverse the trend. In effect, an emerging interest-oriented society has virtually led to the demise of communism as an ideology. What the leadership can do is to rebuild its political system in accordance with the changed and changing reality. Current efforts by the leadership indicate that the CCP has begun to seriously consider how the interests of newly rising classes and social groups can be represented. But it remains to be seen whether the party can succeed in transforming itself by admitting new social classes (see Chapter 9).

5 Bureaucratic reform and market accommodation

Capitalist economic development has facilitated China's rapid transition from a planned economy to a market one. Nevertheless, a full-fledged market economy requires a set of economic institutions compatible with market-led economic activities. Throughout the reform period, the Chinese leadership devoted great effort to building such institutions not only to support but also to spur market growth. Economic institutional building is multifaceted. In this chapter and the next, I provide case studies to show how the leadership has restructured or rebuilt the state economic system to accommodate the market economy. My focus is on the 1990s. Economic reform in the 1980s was characterized by radical decentralization, and national institution-building was not given priority, and most institutional restructuring or rebuilding took place after Zhu Rongji assumed charge of China's overall economic reform in the early 1990s.[1]

This chapter focuses on the restructuring of state economic bureaucracies. It first presents an overall picture of the reform to China's state economic system since the early 1980s, and discusses the failure of several waves of institutional restructuring. It then discusses in detail the building of the State Economic and Trade Commission (SETC). The SETC was set up by Zhu Rongji in early 1993, and by the late 1990s, it had become China's most important and powerful economic bureaucracy. It was regarded as the mini-State Council, in which Zhu Rongji formed and implemented economic reform policies. The case study of the SETC shows how the Zhu administration implemented radical restructuring in order to build an institutional framework for a growing market economy.

The dynamics of bureaucratic restructuring

Bureaucratic restructuring in China essentially refers to efforts to rationalize the bureaucratic state to make it more efficient. John Burns has explained China's bureaucratic reforms from 1978 to 1982 in this vein, and pointed out that these reforms were made in order to reduce, even eliminate, such shortcomings as inefficiency, dysfunction, overstaffing, degeneration, and so on.[2] Furthermore, every bureaucratic restructuring has aimed, more than anything else, to provide an institutional foundation for the development of an increasingly market-oriented economy. Two points underpinning the term "an increasingly market-oriented economy" need to be highlighted. First, China's market economy was not established overnight but developed gradually. Second, in establishing a market economy, Chinese leaders or institutional designers are constrained in planning and restructuring the state bureaucracy. Bureaucratic restructuring is subject to bureaucratic interests and their resistance. Since the reform policy was launched, although every designer of such restructuring has claimed that structuring is to rationalize the state bureaucratic system and to increase its efficiency, the results of every restructuring have been very different. Organizational staffing, structure, and operations not only influence the outcomes of public policy on a wide range of issues but more importantly affect the distribution of political power that has a bearing on such outcome. Restructuring frequently becomes a political game.

Also, every bureaucratic restructuring is subject to individual power interests. Power games in a democratic society are played out through party politics and open popular elections. In China, without democratic methods, power redistribution is carried out by institutional reorganization. Each leader needs his own institutional means to put into effect his own idea on how to govern the bureaucratic system, and to carry out his policies.

John Burns has observed that every major bureaucratic restructuring in China is usually accompanied with the coming of a new "premier-select."[3] Though the leadership collectively designed bureaucratic reform, "the premier-select" plays an extremely important role in planning the restructuring. The premier-select has to consider how to use the restructuring to consolidate and strengthen his power. Although the premier-select does not have much freedom in changing the structure of the state bureaucracy, i.e., the State Council, since other leaders also have a say in the restructuring plan, he has the power to set up new institutions to formulate and implement policies that are more in tune with his own policy orientation rather than those of other leaders. So, under Zhao Ziyang (1982–87) and Li Peng (1988–92), there was the State Commission of Economic Restructuring, and under Zhu Rongji, there was the State Economic and Trade Commission. These institutions not only implement new policies set by the new administration but also constitute organizational power bases for their principal backers.

Bureaucratic restructuring: An overview

Since 1949, Chinese leaders have engaged in efforts to improve the performance, efficiency, or reliability of the state bureaucratic system. Because of the endless political movements in China, the bureaucratic apparatus was extremely unstable in the pre-reform years. With the shift in emphasis from political movement to economic development since 1978, the restructuring of the state bureaucratic system has accordingly shifted from serving "revolutionary" tasks to "constructing" goals.

We can divide the restructuring process since the early 1980s into two distinct phases in tandem with the economic transformation of the country. The first period is during Deng's reform period, i.e., from the early 1980s to 1997, during which each restructuring marked a step in the transition from the planned economy to the "socialist market economy." The second period from 1998 onwards, designed by Premier Zhu Rongji, was characterized by and served the market economy.

The 1982 restructuring by Zhao Ziyang

In the late 1970s and early 1980s, many senior government officials who had been ousted during the Cultural Revolution returned to the political scene. With their reappearance and the need for economic development, more ministries were added to the State Council. In 1978 the State Council had 76 organizations; in 1981, it had 100.

When the leadership started its ambitious bureaucratic reform program in 1982, it wanted to improve both the efficiency and the responsiveness of state institutions. The reforms ran against entrenched local, unit, and factional interests. In that year, the National People's Congress (NPC) passed a proposal for restructuring which reduced the number of vice premiers from 18 to 3 and that of organizations from 100 (52 commissions and ministries) to 61 (43 ministries and commissions).

Overall, the 1982 restructuring reflects the fusing of a planned economy and a market one. Indeed, this was done in accordance with ideological change. In 1982, the CCP held its Twelfth Congress, during which the leadership claimed that China's economic reform was aimed at establishing a mixed economic system, i.e., the planned economy as its main pillar, with the market economy as its supplement.

Table 5.1 lists the commissions and ministries before and after the 1982 restructuring. On the one hand, several ministries and commissions designed for promoting socialist economic development were created either from scratch or through mergers. For instance, the State Economic Commission took over five state commissions, one task group of the State

Table 5.1 Commissions and ministries of the State Council in 1982

Before restructuring: 52	After restructuring: 43
Ministry of Foreign Affairs	Ministry of Foreign Affairs
Ministry of Defense	Ministry of Defense
State Planning Commission	State Planning Commission

State Economic Commission
State Agriculture Commission
State Infrastructure Construction
  Commission
State Machinery Industry Commission
State Energy Commission
Finance and Trade Group of the State
  Council
State Standard Bureau
State Measurement Bureau
State Bureau of Medicine Management
State Patent Office
State Bureau of Constructing Material
  Industry
	State Economic Commission

–	State Comm. for Economic System Restructuring
State Science and Technology Commission	State Science and Technology Commission
Industry Office for National Defense of the State Council	Comm. of Science, Technology, and Industry for National Defense
State Nationalities Affairs Commission	State Nationalities Affairs Commission
Ministry of Public Security	Ministry of Public Security
Ministry of Civil Affairs	Ministry of Civil Affairs
Ministry of Justice	Ministry of Justice
Ministry of Finance	Ministry of Finance
The People's Bank of China	The People's Bank of China
The Agriculture Bank State Foreign Reserve Bureau (Bank of China) People's Construction Bank	(abolished)
Ministry of Commerce Ministry of Food National Supply and Marketing Cooperative	Ministry of Commerce

Table 5.1 (*cont.*)

Before restructuring: 52	After restructuring: 43
Ministry of Foreign Trade Ministry of External Economic Liaison Commission of Foreign Investment Bureau of Export and Import Commodities Inspection	Ministry of Foreign Economy and Trade
Ministry of Agriculture Ministry of Reclamation State Bureau of Aquatic Products	Ministry of Agriculture, Husbandry, and Fishery
Ministry of Forest	Ministry of Forest
Ministry of Water Resource Ministry of Power Industry	Ministry of Water Resource and Power

State Construction Projects Bureau
State Bureau for City Construction
State Survey Bureau
	Ministry of Urban and Rural
	  Construction and Environment
	  protection

Ministry of Geology	Ministry of Geology and Mineral Resources
Ministry of Metallurgical Industry	Ministry of Metallurgical Industry
First Ministry of Machinery Building Ministry of Agricultural Machinery State Bureau for Instrument and Meter Industry State Bureau for Machinery Equipment	Ministry of Machinery Industry
Second Ministry of Machinery Industry	Ministry of Nuclear Industry
Third Ministry of Machinery Industry	Ministry of Aviation Industry
Fourth Ministry of Machinery Industry State Bureau of Broadcasting and Television Industry State Bureau of Information Industry	Ministry of Electronic Industry
Fifth Ministry of Machinery Industry	Ministry of Arms
Sixth Ministry of Machinery Industry	(abolished)
Seventh Ministry of Machinery Industry	Ministry of Aeronautic Industry
Ministry of Coal Industry	Ministry of Coal Industry
Ministry of Petroleum Industry	Ministry of Petroleum Industry

(*cont.*)

Table 5.1 (*cont.*)

Before restructuring: 52	After restructuring: 43
Ministry of Chemical Industry	Ministry of Chemical Industry
Ministry of Textile Industry	Ministry of Textile Industry
Ministry of Light Industry	Ministry of Light Industry
Ministry of Railway	Ministry of Railway
Ministry of Communication	Ministry of Communication
Ministry of Post and Telecommunication	Ministry of Post and Telecommunication
State Labor Bureau State Personnel Bureau State Staffing Commission State Bureau of Scientific and Technological Cadre	Ministry of Labor and Personnel
Central Broadcasting Bureau	Ministry of Broadcasting and Television
Ministry of Education	Ministry of Education
Ministry of Public Health	Ministry of Public Health
Ministry of Culture External Cultural Liaison Commission + 3 State Bureaus	Ministry of Culture
State Sports Commission	State Sports Commission
State Family Planning Commission	State Family Planning Commission

Sources: Su Shangxiao and Han Wenwei, *Zhonghua renmin gongheguo zhongyang zhengfu jigou* (Central Government Organizations of the P. R. C.) (Beijing: Jingji Kexue chubanshe, 1993), pp. 73–82.

Council, and five state bureaus and became a powerful commission in charge of the market economy to counterbalance the State Planning Commission, a symbol of the old planned economy. The Ministry of Commerce also took over two ministries and one cooperative that were products of the planned economy. On the other hand, many ministries that existed under the planned economy remained unchanged, or did not go through any major alteration, or merely had a change of name (e.g. the Ministry of Metallurgical Industry, Ministry of Nuclear Industry, and Ministry of Coal Industry).

The State Commission for Economic System Restructuring was created and headed by Premier Zhao Ziyang. Zhao needed his own institution to design the restructuring of the economic system to develop elements of a market economy. The commission became his think-tank and power base during his term.

The new administration retained the Planning, Economic, and Scientific and Technology Commissions, with a vastly expanded brief going to the State Economic Commission. It absorbed parts of the planning and policy coordination functions of the five abolished commissions – Agriculture, Energy, Machine Building, Finance, and Capital Construction. Long-term capital construction planning, however, went to the State Planning Commission, while the management of capital construction projects went under a new ministry called Ministry of Urban and Rural Construction and Environmental Protection. The hundreds of factories directly under the abolished Capital Construction Commission were attached to this new ministry. These changes made the State Economic Commission responsible for agriculture, industry, capital construction (short-term planning), railroads and transportation, finance and monetary affairs, some aspects of foreign trade, and the drafting of the annual national economic plan.

The streamlining of state commissions (reduced to 7) was only part of the 1982 reform plan. In March 1982, Zhao announced that the number of commissions and ministries would be reduced from 52 to 39, but by May, he revised this figure upward to 41, and by the end of 1982, to 43. This indicated resistance by some ministries. Nevertheless, these changes trimmed the State Council staff by approximately 17,000.[4]

While Zhao Ziyang was not able to change the planned system entirely, he did create many new organs. The old established institutions and the new ones needed time to adapt to each other. For instance, the Auditing Administration and the Ministry of State Security were added in 1983, the Ministry of Supervision and some state bureaus in 1986. Meanwhile, the Ministries of Machinery Building, and of Arms were merged to form a Commission of Machinery Industry.

After the restructuring, there were 61 organizations in the State Council, of which 43 were ministries and commissions. But 5 years later, the number of organizations increased again to 72, of which 45 were ministries and commissions. From 100 organizations in 1981 to 61 in 1982, to 72 in 1987: the restructuring experienced a cycle of contraction and expansion.

The 1988 restructuring by Li Peng

In 1987, the CCP held its Thirteenth Congress during which the party leadership raised a new concept of "combining planned and market economies," and claimed that China was still at an early stage of socialism. The market economy was granted equal status to that of the planned economy in the party's ideology. Li Peng became the premier-select at that congress, indicating that he would succeed Zhao Ziyang in 1988 when the seventh NPC convened.

This change in the CCP's ideology created a political environment conducive to the 1988 restructuring. Nevertheless, Li, the premier-select and architect of the 1988 restructuring, adopted a conservative stand that significantly affected the essence of the restructuring. To be sure, Zhao's market-oriented economic reforms had met with serious difficulty since the mid-1980s, and the conservative faction was in the ascendancy. The ranks of the conservatives in the leadership were further strengthened when, as well as Li Peng, Yao Yilin was recruited into the Standing Committee of the Political Bureau and became the Vice-Premier in 1988.

Table 5.2 shows how the ministries and commissions changed after the 1988 restructuring. The Ministry of Energy was created by merging three ministries. The greater part of the abolished ministries became state companies, for instance, the Petroleum and Gas Company of China. This was a move towards a market economy. The creation of the Ministry of Materials was, however, a step back to the planned economy. This ministry was put in charge of planning the distribution of commanded materials; organizing the orders of the command and important materials and so on.[5]

One particularly significant merger in 1988 was the takeover of the State Economic Commission by an already oversized State Planning Commission of about 1,300 staff. This reorganization, which occurred when Premier Li Peng was working hard to dismantle Zhao's economic reforms, was no doubt partially motivated by the conservatives' desire to throttle the reformist entrepreneurship of the State Economic Commission (SEC). The SEC had led the efforts to expand enterprise autonomy since its formation in 1979, whereas the State Planning Commission had continued to support a planned economy. When the SEC was subsumed under the State Planning Commission, the reform movement lost its highest-ranking bureaucratic advocate.

The 1993 restructuring by Li Peng

After Deng Xiaoping's southern tour in 1992, the CCP's Fourteenth Congress that year formally legitimized the market economy, and established it as the goal of China's economic reform. In line with the political direction set at the very top, a new wave of bureaucratic restructuring was initiated to adjust the state bureaucratic system to meet the demands of a market economy. The Fourteenth Party Congress, however, also decided that Li would have his second term as Premier, and thus Li was in charge of the 1993 restructuring.

Table 5.2 Ministries and commissions in 1988

Before restructuring: 45	After restructuring: 41
Ministry of Foreign Affairs	Ministry of Foreign Affairs
Ministry of National Defense	Ministry of National Defense
State Planning Commission State Economic Commission	State Planning Commission
State Comm. For Economic System Restructuring	State Comm. for Economic System Restructuring
State Education Commission (1985)	State Education Commission
State Science and Technology Commission	State Science and Technology Commission
Industry Office for National Defense of the State Council	Comm. of Science, Technology, and Industry for National Defense
State Nationalities Affairs Commission	State Nationalities Affairs Commission
Ministry of Public Security	Ministry of Public Security
Ministry of State Security	Ministry of State Security
Ministry of Supervision (1986)	Ministry of Supervision
Ministry of Civil Affairs	Ministry of Civil Affairs
Ministry of Justice	Ministry of Justice
Ministry of Finance	Ministry of Finance
Ministry of Labor and Personnel	Ministry of Labor
–	Ministry of Personnel
Ministry of Urban and Rural Construction and Environment Protection	Ministry of Construction State Bureau for Environment Protection
Ministry of Coal Industry Ministry of Petroleum Industry Ministry of Nuclear Industry	Ministry of Energy
State Machinery Industry Commission Ministry of Electronic Industry	Ministry of Machinery and Electronic Industry
Ministry of Aviation Industry Ministry of Aeronautic Industry	Ministry of Aviation and Aeronautic Industry

(*cont.*)

Table 5.2 (*cont.*)

Before restructuring: 45	After restructuring: 41
Ministry of Geology and Mineral Resources	Ministry of Geology and Mineral Resources
Ministry of Metallurgical Industry	Ministry of Metallurgical Industry
Ministry of Chemical Industry	Ministry of Chemical Industry
Ministry of Light Industry State Bureau of Tobacco Monopoly	Ministry of Light Industry
Ministry of Textile Industry	Ministry of Textile Industry
Ministry of Railway	Ministry of Railway
Ministry of Communication	Ministry of Communication
Ministry of Post and Telecommunication	Ministry of Post and Telecommunication
Ministry of Water Resource and Power Industry	Ministry of Water Resource
Ministry of Agriculture, Husbandry, and Fishery	Ministry of Agriculture
Ministry of Forest	Ministry of Forest
Ministry of Commerce	Ministry of Commerce
Ministry of Foreign Economy and Trade	Ministry of Foreign Economy and Trade
–	Ministry of Materials
Xinhua News Agency	(abolished)
Ministry of Culture	Ministry of Culture
Ministry of Broadcasting, Film, and Television	Ministry of Broadcasting, Film, and Television
Ministry of Public Health	Ministry of Public Health
State Sports Commission	State Sports Commission
State Family Planning Commission	State Family Planning Commission
The People's Bank	The People's Bank
Auditing Administration	Auditing Administration

Source: Adapted from Wu Jie (ed.), *Zhongguo zhengfu yu jiegou gaige* (Chinese Government and Institutional Reforms) (Beijing: Guojia xingzheng xueyuan chubanshe, 1998), pp. 393–5.

One would expect that the restructuring after Deng's southern tour would be drastic and most of the state institutions that had supported the planned economy would be abolished and new ones would be established to support and promote the market economy. Yet, such changes did not materialize. As during his first term, Li exerted a conservative influence over the restructuring. Li had by then consolidated his power base, and he was not inclined to make any drastic moves.

Table 5.3 shows that the bureaucratic structure did not alter much after the 1993 restructuring. Some ministries were removed, other were broken into two. The Ministry of Energy, regarded as Li's base, was expanded into two ministries (Coal Industry and Power Industry). The Ministry of Machinery and Electrical Industry, seen as Jiang Zemin's base, was similarly expanded.

The only noticeable development in the move towards the market economy was the creation of the State Economic and Trade Commission (SETC), chaired by a newly appointed Vice-Premier Zhu Rongji. The commission later became the institutional base of Zhu's radical economic reform.

Market-building institutions under Zhu Rongji

Leadership matters. In restructuring the state bureaucratic system, every leader confronts a more or less similar set of constraints, but the results may be quite different. These differences emerge as a result of the individual leader's level of commitment to the market economy and the extent of their power.

Deng Xiaoping once described the relationship between policies and leaders when he said, "Once a political line is established, someone must implement it. Depending on who is in charge of the implementation – those who support the party's line, those who do not, or those who take the middle-of-the-road position – the results will be different."[6]

A market economy does not evolve spontaneously from planned economy. Leadership intervention is necessary and inevitable. To reform or not to reform, both are decisions fraught with political risks. Whatever the leadership does, it affects the existing distribution of power and interest. At the very top, Deng himself has played a major role in pushing ahead with market-oriented economic reform and in establishing a market economy as the CCP's political line. Yet, judging by the restructuring of the state bureaucratic system over the years, China's market economy has not developed evenly under different leaders.

Table 5.3 Ministries and commissions in 1993

Before restructuring: 41	After restructuring: 40
Ministry of Foreign Affairs	Ministry of Foreign Affairs
Ministry of National Defense	Ministry of National Defense
	State Economic and Trade Commission
State Planning Commission	State Planning Commission
State Comm. for Economic System Restructuring	State Comm. for Economic System Restructuring
State Education Commission	State Education Commission
State Science and Technology Commission	State Science and Technology Commission
Comm. Of Science, Technology, and Industry for National Defense	Comm. of Science, Technology, and Industry for National Defense
State Nationalities Affairs Commission	State Nationalities Affairs Commission
Ministry of Public Security	Ministry of Public Security
Ministry of State Security	Ministry of State Security
Ministry of Supervision	Ministry of Supervision
Ministry of Civil Affairs	Ministry of Civil Affairs
Ministry of Justice	Ministry of Justice
Ministry of Finance	Ministry of Finance
Ministry of Labor	Ministry of Labor
Ministry of Personnel	Ministry of Personnel
Ministry of Construction	Ministry of Construction
Ministry of Energy	(abolished)
	Ministry of Power Industry
	Ministry of Coal Industry
Ministry of Machinery and Electronic Industry	(abolished)
	Ministry of Machinery Industry
	Ministry of Electrical Industry

Table 5.3 (*cont.*)

Before restructuring: 41	After restructuring: 40
Ministry of Aviation and Aeronautic Industry	(abolished)
Ministry of Geology and Mineral Resources	Ministry of Geology and Mineral Resources
Ministry of Metallurgical Industry	Ministry of Metallurgical Industry
Ministry of Chemical Industry	Ministry of Chemical Industry
Ministry of Light Industry	(abolished)
Ministry of Textile Industry	(abolished)
Ministry of Railway	Ministry of Railway
Ministry of Communication	Ministry of Communication
Ministry of Post and Telecommunication	Ministry of Post and Telecommunication
Ministry of Water Resource	Ministry of Water Resource
Ministry of Agriculture	Ministry of Agriculture
Ministry of Forest	Ministry of Forest
Ministry of Commerce	(abolished)
Ministry of Foreign Economy and Trade	Ministry of Foreign Trade and Economic Cooperation
	Ministry of Internal Trade
Ministry of Materials	(abolished)
Ministry of Culture	Ministry of Culture
Ministry of Broadcasting, Film, and Television	Ministry of Broadcasting, Film, and Television
Ministry of Public Health	Ministry of Public Health
State Sports Commission	State Sports Commission
State Family Planning Commission	State Family Planning Commission
The People's Bank	The People's Bank
Auditing Administration	Auditing Administration

Source: As for Table 5.2, pp. 414–21.

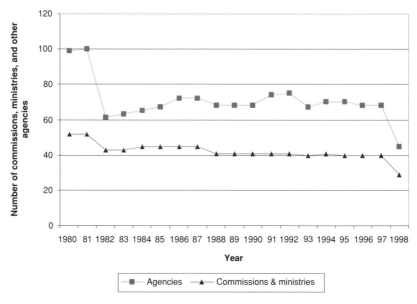

Figure 5.1 Organizational changes in the PRC State Council, 1980–98

Figure 5.1 shows the trend of the restructuring. The two most radical changes took place under Zhao Ziyang and Zhu Rongji. After the restructuring in the early 1980s, the number of state bureaucracies remained relatively unchanged until Zhu Rongji's reform began in 1997–98. Indeed, the restructuring programs under Zhao and Zhu have been regarded as milestones in China's reforms of the state system. However, there is a difference between the two. Zhao Ziyang's reform was achieved by establishing new operational mechanisms in accordance with the market economy, while leaving the old structure largely intact. In contrast, Zhu Rongji's reform was characterized by a rebuilding of the institutional structure to make it appropriate for a market economy. I shall first present an overview of the 1993 restructuring, and then discuss Zhu Rongji's efforts in building a Chinese version of MITI (Ministry of International Trade and Industry), i.e., SETC.

Institution-building, 1998

During its Fifteenth Congress in 1997, the CCP leadership declared that reform of state-owned enterprises (SOEs) would be at the top of the political agenda for the new administration. At that congress, Zhu Rongji became the premier-select for the next NPC in 1998, meaning that Zhu would be the major planner of the 1998 restructuring of the state bureaucratic system. As expected, during the Ninth NPC in 1998, Zhu declared that his new administration would accord highest priority to the reform and reorganization of the State Council and its various ministries. According to Zhu's plan, the existing 40 commissions and ministries were to be cut down to 29, a reduction of 28 percent. The number of civil servants – 8 million – was also to be slashed by 50 percent. Such a large-scale bureaucratic reform had not been seen since the early 1980s.

Accommodating the market

Table 5.4 shows the structure of the State Council before and after the 1998 changes. It is worth highlighting some of the major changes. First, the State Commission for Economic System Restructuring was restructured. The Commission had been set up in 1982 by Zhao Ziyang in order to plan China's economic reform and it soon became an important formal bureaucracy under the State Council. The fact that Zhao Ziyang, Li Tieying, Li Peng and Chen Jinhua all served as directors indicates the importance of the Commission. However, once Zhao Ziyang was transferred to be in charge of party affairs and Li Peng became director, the Commission became very conservative in its orientation. When Zhu Rongji was put in charge of China's economic reform program as Vice-Premier, he could not and did not use the Commission to initiate and implement his reform policies as it was under the control of Li Peng. After Zhu became Premier, he made a conscious decision to sideline the Commission although he was not able to ignore it completely. The Commission was reconstructed not as a formal bureaucracy, but as a high level consultative institution under the State Council. Zhu became its director and various ministers were its members.

The second major change that occurred was to the State Planning Commission (SPC). The Commission was not abolished, but its name was changed to the State Development Planning Commission. The SPC had been a symbol of the old planned economy and reforming it had not been easy. After two decades of economic reform, its importance had waned although it lingered on. Major leaders had disagreed as to how it should evolve and what its function should be. Under Li Peng and Yao Yilin, its position had been strengthened. Under Zhu, its importance was eroded again and, with the name change, it was relegated to being a research institute that focused on China's long-term development plans.

Third, the number of sectoral ministries was reduced from 12 to 3 – a radical change from previous restructuring efforts. This change was

Table 5.4 The 1998 Restructuring of the State Council

Before restructuring: 40	After restructuring: 29
State Planning Commission	State Development Planning Commission
State Science and Technology Commission	Ministry of Science and Technology
State Education Commission	Ministry of Education
Ministry of Foreign Affairs	Ministry of Foreign Affairs
Ministry of Defense	Ministry of Defense
State Economic and Trade Commission Ministry of Power Ministry of Coal Industry Ministry of Metallurgical Industry Ministry of Machine-Building Ministry of Chemical Industry Ministry of Internal Trade Textile Industry Council Light Industry Council General Company of Petroleum and Gas General Company of Chemical Industry	State Economic and Trade Commission
Ministry of Electrical Industry Ministry of Post and Communication Ministry of Radio, Film and Television	Ministry of Information Industry
State Nationality Affairs Commission	State Nationality Affairs Commission
Ministry of Public Security	Ministry of Public Security
Ministry of State Security	Ministry of State Security
Ministry of Supervision	Ministry of Supervision
Ministry of Civil Affairs	Ministry of Civil Affairs
Ministry of Justice	Ministry of Justice
Ministry of Personnel	Ministry of Personnel
Ministry of Finance	Ministry of Finance
Ministry of Construction	Ministry of Construction
Ministry of Railway	Ministry of Railway
Ministry of Communication	Ministry of Communication
Ministry of Water Resources	Ministry of Water Resources

Table 5.4 (*cont.*)

Before restructuring: 40	After restructuring: 29
Ministry of Agriculture	Ministry of Agriculture
Ministry of Foreign Trade and Economic Cooperation	Ministry of Foreign Trade and Economic Cooperation
Ministry of Culture	Ministry of Culture
Ministry of Public Health	Ministry of Public Health
State Family Planning Commission	State Family Planning Commission
People's Bank	People's Bank
Auditing Administration	Auditing Administration
Commission of Science, Technology, and Industry for National Defense Department of National Defense of the State Planning Council Governmental functions of Military Industry Companies	State Science, Technology, and Industry Commission for National Defense
Ministry of Labor Social Security Dept. of Ministry of Personnel Social Security Dept. of Ministry of Civil Affairs Insurance Dept. of Ministry of Public Health	Ministry of Labor and Social Security
Ministry of Geology and Mineral Resources State Land Administration State Maritime Bureau State Survey Bureau	Ministry of Land and Resources
Ministry of Forest – Forest Bureau under SC	(abolished)
State Physical Cultural and Sports Commission	(abolished)
State Commission for Economic Systems Restructuring	(abolished)

Source: Adapted from the Editorial Office of *The Outlook Weekly* (ed.), *Guowuyuan jigou gaige gailan* (A General Survey of Institutional Reforms of the State Council) (Beijing: Xinhua chubanshe, 1998), pp. 7–10.

an element in the plan to separate government from enterprises, an objective which was regarded by reformist leaders as essential to pushing ahead with SOE reforms. Accordingly, a new organization, the Ministry of Labor and Social Security, was created to deal with employment issues as well as to devise a more effective social security program to help those who were unemployed.

Breaking the military links with business

Fourth, a particularly significant reform measure that Zhu Rongji undertook was business demilitarization. The State Commission of Science, Technology and Industry for National Defense (SCSTIND) took over the governmental functions from the military companies, and for the first time since 1949 a civilian official, former Vice-Minister of Finance Liu Jibin, became the director of the Commission. Liu's appointment, fully backed by Zhu, marked the latter's determination to break the military's links with business.

The Chinese military had been involved in various types of businesses such as food production, equipment repair, transport, mining, services, and provision of other day-to-day necessities required by the military since very early days.[7] Most enterprises were run by the General Logistics Department and its local units, but the General Staff Headquarters and the General Political Department also ran enterprises of their own.

The military–business links had increased since the onset of economic reform. The expansion of the military's role in business was initially due to budget constraints.[8] The original purpose of these business enterprises was to serve the needs of the military and promote self-sufficiency and their activities were almost entirely restricted to the armed forces. The 1980s, however, saw major changes in their role. Over the years, the People's Liberation Army (PLA) had become one of the few military establishments in the world that was extensively engaged in a wide range of commercial activities in both domestic and international markets, including mining, footwear and garment manufacturing, pharmaceuticals and chemical products, hotels and vacation resorts, real estate, automotive industry, transportation, telecommunications, and others.

There had been a trend towards the establishment of conglomerates formed from the merging of several PLA-run companies. The PLA's business networks extended all over China, and even abroad. In the 1990s, PLA-owned firms sold millions of assault weapons to American gun collectors and thousands of tons of white fish to American fish-stick food processing companies. It was reported that business companies in the name of corporations owned or controlled by the PLA also owned real estate developments in Thailand and Hong Kong, and in Atlanta and Dallas in the United States.[9]

In many ways, the military–business links greatly reduced the PLA combat capability as a modern military institution. It also raised questions about the professional ethics, degree of internal cohesion, military morale and disciplinary problems within the PLA. But what worried Zhu most was that civilian laws generally did not cover military-related companies, which were mostly controlled by princelings; and that the military–business links had undermined the operation of the national economy and become a barrier to the development of a market economy.

Among other negative effects, the most damaging ramification of the PLA's involvement in profit-making activities was the way that such activities became intertwined with the political economy of cities and towns where such commercial activities were located. It is known that PLA business deals were instrumental in fostering regional and local political and economic powers vis-à-vis the national government. In parts of China, especially in coastal areas, the military's economic welfare was tied closely to local economic development. The symbiotic relationship existed between the local military forces and local governments. Local military forces often helped local government officials engage in shady economic deals. The collusion between the military and local commercial establishments tended to reinforce local defiance against the national government.

Under Zhu, the new administration, supported by the CCP leadership, soon initiated a major wave of campaign to break the ties between the military and business. In July 1998, Jiang Zemin outlined steps to implement the campaign.[10] Major leaders such as Zhu Rongji, Hu Jintao, Wen Jiabao and Wei Jianxing all took part in the process of restructuring the PLA. Zhu Rongji repeatedly stressed that all military expenses needed to be paid from central coffers.[11] In early November 1998, the Chinese leadership set up a task force to tackle the sensitive issue of military–business links. The group was chaired by Zhu Rongji himself, with Hu Jintao and General Zhang Wannian as his deputies. The group reported directly to the Standing Committee of the Political Bureau of the party. Other members of the group included Sheng Huaren, chief of the SETC; Wang Zhongyu, State Councilor and the Secretary General of the State Council; and Zeng Peiyan, Head of the SDPC. The purpose of this powerful task force was to accelerate the process of de-linking the military from business. By the end of the year, the task force announced that the PLA and Armed Police had formally renounced their control of previously owned business establishments.[12]

The development of the Mini-State Council (SETC)

Finally, a far more important change in the 1998 restructuring involved the State Economic and Trade Commission (SETC). The Commission took over seven existing commissions and ministries, two councils and two large state-owned enterprises. The Commission thus became the most powerful organization within the State Council, and came to be known as the Mini-State Council. The formation and development of the SETC was closely associated with Zhu's market-oriented economic reform. An examination of the origins of SETC helps reveal how the reformist Chinese leadership struggled to gain acceptance for, and implement, a pro-market economy state structure.

The ETO and Zhu's initial reform efforts

Zhu was summoned to Beijing by Deng Xiaoping in early 1991 after the Chinese New Year, but his career in *Zhongnanhai* was not as smooth sailing as expected. The State Council was then controlled by conservative political leaders such as Li Peng (Premier) and Yao Yilin (Vice Premier). Zhu was put in charge of initiating new economic reforms but that was not a priority for the conservative leadership. Zhu was asked to oversee several offices under the State Council such as the Office of Production and the Committee for Production Safety; however, these offices were too minor and unimportant to support him in any major reform. Not until June 1991 was Zhu able to find an institution from which to mount his economic reforms. A year later, in June 1992, the central leadership decided to establish a new office – the Economic and Trade Office (ETO) – to be in charge of economic reform.

As discussed earlier, in the 1982 restructuring under Zhao Ziyang, the State Economic Commission was established and it became the institutional base from which Zhao initiated and implemented market-oriented reform policies. Yet, in the 1988 restructuring under Li Peng the importance of the planned economy revived when the State Economic Commission was incorporated into the State Planning Commission. The establishment of the ETO was another step by the reformist leadership to push the country back on the track of economic reform.

Zhu was appointed Director and he was supported by many other reform-minded government officials in the ETO. Table 5.5 lists the people directing the office. Almost half of Zhu's followers came from the State Planning Commission, State Economic Commission or Shanghai, indicating that they were Zhu's former colleagues. Their in-depth knowledge of China's planned economy and their reformist mindsets helped

Table 5.5 Composition of the Economic and Trade Office, 1991

Name	Position	Educational background	Previous experience
Zhu Rongji	Director	Qinghua Univ., electrical engineering	SPC, SEC, and Shanghai Mayor
Wang Zhongyu	Deputy Director	College, economics	Governor of Jilin
Zhang Yanning	Deputy Director	College, chemical engineering	SPC, SEC
Zhao Weicheng	Deputy Director	Qinghua Univ., mechanical engineering	SPC, SEC
Li Xianglin	Deputy Director	Univ.	EPC of the State Council
Yang Changji	Deputy Director	Univ.	Shanghai Pudong Development Zone
Zhu Yuli	Deputy Director	Univ.	State Bureau of Technological Supervision

SPC: State Planning Commission   SEC: State Economic Commission
EPC: Environmental Protection Committee

Zhu to design further economic reform for the country. The establishment of the ETO empowered Zhu and it became his institutional base within the State Council. From this base, Zhu was able to initiate and implement new economic policies through this office without much interference from the conservative leaders.

The SETC (1993)

At the Eighth NPC in March 1993, the ETO was upgraded to the SETC. The goal of the SETC was to adjust the bureaucratic state to accommodate the market economy in the long run, with its immediate task being to restructure China's SOEs. According to the State Council regulations, the SETC was aimed at promoting a market economy via various pro-market methods, including fully utilizing the market in regards to resource allocation, strengthening and improving macro-economic adjustment in accordance with market principles, and standardizing the market economic order. In the short term, the SETC had to focus on speeding up SOE reform, changing the operation system of the SOEs and establishing a modern enterprise system.[13]

Because Zhu Rongji was in charge of China's overall economic reform, the commission was under Zhu's direct leadership. Wang Zhongyu became the first commissioner. Wang was born in Changchun, Jilin province. After graduating from Shenyang Light Industry College, he

Table 5.6 The State Economic and Trade Commission, 1993

Name	Year of birth	Position	Educational background
Wang Zhongyu	1933	Commissioner	Shenyang Light Industry College
Yang Changji	1932	Vice Commissioner	Nanjing Medical Technology Univ.
Xu Penghang	1940	Vice Commissioner	Hubei Univ., mechanical engineering
Chen Qingtai	1937	Vice Commissioner	Qinghua Univ., automobile
Shi Wanpeng	1936	Vice Commissioner	North China Jiaotong Univ.
Yu Xiaosong	1937	Vice Commissioner	Qinghua Univ., civil engineering

worked in a paper factory in his home province and later became a senior engineer. In the early 1980s when China began its economic reform, Wang was promoted to various positions in the provincial government. In 1985, he became Vice Secretary of the CCP Jilin Committee, and in 1989, he was elected Governor of Jilin. Jilin is one of the major locations for China's state-owned enterprises. Wang became one of Zhu's strong advocates for SOE reforms, and his rich experience in SOEs was what Zhu needed, since restructuring SOEs was the SETC's immediate task.

Though Zhu Rongji was supported by Deng Xiaoping and other reformist leaders, he was seriously constrained by the fact that Li Peng continued to be Premier in charge of overall affairs of the State Council. Zhu was not able to play a very influential role in the 1993 restructuring, although he succeeded in creating the SETC. Even then, many economic institutions that were associated with the planned economy remained. Only after 1997 when Zhu became the premier-select could he assume overall charge of restructuring the State Council, and the SETC once again experienced a major transformation.

The SETC (1998)

As mentioned earlier, the 1998 restructuring was the most radical among previous waves of bureaucratic reforms. In particular, the SETC was greatly expanded by taking over many formerly independent industrial ministries and bureaus. All these changes reflected, to a great degree, Zhu's ideas on SOE reforms.

Many factors pushed Zhu and his followers to initiate radical reforms. First of all, it seemed to Zhu that an unwieldy government structure and a slow process of bureaucratic reform were responsible for the lack of SOE reform.[14] Under the planned economy, government intervention in SOEs was the norm. Zhu understood that a precondition to reforming

SOEs was to separate the government from the enterprises. But without liquidating the old institutions that had been involved in SOEs, any measures to reform SOEs would be ineffective. There is a Chinese saying that when the temple is there, the monks will not go away. The only way to get the monks to leave is to pull down the temple. No doubt, it is no coincidence that most ministries liquidated by the 1998 restructuring were economic bureaucracies.

Second, internal and external pressures then demanded a rather radical institutional rebuilding. Internally, with the progress in SOE reform, the numbers of unemployed and "*xia gang*" (literally "off-post") workers were increasing drastically and posed a serious threat to social stability.[15] Externally, the 1997 Asian financial crisis had sent the Chinese leadership a strong signal that without rapid reform of China's SOEs and its financial system, China would not be able to avoid the misfortune that many other Asian countries had experienced.

Third, bold reforms were needed to create a strong and efficient government. For one, the close relationship between government bureaucracies and enterprises would render any anti-corruption measures ineffective. Corruption in turn not only weakened the government's resolve and capacity to implement policies but also seriously eroded the confidence of the people.

Zhu became Premier with a new set of reform ideas, and he wanted to play a new game with new rules. To strengthen his power required the implementation of these new rules, which in turn required a new type of institution in which Zhu could mobilize the resources necessary for this purpose. Reorganization of the State Council, especially the SETC, undoubtedly provided Zhu with an opportunity to construct his own power base to implement his reform policies.

The restructured SETC incorporated six former ministries including Power Industry, Coal Industry, Metallurgical Industry, Machine-Building Industry, Chemical Industry, and Internal Trade. After their incorporation, these ministries were downgraded to bureaus, and were no longer managed SOEs. With this change, the new commission became the most powerful coordinating organ in China. More importantly, by doing so, Zhu wanted the commission to play a role similar to Japan's MITI in leading China's future economic development. China's main strategy in reforming large-scale SOEs was to organize large industrial conglomerates akin to South Korea's *chaebols* (see below). The new Commission was to play an important role in such a transition.

To a large degree, the new commission could be regarded as Zhu's major power base. Table 5.7 shows the composition of the SETC after the 1998 restructuring. Many state entrepreneurs were promoted into the SETC. For instance, Sheng Huaren, former China Petrochemical Corp.

Table 5.7 The State Economic and Trade Commission, 1998

Name	Year of birth	Position	Education and profession
Sheng Huaren	1935	Commissioner	College, manager
Jiang Qiangui (female)	1941	Vice Commissioner	Univ., senior engineer
Wang Wanbin	1949	Vice Commissioner	Postgraduate, senior economist
Zhang Zhigang	1945	Vice Commissioner	Postgraduate, senior economist
Shi Wanpeng	1937	Vice Commissioner	Univ., senior engineer
Yu Zhen	1936	Vice Commissioner	Univ., senior economist
Li Rongrong	1944	Vice Commissioner	Univ., senior economist
Jiang Guangfu	1938	Vice Commissioner	Univ., senior engineer

president, was appointed a commissioner of the SETC. Sheng had been a successful entrepreneur managing one of the largest SOEs in China. The object of the reorganization and expansion of SETC was to implement Zhu's plan of SOE reform. Certainly, Sheng's promotion was aimed at achieving this goal.

Conclusion

This chapter shows how China's bureaucratic reform has been constrained by ideological factors and has proceeded in accordance with shifts in ideological stance on the part of the CCP. Only after the establishment of the "socialist market economy" in 1992 did Chinese leaders recognize how the bureaucratic system should be restructured to embrace a market economy. Yet, Li Peng did not succeed in reforming the state in 1993 because of his predominantly conservative mindset and other factors. Only after Zhu Rongji became Premier and was in full charge of economic reform after 1997 was radical restructuring carried out.

The restructuring of the state bureaucracy was aimed at accommodating a growing market-oriented economy, and at making the bureaucratic system more efficient in governing an increasingly complicated economy. Zhu's restructuring was in accordance with market principles and the state bureaucracy was increasingly geared to market requirements. To a large extent, Zhu and the reformist leadership have done their best to provide an institutional environment in which a market economy can grow.

The restructuring was also a part of the effort by the Chinese leadership to rebuild a modern economic state. Embedded in what Zhu and the reformist leadership have done was the idea that the restructuring would help China modernize its bureaucratic system and make it more efficient in governing an increasingly complicated society. How to maintain central power over the economy and society was a major consideration of the leadership as it introduced major reform measures. This might explain why China's bureaucratic restructuring has been incremental on the one hand and intermittent on the other. Only after the leadership assumed its control over the economy and society did it begin to initiate more radical reforms.

Zhu declared in March 1998 that his administration was going to finish the nationwide bureaucratic restructuring in three years. By the end of 1998, Zhu had succeeded in implementing some of his reform initiatives. The reorganization of the state bureaucracy was completed at the central level, and superfluous government officials were transferred or simply laid off under the euphemism of *fen-liu* (streaming out), as planned. Nevertheless, after the initial success, the reform did not go as smoothly as expected. For example, the Zhu administration planned to complete the restructuring of the state bureaucracy at the provincial level in 1999. But it was not implemented until 2000. Many factors explained such a delay. First, the plan *per se* was regarded as unrealistic. The large-scale lay-offs had a negative impact on the proper functioning of government. In 1999, though the government declared its success in restructuring at the central level, many government employees actually returned (*huiliu*). Many provincial governments grew suspicious about the plan, and did not implement it expeditiously at their level. Second, the Zhu administration was distracted from its restructuring program because it had to cope with other important matters in 1999 such as China's entry into the WTO, the NATO bombing of the Chinese Embassy, and the rise of the Falun Gong movement. Third, local resistance to the implementation of the central plan was strong. The larger size and greater diversity of provincial bureaucracies made the restructuring more difficult.

Despite all these difficulties, the Zhu administration managed to push the restructuring to the provincial level in early 2000. By the end of the year, most provinces had largely met the targets of the reform. For example, administrative bureaus were reduced from 53 to 40 in Henan; from 38 to 32 in Hainan; from 67 to 46 in Beijing, and from 59 to 40 in Guangxi. On national average, provincial bureaus were reduced by 20 percent, and civil servants by 47 percent.[16] Although the bureaucratic restructuring was not implemented exactly as planned at the county and township levels, all these reforms have built a solid institutional foundation for China's growing market economy. Though incremental adjustments can be expected in the future in accordance with changing socio-economic reality, China's bureaucratic system is unlikely to change as drastically as it has previously. This is one of the most important legacies that Zhu has left behind for China's bureaucratic system to deal with globalization and capitalistic development.

6 Building a modern economic state: Taxation, finance and enterprise system

The restructuring of the state bureaucracy deals largely with the relations between the state and market. It does not tell us how the Chinese government has used modern economic means to manage and regulate the economy. This chapter shifts to the latter aspect, focusing on the reforms in the key sectors of taxation, finance, and the enterprise system. In reforming China's fiscal and financial systems, the leadership sought to achieve two main goals. First, fiscal and financial reforms aimed to promote the development of the market economy by changing the relationship between the state and the enterprises, and second, the reforms were expected to build a modern state by managing the economy more efficiently and shifting economic power from local government to the central state. This chapter attempts to link the reforms in taxation, finance, and state-owned enterprises (SOEs) with state-building efforts by the leadership.

Taxation reform and the tax regime

China's fiscal system since the late 1970s has undergone a drastic transformation from a unitary system to a federal one. When the leadership first embarked on economic reform, it recognized that enterprises as well as local governments had to be provided with incentives to support the reform effort. This was achieved through fiscal decentralization. But this process augmented local autonomy at the expense of the center's fiscal capacity. To counter this unhealthy development, the central government initiated and implemented a federal model of the fiscal system to develop and strengthen its own fiscal resources while accommodating the autonomy of local governments.

Fiscal decentralization

In 1978, the Chinese leadership began market-oriented economic reforms by decentralizing the economy. Tax reform was an important part of this reform process and was aimed at providing farmers and SOEs with production incentives, cutting off fiscal dependence of SOEs on government, equalizing tax burdens among enterprises, and promoting fair competition among producers.

Reform measures were first introduced in the rural areas. Agriculture's terms of trade were improved greatly as a consequence of increases in state procurement prices, followed by a freezing of mandatory production quotas and offering farmers a premium price for above-quota production. Meanwhile, the central government made efforts to reduce agricultural taxes.[1]

These measures, coupled with the household responsibility system, resulted in a large and immediate surge in production. But large subsidies on agricultural products, together with other costs such as subsidies on SOEs and the large size of investments, increased the central government's fiscal burden. The government's budget deficit increased and it had to borrow money from banks. The banks in turn issued more currency which led to inflation. As the bulk of the state's revenue came from SOEs, the central government began industrial reform nationwide in 1984 after its relative success in agricultural reform, with the aim of alleviating its budgetary burden.

The 1983–84 Reform: the li gai shui system

In 1983, the central government began the *li gai shui* ("tax for profit") reform. SOEs were divided into two groups, large and small. The corporate income (profits) tax rate for large enterprises was set at 55 percent, while it was progressive for small enterprises. The after-tax profits were divided between enterprises and the state.[2] Two main problems remained. First, there was only one single tax, i.e., the corporate income tax, which did not allow the state to control resource allocation effectively; and second, SOEs were still required to submit part of their after-tax profits to the state and this was a disincentive to better performance. In other words, the state revenues still included both taxes and profits. In 1984, further reform measures were implemented. Enterprises were required to pay only income taxes and their obligation to deliver profits to the state was removed. The process of substituting taxes for profits was completed, and tax revenue became an overwhelming component of the state's total revenues.

The *li gai shui* reform provided enterprises with incentives to make greater profits. Nevertheless, there was still room for improvement in the taxation system. Medium and large firms had to pay not only income tax but also adjustment tax which was enterprise-specific. Many SOEs suffered losses and had to negotiate with the state for subsidies. While the tax rate was high, actual exemptions were large, so tax revenues were not as high as expected.

The 1987 Reform: the contract responsibility system

In 1987 the central government introduced the contract responsibility system (CRS) on the basis of the *li gai shui* system for SOEs. This system was introduced on an experimental basis in the 1980s, and was implemented nationwide after 1987. Under the CRS, SOEs were contracted to pay income tax and adjustment tax on a specific level of profit. If they exceeded the contracted level of profit, they were taxed at a lower rate on their additional profit. The contracted levels were usually based on previous years' profits plus some predicted growth. The CRS aimed to improve enterprise performance by strengthening financial responsibility, emphasizing profitability, and giving enterprises greater autonomy in decision-making.

The shift to this new system affected government revenue collection. Following implementation of the system, government revenue collection of direct taxes on enterprises declined steadily. For example, in 1978, direct taxes accounted for 60 percent of total revenue and 93 percent of direct taxes came from SOEs' profit remittances. In 1989, direct taxes accounted for only 19 percent of the total revenue and only 8 percent of direct taxes were from SOEs' profit remittances.[3]

The CRS generated a strong incentive for enterprises to improve economic efficiency because it gave them greater autonomy in decision-making. But the CRS was also diagnosed as a major cause of fiscal decline because enterprises could retain all or most of their above-quota profits, while the central government had to reduce profit remittance from enterprises if they lost money. Consequently, the central government's fiscal situation deteriorated steadily.[4]

Furthermore, under the CRS, each province had greater autonomy over extra-budgetary revenues. An unintended consequence of the CRS was that it bred a greater sense of localism and led to a rise of economic dukedoms (*zhuhou jingji*). Local governments developed industries, and then the central government tried to bring the industries under its control through the imposition of increased taxes. Conflict between the central and local governments thus deepened.[5]

To increase government revenues, the central government implemented another round of tax reform in 1989, the tax plus profit system (*li shui fen liu*). SOEs were required to pay corporate income taxes first, and then submit a portion of their profits to the state. By doing so, the central government attempted to have a larger share of SOEs' profit since it owned them, and SOEs no longer had the privilege to use the before-tax profits to repay debt caused by wrong investment decisions. To increase enterprises' ability to repay their debts, the state lowered income tax rate for small firms. The tax rate for large and medium enterprises remained at 55 percent, but for small enterprises, the rate was set at 35 percent.

The result of this reform effort was still not satisfactory. Since the CRS had been introduced, negotiations between enterprises and the state, and between central government and local governments on how much tax should be paid, had increased dramatically. SOE managers were more concerned about bargaining with the government to secure the best possible tax arrangement than about competing with other firms. This undermined the rationale behind the government's efforts to reform the SOEs.

The institutional basis of central–local fiscal relations

The central government faced a serious dilemma in implementing fiscal reforms. How was it to increase state revenue by enlisting the support of the provincial governments while retaining some measure of central control over fiscal policy? Traditionally, the provincial government played a significant role in China's administrative structure because they acted as revenue collectors, as instruments of policy implementation, and as institutions with their own interests. The first two roles meant that fiscal decentralization was hardly possible without provincial cooperation. As for their third role, it meant that provincial governments had interests that might not always coincide with those of the central government. The key therefore lay in providing appropriate and sufficient incentives to provincial governments and enterprises alike so that they would be motivated to support the central government's overriding objective of increasing state revenue. This proved to be easier said than done.

China's fiscal system was characterized by interdependence between the center and the provinces. It was a unitary system in theory whereby the central government directed expenditure policy and determined all aspects of tax policy. Almost all taxes were national-level taxes formally accruing to the central government. Provincial governments had few revenue sources of their own, and they shared the revenue they collected with the central government, which held the major responsibility for determining the distribution of revenues among the provinces. In practice, however, the fiscal system was rather decentralized. The central government did not have a unitary nationwide tax collection mechanism. Rather, taxes were collected at the provincial level by provincial governments on behalf of the central government. The central government's revenue thus in fact accrued first to provincial governments, which were acting as collection agents. This reliance on the provincial governments for tax collection complicated China's fiscal system.

Despite playing an indispensable role in collecting revenue, provincial governments could neither levy taxes nor spend revenue as they chose. They had to collect all fiscal revenue in their area of jurisdiction and forward a predetermined proportion to Beijing. The division of the state budget income between the center and provinces was not based on any firm set of rules, but rather on *ad hoc* arrangements. The share of total tax revenue allocated to a province was subject to unpredictable variations annually, and no province had any certainty about future income. The Ministry of Finance had to bargain with provinces periodically to determine the proportion of taxes that provinces should forward to Beijing.[6]

Against this institutional background, provincial governments had no direct interest in increasing their revenue because whether they ran a surplus or deficit did not matter to them. It was the central government's business to balance fiscal income and expenditure. Instead, the provinces were usually dissatisfied with the central government's taxation behavior, just as the central government was unhappy with the provincial governments' taxation behavior. After the economic reform began, the provincial–central fiscal relationship became an increasingly contentious issue. Two aspects of the relationship had to be set right. First, the central government had to devolve more fiscal power to the provincial governments and let them benefit more from their taxation collection efforts. And second, some sort of long-term rules governing central–provincial fiscal relations had to be established, i.e., the relationship between the two needed to be legalized or institutionalized.

As a result, from 1980 onwards, the central government implemented a new fiscal system, "cooking in separate kitchens" *(fenzhao chifan)*.[7] Under this system, the central government no longer planned the expenditures of local governments nor did it issue mandatory fiscal targets. On their part, the provincial governments had the authority to structure their budget by determining their fiscal arrangements with sub-provincial administrations. They could acquire a steady and growing source of revenue by having their share of the industrial and commercial tax fixed for five years.

Between 1982 and 1985, the central government made several major adjustments to the fiscal structure in order to increase its share of national revenues and incorporate extra-budgetary funds into the fiscal management system. First, measures were taken to increase the central government's revenue share, including reducing the central government's deficit by borrowing revenue from the provinces and readjusting the provincial rate of sharing, as well as reducing its subsidies to bail

out enterprises running at a deficit. Second, except for Guangdong and
Fujian, all provinces implemented a system of sharing total revenue, and
they shared most of their revenue sources with the central government
at a single negotiated rate fixed for five years.[8] Third, the central government instituted controls over extra-budgetary funds. Various measures
were taken to curb the use of extra-budgetary funds, including borrowing money from local units, implementing a tight monetary policy which
raised interest rates and encouraged savings, and adopting a strict policy
for releasing funds.

These reforms were expected to generate a more stable fiscal relationship between the center and provinces, but this did not materialize. The
reform failed to bring the central government more revenue. Although the
center could receive a stable revenue income from the provinces, it had
to subsidize increasingly poor provinces and SOEs. Government deficits
increased, becoming a major cause of inflation which led in turn to mass
dissatisfaction.[9]

In order to control the deficit and improve the fiscal situation, the
central government brought in the contract responsibility system (CRS)
in 1987 in some rich areas. A major aim of this system was to require
local governments at all levels to balance their revenues and expenditures. According to an official explanation, the system had a number of
advantages.[10] First, the reform destroyed the old single jurisdiction regarding revenue and expenditure. Revenues were divided between the
center and the provinces. Those provinces that managed enterprises well
could benefit more from their revenues. Expenditures were also divided
between the center and the provinces, with the latter being responsible
for their own budgets.

Second, the reform was expected to institutionalize provincial incentives. The new system streamlined the old hierarchical allocation of fiscal
resources. It no longer defined provincial expenditures in detail. Instead,
provincial officials had autonomy in determining their expenditures.

Third, the new system greatly reduced the need for bargaining between the center and the provinces. Under the old system, fiscal sharing
between the two actors was set annually. But under the new one, once
the base figure was established, it lasted for five years. Accordingly, once
the center's fiscal behavior became more predictable, provincial officials
could make long-term plans.

Nevertheless, these rational calculations did not work due to the nature
of China's fiscal system. The central government wanted to decentralize
financial autonomy to provide incentives not only to the provincial governments but also to the individual enterprises that came under their jurisdiction. But it encountered a predicament: on the one hand, it wanted

provincial governments not to interfere in enterprise activities and let the market influence these activities; on the other hand, it needed provincial governments to effectively manage the economies in their domain to bring in greater revenues for the central government. Moreover, provincial governments had their interests to safeguard, which further complicated the fiscal reform. Provincial officials considered not only whether a given central fiscal policy was favorable to the areas under their jurisdiction, but also what benefits they could gain from such a policy. Decentralizing fiscal power to provinces was no guarantee that provincial officials would follow the priorities set by the central offices. Fiscal reform provided a strong incentive for provincial officials to act like entrepreneurs, using various ways to increase provincial revenues, and the resultant behavior was not always in line with the central government's expectation. Instead, it became an effective tool for local governments to seek greater power in relation to the central government.

The power shift between the center and the provinces

All these fiscal reforms led to drastic decline in state revenue.[11] Consolidated government revenue as a ratio of GDP fell continuously, from 34.4 percent in 1979 to less than 20 percent in 1989.[12] The government's inability to cut expenditures to keep pace with declining revenues created perennial budget deficits.

But when revenue sharing between the center and the provinces is examined, the picture is not so straightforward. The central government's share of collections increased from 20.6 percent of total collections in 1981 to 41.3 percent in 1990 (see Table 6.1). This shift was largely due to the central government's taxation reforms which enabled it to transfer a portion of enterprise profit to the center directly. In 1981, the central government spent 262 percent of the amount it collected, meaning that the central government relied heavily on revenue transfers passed up from the provinces. But in 1990 it spent only 96 percent of collections. This decline in central expenditures was an important change for two reasons. First, it meant that the central government increased its share of revenue collections in the context of a marked overall decline in total collections, and second, provinces reduced their transfers to the central government. The center and the provinces thus became relatively independent fiscally.

On the provincial side, the share of revenue declined to 58.7 percent in 1990 from 79.4 percent in 1981, while the share of expenditures increased to 60 percent from 46 percent during the same time period. These changes meant that the provinces became increasingly independent in that the revenues previously passed on to the center were now retained

Table 6.1 Changing significance of the fiscal arrangements
between the central government and the provinces, 1981–90
(percentage)*

	Central gov. share of		Provincial gov. share of	
	Collection of total	Expenditure of total	Collection of total	Expenditure of total
1981	20.6	54.0	79.4	46.0
1982	23.0	49.9	76.0	50.1
1983	29.8	49.7	70.2	50.3
1984	34.9	47.8	65.1	52.2
1985	37.9	45.3	62.1	54.7
1986	40.6	41.2	59.4	58.8
1987	38.2	42.1	61.8	57.9
1988	39.8	39.2	60.2	60.8
1989	37.5	36.4	62.5	63.6
1990	41.3	39.8	58.7	60.0

* The figures in this table refer to central and local collections and not to actual
revenue, by each level of government, before grants and revenues.
Source: calculated from the State Statistical Bureau, *Zhongguo tongji nianjian
1991* (China Statistical Yearbook 1991) (Beijing: Zhongguo tongji nianjian
chubanshe, 1991), p. 221.

at the provincial level. As a result, the central government's fiscal burden
increased although its collection capacity grew. The primary cause of the
increasing deficit was due to the central government's huge subsidies of
various types.

Fiscal decentralization also led to wide disparities in per capita revenue collections and expenditures among the provinces (see Table 6.2).
In 1985, the per capita revenue collection in Shanghai was 1,492 yuan
while it was 40 in Tibet, and 49 in Guizhou. There was a correlation
between a higher level of revenue collection and higher levels of economic development. Four provinces – Shanghai, Beijing, Tianjin and
Liaoning – collected 31 percent of revenues even though they accounted
for 6.4 percent of the national population.[13] Similarly, there were disparities on the expenditure side. In 1985, the per capita expenditure was 346
yuan in Shanghai and 344 in Beijing while it was 63 in Sichuan, and 66 in
Anhui. The same four high income provinces accounted for 15.2 percent
of total expenditures.

Compared to the expenditure side, the collection side displayed much
smaller disparities.[14] Tax collections were higher in the provinces where
income was higher. Higher income provinces, however, did not make
greater efforts to collect taxes and thus raised less revenue than might

Table 6.2 Collection and expenditure disparities among the provinces, 1991 (ranking)

	Per capita revenue	Per capita expenditure		Per capita revenue	Per capita expenditure
Shanghai	1	3	Xinjiang	16	7
Beijing	2	2	Hubei	17	21
Tianjin	3	4	Shandong	18	25
Liaoning	4	8	Hebei	19	27
Guangdong	5	14	Ningxia	20	6
Zhejiang	6	17	Hainan	21	10
Yunnan	7	11	Henan	22	26
Helongjiang	8	13	Shaanxi	23	19
Jilin	9	12	Guizhou	24	23
Shanxi	10	16	Guangxi	25	20
Fujian	11	15	Sichuan	26	29
Jiangsu	12	22	Jiangxi	27	24
Qinhai	13	5	Hunan	28	30
Inn. Mongolia	14	9	Anhui	29	28
Gansu	15	18	Tibet	30	1

Source: Ma Hong and Sun Shangqing (eds.), *Zhongguo jingji xingshi yu zhanwang* (China's Economic Situation and Prospects, 1991–1992) (Beijing: Zhongguo fazhan chubanshe, 1992), p. 156.

be expected. In other words, richer provinces tended to become weak in their revenue efforts even though they collected more revenue than poorer provinces did.[15]

The 1994 Reform and fiscal federalism

As of the late 1980s, the momentum towards the development of the revenue-division system (*fen shuizhi*) or fiscal federalism gathered speed. For the central government, the implementation of fiscal federalism was expected to achieve at least three aims. First, enterprises would be treated equally regardless of whether they were owned by the central government, provinces or any other actors. Under the CRS, enterprises were treated extremely unequally, which often led to unfair competition among different enterprises. Because fiscal federalism applied the same tax rate to different enterprises, provincial governments were expected not to treat the enterprises owned by the central government in a discriminatory manner.[16] Second, fiscal federalism would institutionalize the center–province relationship. The central government would not step into provincial taxation affairs once the overall allocation had been negotiated. Provincial governments would have real autonomy in determining provincial tax affairs, and they could implement different fiscal policies which were appropriate to their own circumstances. Third, under the new system, there were separate revenue sources for the central and local governments. Provincial governments had authority to determine the tax rate and to reduce tax within their domains, and thus could use fiscal policies to regulate their provincial economies. On the other hand, because the central government had its own fixed revenue sources and retained authority over revenue sharing (between the central and provincial governments), the center's fiscal capacity was expected to increase and stabilize.[17]

In 1994, the central government established a new, federal style taxation system, and introduced some major institutional changes into the relations between the center and the provinces. First of all, under the new system, taxes were divided into three categories: central, local, and shared. Central taxes would go to the central coffers, local taxes would go to local budgets, and shared taxes were to be divided between the center and the provinces according to previously established agreements (see Table 6.3 for detail).

Second, a central tax bureau (*guo shui ju*) and local tax bureau (*di shui ju*) were established as two separate entities. Instead of authorizing local tax offices to collect virtually all taxes, the center now collects taxes with its own institutions independent from the provinces. Third, the new system recognizes independent provincial power, that is, provincial authorities can collect several types of taxes without central interference. A system of "central to local tax rebate (*shuishuo fanhuan*)" was also established, and shared taxes are collected by the central government first, then divided between the center and the provinces.

These institutional changes shifted fiscal power from the provinces to the center to a great degree. As shown in Table 6.4, total government revenue has increased quite dramatically since 1994. Total government revenue has increased consistently since the reform. Central collection as a proportion of total tax collection has increased from less then 30 percent to around 50 percent. If the locally collected revenue that the local governments are obliged to remit to the central coffers are included, then the central government's share reaches about two-thirds of total government revenue.

Yet, under the system of "central to local tax rebate," the central government has to return a proportion of the revenue to the provinces. But because the center collects and redistributes the bulk of the revenues, the fiscal dependence of the provinces on the central government increased substantially. Before 1994, the central government tended to rely heavily on such coastal provinces as Shanghai, Shandong, Zhejiang, Jiangsu, and

Table 6.3 Revenue bases under the 1994 tax sharing system

Central fixed revenue base	Local fixed revenue base	Central–local shared revenue base
• Profit remittances by and income tax on center-owned state enterprises, local and foreign banks, and other financial businesses • Tariffs • Consumption and value-added taxes collected by the customs • Tax refunds to external trade enterprises • Business taxes, income taxes, and urban maintenance and construction taxes of Railway Department, main banking branches, and insurance companies • Consumption taxes	• Business taxes and income taxes of local state enterprises • Personal income tax • Urban land use taxes • The Stamp tax • Vehicle utilization tax • The animal slaughter tax • The title tax • Agricultural and husbandry taxes; tax on agricultural special products • Tax on alternative use of arable land • Inheritance and gift taxes • Capital gains tax on land • State land sales revenues	• Value-added tax (extended to incorporate the product tax; 75% going to the center, and 25% to localities) • Resources tax (incorporating salt tax; most of it would be retained by the localities, with the exception of ocean petroleum tax) • New securities trading taxes (divided evenly between the center and localities)

Sources: Christine Wong, *Financing Local Government in the People's Republic of China* (Hong Kong: Oxford University Press, 1997), pp. 34–5; Tsang Shu-ki and Cheng Yuk-shing, "China's Tax Reforms of 1994: Breakthrough or Compromise," *Asian Survey*, 34: 9 (September 1994), p. 775.

Guangdong for revenue contribution. Now it is the provinces that rely on the central government for revenue.

Financial liberalization and centralization

A modern financial system is essential for a modern economic state. A modern financial system is composed of a banking system and a capital market, which serve to channel financial resources and to discipline the use of these resources. China's financial system has been dominated by banks, though a capital market is developing. As of the late twentieth century, banks accounted for 90 percent of all financial intermediation between savers and investors.[18] As such, my discussion here focuses on the development of the banking sector. Since how the central bank

Table 6.4 Revenue and expenditures by central and provincial
governments (100 million yuan)*

	Total Revenues				Total Expenditures			
Year	Local gov.	Central gov.	Central gov. %	Total	Local gov.	Central gov.	Central gov. %	Total
1970	480.0	183.0	27.6	662.9	267.0	382.4	58.9	649.4
1975	719.0	96.6	11.8	815.6	411.5	409.4	49.9	820.9
1976	677.7	98.9	12.7	776.6	428.6	377.2	46.8	806.2
1977	760.6	113.9	13.0	874.5	449.8	393.7	46.7	843.5
1978	956.5	175.8	15.5	1132.3	590.0	532.1	47.4	1122.1
1979	915.0	231.3	20.2	1146.4	626.7	655.1	51.1	1281.8
1980	875.5	284.5	24.5	1159.9	562.0	666.8	54.3	1228.8
1981	864.7	311.1	26.5	1175.8	512.8	625.7	55.0	1138.4
1982	865.5	346.8	28.6	1212.3	578.2	651.8	53.0	1230.0
1983	876.9	490.0	35.8	1367.0	649.9	759.6	53.9	1409.5
1984	977.4	665.5	40.5	1642.9	807.7	893.3	52.5	1707.0
1985	1235.2	769.6	38.4	2004.8	1209.0	795.3	39.7	2004.3
1986	1343.6	778.4	36.7	2122.0	1386.6	836.4	37.9	2204.9
1987	1463.1	736.3	33.5	2199.4	1416.6	845.6	37.4	2262.2
1988	1582.5	774.8	32.9	2357.2	1646.2	845.0	33.9	2491.2
1989	1842.4	822.5	30.9	2664.9	1935.0	888.8	31.5	2823.8
1990	1944.7	992.4	33.8	2937.1	2079.1	1004.5	32.6	3083.6
1991	2211.2	938.3	29.8	3149.5	2295.8	1090.8	32.2	3386.6
1992	2503.9	979.5	28.1	3483.4	2571.8	1170.4	31.3	3742.2
1993	3391.4	957.5	22.0	4349.0	3330.2	1312.1	28.3	4642.3
1994	2311.6	2906.5	55.7	5218.1	4038.2	1754.4	30.3	5792.6
1995	2985.6	3256.6	52.2	6242.2	4828.3	1995.4	29.2	6823.7
1996	3746.9	3661.1	49.4	7408.0	5786.3	2151.3	27.1	7937.6

* The figures do not include the revenues from issuing debt, interest payment or basic
construction expenditures financed by foreign debt.
Sources: The State Statistical Bureau, *Zhongguo jinrong nianjian* (The Finance Yearbook of
China) (Beijing: Zhongguo tongji chubanshe, 1997), pp. 461, 462.

works determines whether the central government is capable of exercising
its control over the financial sector, the discussion will examine in detail
the evolution of China's central bank, People's Bank of China (PBOC).

Prior to 1978, China operated a monobanking system. The People's
Bank of China functioned as both a central bank and a commercial bank.
International business was handled by the Bank of China (BOC), which
served as the foreign exchange arm of the PBOC. Under the monobanking system, government and enterprise financing needs were fulfilled by
the annual budget and annual credit plans, which regulated the direct allocation of financial resources. Government and enterprise transactions
were reflected as book entries of the PBOC, which functioned much like

the government cashier. Under central planning, there was no need for financial intermediation; nor was there debt financing. Interest rates and money supply were fixed administratively as part of the state plan. Monetary policy was essentially an adjunct of fiscal policy.

Economic reform and banking institution-building

Institution rebuilding in the financial sector has been closely associated with economic reforms in China, as it has elsewhere. The development of the banking sector reflects not only the needs resulting from market-oriented economic reforms, but also the willingness of the Chinese leadership to lead economic reforms and rebuild the infrastructure of China's economic state.

After market-oriented reform was initiated in the late 1970s, the financing of enterprises started to shift from direct state allocation to loans, and a greater range of financial services was required. Since economic reform was first initiated in the agricultural sector, the Agricultural Bank of China (ABC), which focuses on deposit and lending activity in rural areas, was established in 1979. In the same year, two other banks were established. The Bank of China (BOC) was separated from the People's Bank and became an economic entity directly subordinated to the State Council. The bank's business scope was expanded rapidly to support the country's opening to the world. Furthermore, the Construction Bank of China (CBC), which was previously under the administrative control of the Ministry of Finance, became directly subordinated to the State Council, in the same administrative rank as China's other banks.

In 1980, China joined the World Bank and the International Monetary Fund. To meet these changes, the China Investment Bank (CIB) was formally created in 1981 to control the disbursement of project funds provided to China by the World Bank. Again, after China became a member of the Asian Development Bank in 1986, the CIB assumed responsibility for the disbursement of funds from that bank.

Several other important changes took place in the 1980s, the most important of which was the creation of China's central bank in 1984. After PBOC became the central bank, its deposit-making and lending functions were taken over by the Industrial and Commercial Bank of China (ICBC). The ICBC was created through a reorganization of the branch network of the PBOC.

Ten years later in 1994, the leadership introduced a rather radical reform program in the banking sector. The main thrust of this reform was 1) to set up a strong and independent central bank, with the primary responsibility of maintaining monetary and exchange rate stability, and 2) to commercialize the banking system in which the state-owned specialized banks would operate on a commercial basis, leaving unprofitable "policy lending" to three newly created "policy banks": the State Development Bank of China, the Agricultural Development Bank of China, and the China Import and Export Bank. This kicked off the transformation of the four state banks – the ICBC, ABC, BOC, and CBC – into commercial banks.

In 1995, China enacted the Central Banking Law to confirm the status of the PBOC as the central bank of China. This was shortly followed by the promulgation of the Commercial Bank Law, the Negotiable Instrument Law, and the Insurance Law, which together provided the rudimentary legal framework for financial supervision and the proper functioning of the financial sector.

Meanwhile, competition was gradually introduced into the banking system and this helped to speed up the development of China's financial sector. Broadly speaking, this was done in several ways. To begin with, the division of business among the four state banks was at first quite blurred. The four state banks were established originally for different business areas and were not allowed to compete head-on with each other. For example, foreign exchange business was once monopolized by the BOC. Subsequently, however, the other three state banks, along with the newly established banks, and trust and investment companies (TICs), were allowed to engage in foreign exchange business. The increased competition reduced the foreign exchange business share of BOC from virtually 100 percent in 1979 to about 40 percent by 1996.[19]

After the mid-1980s, many banks and TICs were established, with the China International Trust and Investment Corporation (CITIC) the first to be set up. Other new national banks included the Bank of Communications, the Everbright Bank, the Huaxia Bank, and the Minsheng Bank (China's first non-state-owned bank). These banks are not subject to any geographic restrictions and can establish branches nationwide, subject to the approval of the central bank.

Meanwhile, some large regional banks were established, including the Guangdong Development Bank, the Shenzhen Development Bank, Merchants Bank, the Fujian Industrial Bank, the Bengbu Housing Savings Bank in Anhui province, the Hainan Development Bank, and the Yantai Housing Savings Bank in Shangdong province. The entry of new financial institutions created a more level playing field for all financial institutions, both state and non-state alike.

Over the years, some regional banks have expanded rapidly beyond their regional orientation. The Shenzhen-based Merchants Bank and Shanghai Pudong Development Bank, for example, have established branches outside Shenzhen and Shanghai, respectively. Many urban cooperatives have been converted into urban cooperative banks. Of greater significance, banks have started to become more consumer-oriented, offering consumer loans for automobile hire purchases and mortgages for state-owned housing schemes. The big state banks have taken steps to promote e-banking. In particular, the ICBC has started to spread its online banking business to enterprises throughout the country.

Above all, the banking sector has gradually opened up to foreign participation. Initially, in the 1980s, a few foreign financial institutions were allowed to set up branches only in the Special Economic Zones. In 1990, Shanghai became the first coastal city to open to foreign banks. In 1996, several foreign banks in Shanghai were granted licenses to conduct renminbi business on a limited basis. In 1998, more of such licenses were issued. In 1999, both operational and geographical restrictions were further relaxed, so as to allow foreign banks to engage in domestic currency business in more cities and more provinces.

As a result of the gradual process of reform, along with the dynamic growth of China's economy and foreign trade, China's financial sector experienced remarkable growth in the 1990s. By the end of 1999, China could boast a fairly comprehensive banking and financial structure. It consisted of 4 wholly state-owned commercial banks, 3 policy banks, 10 joint-equity commercial banks, 90 city commercial banks, 836 urban credit cooperatives, 41,755 rural credit cooperatives, 230 trust and investment corporations, 70 finance companies, and 15 leasing companies.[20]

The Asian financial crisis and financial centralization

The Asian financial crisis had a major impact on the regional and the world economy, including China. The crisis triggered a new wave of multifaceted financial reforms in China. Among others, the reform of the central bank, more than anything else, reflects how the central government has attempted to exercise its control over China's economy through the greater use of financial instruments.

In the pre-reform period, the PBOC was hardly a financial institution with its own autonomy. Initially, it was a separate entity under the State Council, with the same administrative rank as the Ministry of Finance and other planning agencies. After the Great Leap Forward (1957–58) and until the mid-1970s, the PBOC was subordinated to the Ministry of Finance and its role then was more fiscal in orientation rather than financial. Though the PBOC was separated from the Ministry of Finance in 1976, it remained a weak financial institution.

After the leadership initiated economic reform, changes were introduced in the PBOC. In 1984, the PBOC formally assumed the function of a central bank. In 1985, the PBOC began to be responsible for issuing currency, managing credit, setting interest rates, and supervising China's foreign exchange business. It set reserve requirements for the specialized banks, promulgated credit targets, and adjusted the flow of funds across banks. It also assumed the supervisory and regulatory roles associated with central banks elsewhere. In 1985, the PBOC established a Department of Examination and Supervision, and in 1986, the State Council issued a formal regulation legalizing the central bank's supervision of specialized banks, rural credit cooperatives, and other financial institutions.[21]

All these changes reflected central government attempts to build the PBOC into an effective financial institution in China's economy. Nevertheless, it was not until Zhu Rongji's economic reform in 1993 that the PBOC was able to exercise its central bank role more effectively. Among other factors, the structure of China's central–local relations constrained the working of the PBOC as the central bank.

Central–local relations and the central bank

The reform leadership expected the banking system to become an indirect instrument to manage China's economy. Additionally, if the bank could become an independent enterprise whose goal was to make profit, it would be capable of both providing enterprises with financial resources and achieving effective use of those resources. Facing financial demands from enterprises, the bank would have autonomy to collect financial resources, and to issue loans to enterprises. With increasing competition among enterprises, the banking system was required to be an independent profit maker.[22]

In order to increase its autonomy, political decentralization measures were introduced into the banking sector, especially in regards to the PBOC. This was reflected in changes in the nomenclature system. After the 1984 nomenclature reform, in the PBOC system, the number of posts on the Central Committee's nomenclature fell by at least 87 percent. Only a handful of the top positions in the bank headquarters appeared on the list, and most of the positions previously on the central nomenclature are now on the bank's own nomenclature.[23]

By doing so, the central government attempted to empower the PBOC vis-à-vis other state administrative organizations. But there was also a central–local issue regarding the PBOC, which greatly constrained the power of the PBOC. The provincial branches of the PBOC were subordinated to local party and government officials. The provincial party committee had the power of appointment, dismissal, transfer, and promotion of personnel of banks operating within their geographic jurisdictions.

This structure undermined the ability of the head office of the PBOC in Beijing to implement its policies at local levels. In effect, local branches could hardly make their own decisions on mundane matters such as the extension of credit. Instead, their decisions were responses to the requests by local party and government officials.

In order to cope with strong local resistance, the PBOC sought the power of appointment of personnel in its provincial branches in the 1980s, but with little success. Only in 1988 was the PBOC formally vested with the power to appoint and remove provincial and lower level branch managers. Nevertheless, the PBOC still had to consult local party officials, who held veto power over personnel appointments.

In the aftermath of the 1989 crackdown on the pro-democracy movement and the collapse of communism in Eastern Europe, a wave of conservatism swept across the country. Deng Xiaoping's southern tour in 1992 triggered a fresh wave of investment expansion. The rapid and huge influx of investment led to high inflation, which posed a threat to China's political and social stability. The central government made a great effort to cope with an overheated economy.

In 1993, Zhu Rongji, who was already Vice Premier, assumed the additional role as President of the PBOC. This position enabled him to appoint and remove the heads of PBOC branches in each province. Beginning in 1994, the PBOC, for the first time in its history, refused to lend money to the Ministry of Finance to cover the state's budget deficit. This act was formally justified in the provisions of the Central Bank Law in 1995. The head office of the PBOC in Beijing gained full control of the bank credit extended to financial institutions. In other words, the authority for all PBOC lending and allocation of credit quotas was centralized.[24]

Banking centralization after the Asian financial crisis

China was one of the few economies in Asia that were largely spared from the adverse impact of the 1997 Asian financial crisis. Its success in staving off the crisis was believed to be due to a number of factors. First of all, Zhu Rongji had successfully achieved a soft-landing of the Chinese economy with his radical financial reform before the crisis. By 1997, macroeconomic fundamentals, in terms of higher growth and lower inflation, were far stronger in China than in other Asian economies. What made China different from the crisis-ridden Asian economies was China's healthy and stable external economic position. On account of its strong export performance and rising trade surplus, China did not have current account deficits.

Second, in other Asian countries, much of the foreign investment was hot money, i.e., short-term portfolio investment and debt. By contrast, the capital inflows to China were predominantly foreign direct investment (FDI), which was much less volatile. China had been highly successful in attracting FDI so its external debt was relatively small, especially in terms of its exports and its existing foreign reserves. In other words, China had not over-borrowed as Thailand and South Korea did.

Third, there was a high degree of government intervention in the financial system in terms of capital controls. The renminbi was not easily convertible for capital transactions. It was not possible for international currency speculators to "short sell" the renminbi outside China. Nor was it possible for outside panic to spark off a massive capital flight from China.[25]

Even though China had emerged relatively unscathed from the regional financial crisis, the Chinese leadership realized that China's economic system was also plagued by problems similar to those in Thailand, Indonesia, Malaysia, and South Korea. Bank dominance of the financial system, lack of central bank autonomy, policy and political lending, accumulation of bad loans, absence of a strong and disciplined equity market, weak regulation of commercial banks, nepotism and corruption, all these factors had contributed to the financial crisis, and they all, for better or worse, existed in China's economic system. The Chinese leadership made greater efforts to reform the country's financial system, especially the central bank.

In November 1997, China's leadership convened a national financial work conference in Beijing to discuss the implications of the crisis for China. Jiang Zemin, Li Peng, and Zhu Rongji spoke at the conference. Other members of the Standing Committee of the Political Bureau were present. Such a high level conference was unusual, and it reflected the leadership's concern about the implications of the crisis on China. The meeting focused on the similarities between China's weak financial institutions and those in other Asian countries. Analyses were made on how the weak financial systems in these countries led to the crisis. Particular attention was paid to why the central bank in these countries was not able to exercise adequate prudential supervision over commercial lending.[26]

Meanwhile, heated discussions took place among Chinese researchers and think tanks. While many lamented the power of international financial capital and its threat to the national sovereignty and national economic security in developing countries, others believed that the financial crisis was deeply rooted in the domestic institutions of those countries.[27]

Whatever their arguments, they all believed that economic globalization was inevitable, and the only way for China to prevent such a crisis was to engage in deep financial reforms.[28]

The Asian financial crisis and its domestic reaction created a favorable atmosphere as well as pressure for the leadership to introduce some radical reform measures to the country's financial system. The most important was the restructuring of the PBOC, with its 32 provincial and city branches being merged into 9 regional branches. The new banking system resembled the US Federal Reserve system, and was supposed to have autonomy and be free from local political intervention.[29] The new system began to function in 1999.

Moreover, serious measures were introduced into non-bank financial institutions aimed at curbing illegal behavior in this sector. The most notable action was the closing and bankruptcy of the Guangdong International Trust and Investment Corporation (GITIC), China's second largest trust and investment company.[30] Prior to GITIC's closure, the government had taken steps to liquidate the Hainan Development Bank in June 1998, and two other TICs. Subsequently, 21 urban credit cooperatives and 18 rural credit cooperatives were closed as part of government efforts to prevent contagion in the financial system. In August 2000, the debt-ridden China Education, Science and Technology Trust and Investment Corporation was closed down.[31]

The government also made greater efforts to strengthen central regulation on the financial system. In June 1998, the CCP Central Committee established a Financial Work Committee headed by Political Bureau member Wen Jiabao. The committee was designed to institute vertical leadership over the financial system. Meanwhile, a Financial Discipline Committee was set up to step up the fight against corruption. Similarly, the government took action to strengthen the vertical control of the securities industry through China Securities Regulatory Committee. In November 1998, China Insurance Regulatory Committee was established.[32]

Financial reform and a market economy

China's leaders have made greater efforts to reform the country's financial system, especially the banking system. The financial reform has consisted of strengthening the independence of the central bank, converting state-owned banks into genuinely commercial entities, and the development of a disciplined capital market. All reform measures introduced so far were aimed at increasing the role of the "invisible hand" of the market in the allocation of resources and thus laying down an institutional framework for a market economy.

Despite all these efforts, challenges still remain. To begin with, the state commercial banks have still to be restructured. Prior to the 1994 reform, these banks were not run as truly commercial banks, and they inherited a bureaucratic management style whereby bank branches were under the dual leadership of the bank headquarters and the local government. The banks were pressured to make loans to loss-making SOEs, usually against commercial considerations. Though such pressures have been reduced with reform measures such as the establishment of the three policy banks, the state commercial banks are still pushed by the government to make unprofitable loans.

Furthermore, there are internal problems in the banking system. The management of the banks and their branches are usually political appointees (i.e., the party cadres) who are not held responsible for the banks' commercial performance. Problems such as weak internal control, poor discipline, and lack of well-trained professional staff, all have plagued the financial sector.

More importantly, it is still uncertain whether the central bank, the PBOC, will be able to develop sufficient independence to carry out its role effectively. The Central Bank Law, passed in 1995, stated that the PBOC should independently implement monetary policies and be free from any intervention. Nevertheless, as Nicholas Lardy pointed out, many factors have seriously undermined its presumed independence. For example, the law stated that the PBOC exercised its power under the leadership of the State Council. This implied that the bank was not the final authority on important matters, and that it had to refer to the State Council for approval. Furthermore, the PBOC continued to lend to industrial enterprises and other commercial activities, and this undermined the bank's independence.[33]

The leadership has attempted to restructure the central bank along the lines of the Federal Reserve Bank in the United States. To achieve this goal, the central bank has to gain autonomy vis-à-vis other ministerial level units under the State Council, as well as vis-à-vis party and government leaders in the provinces. As Lardy pointed out, the central bank has to have sufficient independence and political power to achieve two objectives. First, it must be able to insulate banks from demands from political leaders to extend loans to projects that do not meet commercial lending standards. Second, it must ensure that any subsidies for policy lending are financed through the budget, rather than borne by the banking system.[34] As yet, the presumed autonomy of the central bank has certainly not been realized.

Building a modern enterprise system

A third important aspect of building a modern Chinese economic state involves the establishment of a modern enterprise system through SOE reforms. SOEs are essentially products of the old planned economy. In China, they used to function primarily as socio-economic entities rather than as production units only. The objective function of many large SOEs is not limited to the maximization of profits. Their operations include the provision of a number of social and welfare services normally considered "public goods" such as education, medical services, housing, child-care services and pensions. Indeed, many large SOEs exist much like "mini-welfare states;" and not surprisingly, they operate under "soft budget constraints," with the government always ready to subsidize their losses.

Official statistics showed that as of 1996, China had about 320,000 SOEs, of which some 240,000 were commonly classified as "small."[35] Of the 320,000 SOEs, only about 118,000 were engaged in industrial production, and about 16,000 were classified "large and medium."[36]

In 1978, SOEs accounted for 78 percent of China's total industrial output. By 1996, the share had declined to 29 percent.[37] But the lower output share of the state sector should not be misconstrued as a sign of diminishing economic importance, since 108.5 million or 74 percent of the urban working population still relied on the SOEs to provide them with some form of "cradle-to-grave" employment.[38] Furthermore, the state sector as a whole still controlled approximately 61 percent of total state assets and constituted some 55 percent of total domestic sales. In terms of foreign trade, about 67 percent of China's exports and 50 percent of imports in 1995 were conducted through the foreign trading arm of state firms. The economic importance of the state sector in the Chinese economy was reflected in its traditional role as a major source of central government tax revenue (Table 6.5). In fact, SOEs still predominate in key heavy industries such as iron and steel, coal, metallurgy, chemicals, energy production, and petroleum exploration, which operate on economies of scale and are generally shunned by the TVEs, or to which foreign investors are denied access.

Since the mid-1990s, the leadership has started to publish its own "Fortune 500," most of which are SOEs, including the annual best performing "Top Three."[39] In addition, there are those "Red Chips" enterprises, which have already been listed as "H shares" on the Hong Kong Stock Exchange and the "N shares" on the New York Stock Exchange. But this picture of China having many "good SOEs" can be misleading.

Table 6.5 Profits and taxes of state enterprises, 1978–94 (RMB billion)

Year	Total government tax revenue (A)	SOEs' total profits & taxes		Ratio of C/A (%)
		Profits (B)	Taxes (C)	
1978	51.93	73.35	33.13	63.8
1980	57.17	66.92	38.24	66.9
1981	62.99	64.31	40.77	64.7
1982	70.00	63.15	43.88	62.7
1983	77.56	69.65	45.55	58.7
1984	94.74	78.89	51.47	54.3
1985	204.08	99.88	69.49	34.1
1986	209.07	79.51	74.52	35.6
1987	214.04	98.15	86.51	40.4
1988	239.05	116.49	105.06	43.9
1989	272.74	100.12	123.23	45.2
1990	282.19	49.15	123.10	43.6
1991	299.02	74.45	139.29	46.6
1992	329.69	95.52	155.54	47.2
1993	425.53	166.73	197.58	46.4
1994	512.69	160.80	223.63	43.6

Sources: The State Statistical Bureau, *The Statistical Survey of China 1996* (Beijing: Zhongguo tongji chubanshe, 1997); and *China Statistical Yearbook 1996* (Beijing: Zhongguo tongji chubanshe, 1997).

In 1993, the Chinese government announced that about one-third of its SOEs were reported to have made losses, with another one-third just breaking even. The proportion of loss-making SOEs has since been increasing and by the first half of 1997, 47 percent of all SOEs were reporting losses.

In the 1980s, the reform of SOEs in China was focused mainly on improving enterprise governance with the emphasis on a progressive increase in managerial autonomy and accountability. However, no substantive results were achieved. By the early 1990s, the basic socialistic *modus operandi* of China's SOEs, particularly for the large ones, remained unchanged. But a new economic crisis was confronting the SOE sector. As a result of the government's post-Tiananmen credit crunch, many SOEs came to grief after having made heavy losses. Many more were trapped in a serious "triangular debt" involving both enterprises and state banks.[40] Apart from being a serious threat to the financial sector, these debt-ridden SOEs also imposed high fiscal burden on the government, which is obliged to subsidize their losses.[41] The Chinese leadership, therefore, had no alternative but to make new efforts to deal with the SOE problem.

Zhu Rongji's initial attempt

One of the challenges that Zhu Rongji had to contend with in his early years as Vice Premier was to address the "triangular debt" problem. Zhu attempted to end the vicious cycle by injecting large sums of money into the system. But as soon as the old debt chain was eliminated, new ones started to appear. Zhu realized that the "triangular debts" could not be stopped if a "hard budget constraint" was not imposed on the SOEs. But without other radical reform measures, "hard budget constraint" would not become reality. Zhu had to search for other ways to deal with the problems of the SOEs.

Once the Economic and Trade Office was established, Zhu began to put into operation his ideas on economic reforms, and his reform initiatives were supported and encouraged by Deng's southern tour in 1992. In the amended Constitution approved by the Eighth National People's Congress in March 1993, the name "state enterprise" or *guoying qiye* (literally, "state-run enterprise") was formally changed to *guoyou qiye* (literally, "state-owned enterprise"). This simple change in name was significant as it distinguishes between enterprise ownership and enterprise management, with the clear implication that the government is no longer obliged to be directly involved in enterprise management. SOEs are officially owned by the state but technically, they are to be managed by themselves. In other words, SOEs can now incorporate various market-oriented systems.

Corporatization attempts 1993–97

During the period 1993–97, the main thrust of the SOE reform efforts was towards the establishment of a "modern enterprise system," which was incorporated into the comprehensive economic reform package adopted by the Third Party Plenum in November 1993. Specifically, apart from promoting further improvement in enterprise governance, the government emphasized corporatization. Thus, SOEs were encouraged to develop into a profitable "modern enterprise system" by restructuring their internal operations and incentive structures, or to form new enterprise groups (or *qiye jituan*) through mergers and acquisitions or other forms of integration. Meanwhile, the experimentation of the shareholding system was stepped up. In fact, reformist leaders looked towards the Japanese *keiretsu* and South Korean *chaebols* as models. Above all, the Company Law was enacted in July 1994 in order to provide a modern legal framework for the corporatization drive.

In early 1995, Zhu's SOE reform efforts crystallized further into a more explicit strategy of *Zhuada fangxiao* or "nurturing the big into giant conglomerates while letting the small SOEs face the forces of the market." Reformist leaders believed that while they could "let go" of the 240,000 or so small, mainly local-level SOEs via various forms of restructuring including reorganization, mergers and takeover, leasing and management contract, conversion into shareholding companies, or even outright closure, they had to retain the 1,000 large SOEs belonging to the central government, for obvious economic and social reasons. These key SOEs are still of strategic importance as they constitute the backbone of China's industrial economy in terms of total capitalization and employment.

With all these reform measures, it was reported in the 1997 "Government Work Report" that in 1996, of the 1,000 targeted SOEs, 300 of them had improved their performance after the further injection of state bank loans along with tighter financial control, and an additional 57 SOEs had formed into modern enterprise groups.[42] Nevertheless, according to a survey of 124,000 SOEs in 1997, the asset–liability ratio of SOEs lay between 71.5 percent and 83.3 percent.[43]

Reform of SOEs after 1997

Before the Fifteenth Congress of the CCP, the question of how China's SOEs could be reformed further became a heated topic. The focus was on whether China should go ahead with privatization. It was an ideological taboo in China to openly advocate "private ownership," which would immediately evoke strong reaction from the conservative party ideologues and spark off the old debate on the relative virtues of socialism and capitalism. In the past, SOE reform strategy had deliberately avoided a direct attack on the "state ownership" issue by playing down the "privatization" aspects of the reform, so as not to cross into areas that were ideologically off-limits. To initiate further reforms in SOEs, the leadership had to establish the ideological groundwork first.

What the leadership did was essentially to urge people to put aside futile debates over the "public vs. private ownership," and to remind the leftist critics that China was still at the transitional "early stage of socialism," which would therefore warrant having "diverse forms of ownership to develop side by side" and "diverse economic sectors to develop side by side."[44] This implied flexibility in changing the ownership structure of SOEs, thus filling an important gap in the previous reform efforts, which encountered difficulty in coping with SOEs' weak internal incentive mechanism associated with ownership and controls.

In 1998, the government formally introduced a new concept, the shareholding system. It technically was a Chinese form of "privatization in disguise." The shareholding scheme was able to address the crucial state ownership issue more effectively, i.e., without owning a stake in the enterprise, workers and management did not have an inherent incentive to perform well.

These conceptual adjustments enabled Zhu Rongji to initiate the above-discussed radical restructuring of the state system in accordance with market principles. Nevertheless, in regards to SOE reform, not much of the policy initiative was new.

The basic strategy was still the *Zhuada fangxiao*. Even though the Asian financial crisis struck South Korea's chaebols severely, the leadership decided to go ahead with the original plan.[45] For the large and medium SOEs, the reform attempted to improve enterprise governance but the emphasis was on "corporatization" or transforming the SOEs into independent modern corporations. Thus, some merged, some broke up, some sought foreign partnership, and some were listed on stock exchanges at home and abroad.

For the numerous smaller SOEs, the main reform strategy remained pretty much the same. But the government was much more willing to "let go" of them, virtually allowing them to pick whichever mode suited them best: restructuring and reorganization, merger and/or takeover, leasing and management contract, conversion into shareholding companies or even a sell-off. Since private ownership was no longer such an ideological minefield, more SOEs could be converted into shareholding companies this time. It became easier for firms to declare bankruptcy and be sold, even to foreign partners. These smaller SOEs were given more options and greater flexibility to choose their reform paths. Many of them began to engage in potentially competitive activities that did not need the presence of the state.

Zhu Rongji and the reformist leadership have done their best in reforming China's SOEs in accordance with market principles. Nevertheless, economic reform is as much a political exercise as an economic one. In initiating and implementing reform policies, the leadership has to carefully calculate the risks and costs resulting from the SOE reform. The unemployment problem is getting more serious in the country, especially in the urban areas. Herein lies a great challenge for the leadership.

Given the current dominance of the state sector, in terms of physical, financial and human resources, and its social responsibilities and contribution to government revenue, it will take a longer time for the reform process to reap visible and real benefits for both the enterprises and the economy. China's SOEs are plagued not merely by "hard problems" such as capital shortage and outdated technology and equipment, but also by a host of equally serious "soft problems" such as corruption, nepotism, and a socialistic style regarding management and work habits, which defy simple technocratic solutions. China will require many years to put in place a functioning legal framework. It takes time for the reformed SOEs to learn to behave as competitive business units.

Economic nationalism and state-building

This chapter has argued so far that all the reforms that the Chinese leadership introduced in the taxation, finance and enterprise sectors aimed to build not just the market economy, but also a modern economic state. In other words, embedded in all these reform efforts is the idea that a modern economic state has to be rebuilt alongside a growing market-oriented economy. Therefore, associated with all these reforms was the rise of Chinese economic nationalism.

Economic nationalism came into being in the late 1980s to justify various centralization measures introduced by the central government. Many government officials and intellectuals began to reflect on the political consequences of economic decentralization. The decentralization strategy, which dominated China's economic reform in the 1980s, met with serious criticism because it was believed to have led to the rise of local power centers, thus putting the central government in a weak position when it came to implement its development policies. After comparing China to other countries, Wang Shaoguang, whose works became very influential in the early 1990s, warned that the weakening of the state capacity in China should not be read as a good sign: rather than bringing about Swedenization, as most of us have hoped, it may, at best, lead to the creation of a stable but weak democracy, or Indianization; at worse, the collapse of the central authority may even lead to the disintegration of the nation, or economic Africanization, plus political Lebanonization.[46] Wang Huning, a political scientist and who later became Jiang Zemin's advisor, regarded decentralization as a "mistake."[47]

Economic nationalism aimed to achieve rationality through state planning. It did not reject marketing, but emphasized that state planning had to direct the operation of marketplaces. In China, this ideology was embedded in the works of Chen Yun, one of the founders of China's economic system.[48] After the reform began, Chen consistently emphasized the importance of state planning and argued that both economic reforms and political reforms had to operate within the context of state plans. In other words, the most important aim of any reform was to strike a reasonable balance between market force and state planning.

Ideologically, the concept of economic nationalism largely followed Chen's thoughts on this issue. It assumed that the past reform had given rise to greater local autonomy, while the central government's autonomy had been declining fast. According to economic nationalism, and from the perspective of the central government, greater local autonomy had led to at least three serious "mistakes." First, local autonomy was characterized by its rejection of central power. The central government was incapable of penetrating into provinces and using macroeconomic policy to coordinate its economic actions. As a result, investment expanded excessively, and the central government's revenue declined rapidly. Second, because of the rapid withdrawal of the center from local economic affairs and the decline of the central government's revenue, the center was incapable of providing enough national "public goods." Meanwhile, local capacity in supplying "public goods" within the jurisdiction of the local government had increased quickly. This fact had great political significance. Citizens had developed strong local identity, and, together with local officials, resisted central policies. Third, decentralization shifted national development priority to coastal areas, and provided a great incentive for those areas to develop their economies. But there was a growing development gap between these areas and the rest of China. As a result, a neo-authoritarian regime was widely perceived as necessary, and the central government was believed to be the one which should play an important role in building a national market. Many argued that unlimited decentralization of decision-making would lead to the break up of the Chinese economy.[49] Recentralization was seen as imperative in fiscal matters. According to Chen Yuan, a crucial problem facing the Chinese economy was "whether the central government is able to centralize necessary power, especially fiscal capacity organized around economic power" in a relatively short period because in any modern economy, fiscal and financial power had to be centralized in order for the central government to implement macro management policy.[50]

According to economic nationalism, there would be no pure market economy in China, and the state had to play an important role in maintaining national integrity. Strong local autonomy had made it impossible for the central government to make and implement macroeconomic policies, and the central government therefore had to recentralize its economic power to constrain an already overly decentralized local autonomy.

Moreover, continuous economic growth depended on whether or not China could create a nationwide market, integrating China's economy. The central government had to be responsible for building such a market. Local autonomy caused the Chinese economy to take on a cellular quality, and this was a major barrier to the formation of a national market. The central government thus had to recentralize its power to constrain or even "destroy" localism.

Economic nationalism was embedded in government efforts of recentralization discussed in this chapter. What happened in the 1990s was well described by Ren Zhongping in *People's Daily* in 1994, when he argued for recentralization:

In the 1980s, the reform was "pushed" by decentralization of decision-making and fiscal power initiated by the central state and "pulled" by local initiatives. During that period, the main forces that attacked and undermined the old economic system were largely from the localities and grassroots. But now the situation is different. We need to make enormous efforts to establish a new economic system. Different units need to be coordinated. The establishment of a new fiscal system, financial system, foreign trade system, investment system and other institutions cannot be achieved from below. A strong central government is imperative to initiate and implement such reforms.[51]

7   State rebuilding, popular protest and collective action

State rebuilding is not an uncontested enterprise. Even though China remains an authoritarian state, the leadership cannot rebuild the state at will. Not only did the state rebuilding efforts produce enormous unexpected consequences but they also encouraged different social groups to jostle for participation in the new state. All these factors affected the leadership's efforts in state rebuilding. The next two chapters will discuss these aspects of state rebuilding.

This chapter focuses on how state rebuilding has led to the rise of social movements and collective action.[1] While social protests are not new in China, some forms of protests are related to state rebuilding. The term "state-building" can be defined in different ways. As I have examined in previous chapters, state-building refers to, first, the efforts of recentralization and, second, the efforts to transform China's enterprise system from a socialist-oriented one to a capitalist-oriented one. Although "state-building" often overlaps "reforms," not every measure of reform can be regarded as state-building. Economic decentralization such as financial and fiscal decentralization is not regarded as state-building. Similarly, many measures for restructuring China's enterprise system are not state-building, and only those efforts of systematic transformation aimed at strengthening the power of the central state in regulating enterprise behavior are considered state rebuilding.

A caveat has to be added here. Social movements, as Doug McAdam, John McCarthy and Mayer Zald have pointed out, can be analyzed by three broad sets of factors: political opportunities, mobilizing structures and framing processes.[2] Since this study is not about social movements in China, my discussion is not about the internal dynamism of social movements. In other words, the discussion does not focus on "mobilizing structures and framing processes," even though it will touch on these factors. Instead, the discussion will focus on the first factor, i.e., how state rebuilding has created opportunities for social movements to surface and why social movements are a part of state rebuilding.

State-building and social movements

According to Sidney Tarrow, social movements can be defined as "collective challenges by people with common purposes and solidarity in sustained interaction with elites, opponents and authorities."[3] Why do social movements take place? A social movement is not determined by a single factor, but many scholars have highlighted the role of the state. Charles Bright and Susan Harding found that social movements have been associated with state-making or building.[4] This is especially true in Europe where "the coming of the national state coincided with the birth of national movement."[5] Then, how are social movements and state-making correlated? This has been a central question for scholars on social movements such as Charles Tilly, Doug McAdam and Sidney Tarrow.[6]

Among early scholars, Tocqueville once tried to explore the impact of the state on social movements by showing how differences in state centralization produced differences in the opportunity structure of social movements. Tocqueville argued that the stronger the state, the weaker its encouragement of institutional participation and the greater the incentive to violence when collective action did break out.[7] Though it is questionable if this statement can be applied to different states, as Tarrow pointed out, what is important in Tocqueville's analysis is his search for linkages between the state structure and social movements. Tocqueville suggested that state-building created an opportunity structure for collective action of which movements took advantage.[8] Indeed, his efforts in this regard remain influential among contemporary scholars on social movements.

To many scholars, the roots of social movements are found in the process of state-making. State-making is a process of interaction between state and society. In the "statist" paradigm, the state is regarded as "an autonomous, irreducible set of institutions."[9] Nevertheless, scholars have also found that the state is a part of society, and it is not an "internally rationalized bureaucracy immune to popular influences or governed by self-generated rules;" instead, the state, as Bright and Harding pointed out, can be regarded "as the arena of routinized political competition in which class, status, and political conflicts, representing both elite and popular interests, are played out."[10]

From this point of view, state-making "not only involves states' initiatives and the reactions of social groups towards them, but also social mobilizations which target the state and trigger responses by its governors."[11] Even though the state serves as a major actor of socio-economic transformation, it cannot do so without encountering social challenges that affect the state itself. Instead, "statemaking does not end once stately institutions emerge, but is continuous . . . . [C]ontentious processes both define the state vis-à-vis other social and economic institutions and continually remake the state itself."[12] In other words, "the boundaries between legitimate state politics and the activities of challengers, dissidents, and rebels 'outside' the sphere of the state are defined and redefined by contestatory actions."[13] Therefore, popular protests can be better understood by looking at the interplay between the state and society in the process of state-making. The state defines or redefines itself in accordance with changing relations between state institutions and society.

State-making creates opportunities for social movements. According to Tarrow, modern state-building involved three basic state policies, i.e., making war, collecting taxes and provisioning food. Opportunities for social movements are embedded in these policies. Tarrow said that, "states made war and collected taxes; war and taxes required the infrastructure of a consolidated state; social movements emerged from the conflicts and opportunity structures surrounding the process of state consolidation."[14] Surely, the state engaged in all three policies not to support social mobilization but to assure and expand its power. Nevertheless, "each new policy initiative produced new channels of communication, more organized networks of citizens and more unified cognitive frameworks around which insurgents could mount claims and organize."[15] Tarrow concluded that, "these policies shaped arenas for the construction of social movements, and these movements – or the fear of the movements – shaped the way the national state evolved."[16]

According to Tilly, while state-making provided social actors with opportunities for collective action, the modern state was forged by tremendous contention not only in the countless wars fought among various emergent states, but also in the struggle between state managers and the population during the process of subjugation. As state structures were nationalized and electoral politics evolved, popular agitation also underwent profound changes. Different and deliberately constituted groups came to make claims on the state, presenting organized, sustained and self-conscious challenges to state authorities. As popular movements managed to gain access to and control over state resources, they also reshaped the political arena and altered the activities of the state itself.[17]

State rebuilding and its discontents in China

The rise of social movements in China has caught the attention of many scholars.[18] I argue that social movements in an era of capitalistic development and globalization can also be explained in the context of state rebuilding. This does not mean that the state intended to cause the rise of social movements. In the pre-reform era, Mao Zedong initiated tirelessly waves of social movements to build a socialist state or to attack his political enemies. After Deng Xiaoping came to power, however, the leadership made great efforts to demobilize society. In the former Soviet Union, *perestroika* and *glasnost* opened new opportunities for collective action and led to protest movements. In China, the leadership has accorded the highest priority to stability and economic development, and it has ruthlessly cracked down on any social movements, especially organized ones that posed serious challenges to the regime, as exemplified by the crackdown on the pro-democracy movement in 1989 and the Falun Gong (FLG) movement in recent years. Here, the issue is why popular protests rose so frequently despite tight political control by the government. In other words, why was the government not able to control the rise of popular protests despite its commitment to maintain stability?

Like elsewhere, popular protest has been an integral part of state rebuilding in China. The state has played an important role in leading China's economic and social transformation. In doing so, the state has initiated new policies (e.g., de-emphasizing the role of ideology, and uneven development policy) and engaged in various development programs (e.g., information society). While all these new policies and programs effectively promoted socio-economic transformation, they also provided tools and created opportunities for popular protests.

Information society and collective action

China has rapidly developed an information society (Chapter 1). How does the information society affect social movements? Many scholars believe that there are positive linkages between the rise of the information society and social movements. While many have argued that the information society is favorable towards the formation of the public sphere, others emphasize the impact of the information society on popular democratic political participation. According to scholars writing about the public sphere, civil society is an integral part of democracy,[19] and information technologies, especially the Internet, provide important tools for the formation of civil society.[20] Indeed, communication has been essential for the rise of the public sphere,[21] and information technologies have given rise to an "electronic public sphere."[22] Furthermore, information technologies also facilitate political participation and help transform traditional elite democracy to popular direct participation.[23] The Internet encourages direct links between the ruler and the ruled, and between the government and the people.[24]

This is certainly true in China. Information technologies have provided tools and resources for social movements, especially religious movements as exemplified by the FLG movement in recent years.[25] On April 25, 1999, over 10,000 FLG followers in Beijing grabbed the headlines of the international news media by "laying siege" to the Communist leadership compound, *Zhongnanhai*, and staging a "sit-in" to complain about the persecution of FLG followers in Tianjin and demand official recognition of its status as a respectable body. The top leadership was unnerved by such a development which its public security services had failed to pre-empt.

After 1978, the Chinese government gradually loosened restrictions on religious practice. The revival of religious movement, however, started in the 1990s when China became more advanced technologically. Without modern information technologies, the FLG would not have been able to mobilize its followers so efficiently. To a great degree, the FLG had formed a worldwide network connected by modern communication techniques. After the sit-in, the Chinese government found that the FLG was not really a simple organization as its followers had claimed, but a highly structured one linked together via modern communications such as the Internet and mobile phones. To an outsider and even its numerous new converts, FLG appeared to be a loose and informal organization based on voluntary participation, with followers paying no membership fees and reporting to no specific administrative outfit. But the Chinese leadership was soon "alarmed by the cult's tight, secret society-type organization, which bears some resemblance to that of the underground CCP in the 1930s and 40s."[26] At the grassroots level, members are grouped into loosely constituted "cells," 1,900 instruction centers and 28,000 practice sites throughout China through electronic communications.[27] Though the siege of *Zhongnanhai* immediately led to a nationwide crackdown by the Chinese government, it seems that there is no way for the government to stop FLG followers from communicating with each other worldwide. The only significant impact that the government appears to have made is to force the FLG underground.

There are also frequent reports of authorities shutting down dissident websites.[28] The *People's Daily* regards the Internet as a platform for undesirable elements to sway public opinion, and has warned that "enemy forces at home and abroad are doing all they can to use this field to infiltrate us."[29] Realizing that the Internet can be used as part of public discourse against the regime, the Chinese government has made enormous efforts to control Internet traffic, including monitoring and closing down critical websites. From 1994 to 2000, the government issued 8 regulations to manage Internet activities, two regulations on computerized information security, two on domain registration management, two on Internet physical connection and access, one on telecommunication including Internet, and one on Internet services. The 2000 regulation set guidelines on what constituted undesirable Internet behavior such as articles against the Constitution, against state interests, harming state reputation, causing ethnic conflict, promoting evil cults, causing social instability, spreading pornography, violence, terrorism, and gambling contents, slanderous remarks, and other activities covered by criminal and civic laws and regulations.[30] The government has even attempted to set up "net police" in order to control Chinese "netizens."[31]

Income disparities and social grievance

Since state rebuilding is a process of interest redistribution, it produces distributive conflict among different social groups and regions. Some groups and regions benefit more than others, with some becoming winners and others losers. In other words, social groups and regions have unevenly benefited from an increasingly market-oriented economy and globalization. While those who are able to participate in the process have gained benefits, those who have not become disadvantaged.

Who are these losers? Table 7.1 reflects perceptions among Chinese government officials and urban residents about the winners and losers of China's reforms undertaken in the 1990s. Although government officials and urban residents generally disagreed with one another, they did agree that farmers and SOE workers were the biggest losers in this process. It would also be reasonable to say that government employees and migrants were also among the losers. The question then arises: Why and how do they become losers?

Among other reasons, one major factor contributing to this situation was a dramatic widening in income disparities. Economic reform policies gradually dismantled the Maoist egalitarian policy and drastically promoted China's economic growth, accompanied by substantial gains in poverty reduction. Nevertheless, both welfare increase and poverty reduction were extremely uneven, meaning these reforms were not able to reduce income disparities among different social groups and regions. The World Bank estimated that, in 1981, China's Gini coefficient was 28.8, but by 1995, it was 38.8. It was still lower than in most Latin American, African, and East Asian countries and similar to that in the United States, but higher than in most transition economies in Eastern Europe and many high income countries in Western Europe.[32] According to many studies, income disparities worsened since the mid-1990s, as shown in Table 7.2.

Table 7.1 Perceptions of winners and losers from China's reforms during the 1990s

A	Perceptions by government officials	
Benefit most	**Benefit least**	

The October 1997 Survey	
1 Private business owners	1 SOE workers
2 FDI employees	2 Farmers
3 Farmers	3 Government employees

The October 1998 Survey	
1 Private business owners	1 SOE workers
2 Artists	2 Farmers
3 FDI employees	3 Government employees

The November 1999 Survey	
1 Private business owners	1 Unemployed workers
2 Artists	2 Farmers
3 FDI employees	3 SOE workers & rural enterprise workers

The October 2000 Survey	
1 Private business owners	1 Farmers
2 Artists	2 SOE workers
3 FDI employees	3 Government employees & rural enterprise workers

B	Perceptions by urban residents	
Benefit most	**Benefit least**	

The November 1997 Survey	
1 Private business owners	1 SOE workers
2 Artists	2 Farmers
3 Bank employees	3 Migrants

The December 1998 Survey	
1 Artists	1 SOE workers
2 Corrupted officials	2 Farmers
3 Private business owners	3 Migrants

The August 1999 Survey	
1 Artists	1 SOE workers
2 Corrupted officials	2 Farmers
3 Private business owners	3 Migrants

Sources: Compiled by Wang Shaoguang, based on Ru Xing, Lu Xueyi and Shan Tianlun (eds.), *Shehui lanpishu: Zhongguo shehui xingshi fenxi yu yuce* (Social Bluebook: Analysis and Forecast of Social Situation in China) (Beijing: Shehui kexue wenxian chubanshe, 1998, 1999, 2000, 2001). See, Wang Shaoguang, "Kaifang xing, fenpei xing chongtu he shehui baozhang: Zhongguo jiaru WTO de shehui he zhengzhi yiyi" (Openness, Distributive Conflict and Social Assurance: The Social and Political Implications of China's WTO Membership), Working paper, The Department of Government and Public Administration, The Chinese University of Hong Kong, 2002.

Table 7.2 China's inequality, comparisons with other countries and regions (Gini coefficient)

Region or country	1980s	1990s
Eastern Europe	0.250	0.289
High-income countries	0.332	0.338
South Asia	0.350	0.319
East Asia and the Pacific	0.387	0.381
Middle East and North Africa	0.405	0.380
Sub-Saharan Africa	0.437	0.470
Latin America and the Caribbean	0.498	0.493
China	0.299	0.388
China (Zhao Renwei)	0.382 (1998)	0.445 (1995)
China (Qiu Xiaohua)		0.450 (1997)
China (Li Qiang)		0.458 (1997)
China (Cheng Zongsheng)		0.403 (formal economy, 1997)
China (Cheng Zongsheng)		0.515 (including informal economy, 1997)

Source: Wang, "Kaifang xing."

Rural disparities

In rural China, various surveys in the late 1980s found that the income of more than 80 percent of the Chinese farmers was below the national average. In other words, less than 20 percent of rural residents had an income much higher than the rest of the rural residents.[33] The gap between the low income and high income groups was widening. The rural Gini coefficient increased from 24.2 in 1981 to 33.3 in 1995.[34]

According to Wang, the worsening employment situation contributed most to widening income gaps in rural areas. The rapid development of China's village and township enterprises had created enormous employment opportunities for rural Chinese, but since the mid-1990s, this was no longer happening. According to an estimate, in 1995, of 500 million rural laborers, the market could take only 325 million, the rest were redundant.[35] Official statistics also revealed that the employment in village and township enterprises declined drastically in the late 1990s. For instance, it declined 4.8 percent in 1997 and 18.7 percent in 1998.[36]

Urban disparities

In urban areas, many households experienced a decline in their real income since the mid-1990s. According to official data, the urban Gini

Table 7.3 Growing inequality in urban China, 1990–98

Year	Income of top 20%/income of bottom 20%	Bottom 20%'s share of total income	Top 20%'s share of total income	Top 10%'s share of total income
1990	4.2 times	9.0%	38.1%	23.6%
1993	6.9 times	6.3%	46.5%	29.3%
1998	9.6 times	5.5%	52.3%	38.4%

Sources: Xu Xinxin and Li Peilin, "1998-1999 nian Zhongguo jiuye shouru he xinxi chanye de fenxi he yuce" (Employment, Income, and IT Industry: Analysis and Forecasts, 1998-1999), in Ru Xin, Lu Xueyi and Shan Tianlun (eds.), *Shehui lanpishu*, p. 34 Also, Wang, "Kaifang xing."

coefficient increased from 17.6 in 1981 to 27.5 in 1995.[37] In 1996, of the bottom 20 percent of households, nearly two-thirds of them found that their income had fallen. Among the next 20 percent of households, almost half the families found their income had declined. In contrast, the top 20 percent of urban households enjoyed an increase in their income.[38] In 1990, the average income of the top 20 percent of households was only 4.2 times higher than that of the bottom 20 percent. By 1998, the ratio had jumped to 9.6 times. The share of the richest 10 percent of households of the total income increased from 23.6 percent in 1990 to 38.4 percent in 1998. On the other hand, the share of the bottom 20 percent of households of the total income declined from 9 percent to 5.5 percent during the same period of time (Table 7.3). Urban residents used to enjoy the safe haven of the cities, cut off from the hundreds of millions of have-nots in the vast countryside. But after more than two decades of economic reform, about 30 million urban residents were living in poverty and their incomes were no more than one-third the national average.[39]

Urban–rural disparities
Reforms also led to huge income disparities between the cities and rural areas. The urban–rural divide is not new. When China began its economic reform, the per capita income of the urban resident was 2.6 times that of the rural resident.[40] In the early years of reform, the urban–rural disparities were reduced because reforms were first implemented in rural areas. However, once the urban reform began in 1984, the gap has widened continuously. According to the World Bank, China's rural–urban gap is large by international standards. In other countries, urban income is rarely more than twice the rural income. In most countries, rural income

is 66 percent or more of urban income. In China, rural income was only 40 percent of urban income in 1995, down from a peak of 59 percent in 1983.[41] In 1999, on average, a peasant has a per capita income of 2,162 yuan, while in the cities, the average per capita income of a worker is 7,668 yuan.[42]

Regional disparities

According to the World Bank, regional disparities were moderate compared to inequality within provincial borders. For example, in 1992, average income in coastal China was 50 percent higher than in interior provinces but in the same year, the rural–urban income gap was twice as large.[43] In contrast, Wang and Hu have given us a more pessimistic picture. In a detailed study on regional disparities, they reached three conclusions. First, inter-provincial inequality had been widening; second, regional gaps were unusually large; and third, regional inequality was a multidimensional phenomenon.[44] Income disparities in per capita GDP between China's coastal and interior provinces has been on the rise since 1983 and has accelerated since 1990. All the coastal provinces, except Guangxi, had per capita GDP higher than the national average. Shanghai was 4.5 times the average. At the other extreme, Guizhou's per capita GDP was equivalent to only 37 percent of the national average. Apart from Heilongjiang, none of the central and western provinces had per capita GDP higher than the national average.[45]

Corruption and moral decay

Capitalistic economic transformation has led to an increasingly diversified society, which is becoming more difficult for the Chinese state to govern. More importantly, this same process has also weakened the state itself and eroded people's confidence in the government. When there is a decline in the state's capacity to maintain and deliver public goods to its people, their worries mount, and similarly, their motivation for collective action is increased.

It is certainly true that the Chinese state has played an extremely important role in pushing the process of economic transformation. But during this process, the state became increasingly corrupt. The close linkages between the government and businesses have led to widespread corruption among party cadres and government officials. Table 7.4 shows official statistics on corruption committed by leading party cadres at different levels.

Corruption fanned people's unhappiness about the inability of the CCP to ensure fairness and led to doubts on its legitimacy to rule the country.

Table 7.4 The development of corruption among leading cadres in the 1990s

		1993	1994	1995	1996	1997	Jan.–Sept. 1998	1999
Punished by	Provincial level	6	17	24	23	7	10	17
party & gov.	Prefectural level	205	309	429	467	576	219	327
disciplines	County level	2,793	3,528	4,880	5,868	6,585	2,955	4,029
Investigated by	Provincial level	1	1	2	5	3	3	3
procuratorial	Prefectural level	7	88	145	143	148	85	136
organs	County level	1,141	1,826	2,306	2,551	2,426	1,462	2200
Sentenced by	Provincial level		1		1	5	2	2
law	Prefectural level	7	28	35	43	58	30	65
	County level	69	202	396	364	403	271	367

Source: The Research Group of the Department of Organization, the CCP Central Committee (ed.), *2000-2001 Zhongguo diaocha baogao: xin xingshi xia renmin neibu maodun yanjiu* (China Investigation Report, 2000-2001: Studies of Contradictions Within the People under New Conditions) (Beijing: Zhongyang bianyi chubanshe, 2001), p. 86.

Various surveys show that since the early 1990s, "serious corruption committed by government officials" and "public disorder" were among the issues of concern to ordinary citizens in China.[46] When a government is perceived as corrupt and there is a breakdown of public order, people tended to become worried. According to a 1998 survey, nearly 93 percent people did not regard China as a country ruled by law. When asked what they would do if conflicts or disputes with others happened, 74.7 percent said they would turn to legal means for a resolution. Nevertheless, they also believed that such means would be ineffective since power was still above the law in China; so they would appeal to non-legal means. About 49 percent believed that they would seek help from the media, and 24.7 percent from individual leaders. Furthermore, about 16 percent of the people were likely to turn to some form of collective action to seek justice such as petitions, demonstrations, or collective visits to higher authorities to ask for their intervention (*shang fang*).[47]

Serious corruption in the public sector has greatly affected social morale. Ordinary citizens see the abundance of wealth accumulated by party cadres and government officials, and find it difficult to accept that they should restrain themselves. Over time, they have come to regard the system in which they live in as being unfair to them. Meanwhile, government officials at different levels have also found that it is increasingly

difficult to maintain a sense of moral and social community among both
the urban and the rural residents. As corruption among party cadres
and government officials becomes rampant, crime has also become
widespread among ordinary citizens.[48] Robbery and armed assault, which
were unthinkable during Mao's time, have become a part of people's daily
life.

The rise of social protests: farmers and workers

Social protests by peasants and workers have virtually become a norm in
China. No nationwide statistics are available due to the sensitivity of the
issue. It is worth quoting a Chinese report (1998) at length:

Various events leading to social instability have taken place in recent years, and
some are really severe and have had a negative impact on social stability as a
whole. These events take many forms such as workers' strike, teachers' strike,
collective visit to higher authorities, petition and protest march, violent conflicts, sit-in demonstration, lying on the rails, hunger strike, perniciously harming
others, damaging, and collective robbing. The most frequent are workers' and
teachers' strikes, collective visit to higher authorities, and petition and demonstration. Some major characteristics are as follows. First, the increase in intensity.
In some regions, [protestors] laid siege on government organs, blocked vital communication lines, attacking government officials, and shouting slogans [against
the government]. In one city, within a month, protestors attacked the government
compound twenty three times. In some provinces, there were bombing events.
Second, drastic increase in the events involving collective action. Take collective
visit to higher authorities for example, the annual growth rate was 27 percent in
recent years. In a county in southern China, there were 13 collective visits by
farmers who felt too heavy burden within a month. Every visit involved hundred
of protestors, and there were more than 10,000 protestors in total. Nowadays,
such collective visits often involved hundreds of protestors from different villages
and different towns. Protests are great in strength and momentum, and partic-
ipants drove cars, raising banners and placards, and shouting slogans. Third,
rapid increase in events resulting from tensions between mass and government
officials.[49]

The report, written by Wang Chunguang, a scholar from the State
Council, advised the government that something had to be done to cope
with rising social protests in the country. Another report in 2001 also
recognized a spreading pattern of collective protests and group inci-
dents arising from economic, ethnic and religious conflicts in China.
The report, produced by a research team organized by the Department

of Organization of the Central Committee of the CCP, warned that the coming years of rapid change, driven by China's opening of markets to foreign trade and investment, were likely to cause greater social conflict. The report made urgent recommendations for changes to save the party and the nation by reducing popular grievance.[50] This section aims to highlight the linkages between social protests and state rebuilding by focusing on farmers' protests and labor disputes in the reform era.

Taxation reforms, rural burdens and farmers' protests

Farmers' protests are not uncommon in China. According to an official report, "To organize themselves to resist various forms of non-policy and illegal matters by local state organizations and communities has become farmers' conscious and unconscious action."[51] Another research in 2000 reported that:

> in recent years, as tensions between cadres and masses have intensified, social conflicts have skyrocketed. Individual and collective visits to higher authorities have increased dramatically. There are underground training classes for such visits organized by the farmers themselves in some regions, while in other regions, such handbooks as *Guide for Visits to Higher Authorities*, and *Handbook for Visits to Higher Authorities* have been widely circulated.[52]

Most scholars would agree that farmers' protests are closely associated with the heavy burdens imposed on them by different levels of government.[53] This is officially called "*nongmin fudan*" (peasant burdens), which refers to various types of taxes and fees and charges that the government of different levels and other administrative organs extracts from peasants, including:

1 State taxes: Agricultural tax and surcharge; special products tax; slaughter tax; farmland utilization tax; education surcharge.
2 Township and village levies (*xiang tongchou* and *cun tiliu* or *santi wutong*): Villages collect three items – collective investments, welfare, cadre compensation; townships collect five – schools, family planning, support for veterans, militia, and road construction and maintenance.
3 Collective contracting fee for land: 5–10 days of labor on flood prevention afforestation, roads or school construction; 5–10 days on "accumulation labor" on state water conservancy of afforestation projects.
4 Fees, assessments, and fundraising: For road or school construction and other local improvement projects; newspaper subscriptions, purchase of insurance, marriage certificates, etc.

5 Fines: Collected by numerous government agencies for infractions such as birth control violations.
6 "Hidden burdens": Compulsory grain sales to state at below market prices; scissors differential between industrial and agricultural prices.[54]

While not all burdens are illegal, it is equally true that not all burdens are resisted by peasants. Many studies found that generally, peasants are willing to accept the first two items but have enormous complaints against and are resistant to the last four items. The first two items, i.e., formal state taxes and the village and township levies, were set by laws and regulations, and thus are managed by higher authorities. But the central government does not have any laws and regulations for the last four items, and local states and other administrative organs often misuse their power in collecting these items. Consequently, the real extraction of funds often exceeded the prescribed level. For example, the combined village and township tax was not supposed to exceed 5 percent of the preceding year's average net per capital income of the township residents, but the real figure was far above it. According to a survey of 1,000 rural families in Sichuan province, the rate was 12.7 percent in 1991.[55] A study of four villages in Guizhou province showed that it was 13.8 percent in 1992.[56] Another study of one county in Anhui province indicated that the figure was above 25 percent in the mid-1990s.[57] The situation indeed tended to become worse after the mid-1990s. A study group from the Suzhou University found that the total burden on peasants nationwide amounted to 30–50 percent, and among these burdens, 20–40 percent were regarded as illegal or illegitimate.[58]

So, why did the Chinese peasants face increasingly heavy burdens? Scholars have different views on this. Some argued that it was because of the corrupt local government officials' greediness,[59] others believed that it was a result of rapid expansion of local government organizations,[60] and still others ascribed it to the shrinking income sources at local levels.[61] Each argument has its own rationale but hardly addressed the fundamentals of the issue. Government officials' greediness led to illegal and illicit levies on peasants. But not all levies were for their personal benefits. Instead, these levies were meant for local public goods such as road construction, school building and reforestation. Shrinking income resources were an important factor contributing to the imposition of illegal and illicit levies, especially in the poor areas in western regions. But it is hard to explain why peasants in rich coastal areas also faced a heavy burden since the mid-1990s. The rapid expansion of local administrative organs did contribute to an increase in peasant burdens but as various

Table 7.5 Shares of provincial budgetary revenue (percentage)

	Share of remitting provinces	Share of subsidies-receiving provinces	Share of all provinces	Shared budgetary revenue as % of GDP	Total budgetary revenue as % of GDP
1985	61.8	131.7	96.4	14.4	23.7
1986	67.1	141.7	104.3	15.7	22.2
1987	70.1	140.8	107.1	15.1	19.7
1988	75.9	126.1	102.8	13.5	17.8
1989	79.8	122.2	103.0	14.1	18.0
1990	79.4	122.0	104.4	13.1	17.9
1991	81.0	118.8	102.6	12.3	16.0
1992	81.3	118.2	101.4	10.6	14.2
1993	85.8	112.7	98.5	10.8	13.5
1994	78.7	96.0	88.5	9.7	11.8
1995	76.5	95.3	87.0	8.9	11.2
1996	77.9	94.5	87.3	8.9	11.3
1997	66.1	89.2	79.6	8.7	12.0
1998	61.8	86.3	74.4	9.6	12.8

Source: Kang Chen, Arye L. Millman and Qingyang Gu, "From the Helping Hand to the Grabbing Hand: Fiscal Federalism and Corruption in China," *EAI Working Paper* No. 67, East Asian Institute, National University of Singapore, February 2001.

studies showed, most of the peasant burdens came from fees and charges for the abovementioned local public goods, not personnel costs imposed by local states; and further, most personnel costs went to local school teachers.[62]

A more fundamental source of the problem was the 1994 taxation reform and its impact on rural residents. Chapter 6 shows that the 1994 taxation reform is an important part of the leadership's state rebuilding efforts, aimed at centralizing fiscal power and constraining rising localism. As discussed in Chapter 6, the new system was quite effective. It was able to arrest the downward trend of the budgetary revenue to GDP ratio, and to increase the share of the central revenue in total budgetary revenue. As shown in Table 7.5, the total budgetary revenue was 12.8 percent of GDP in 1998, only slightly below the 13.5 percent in 1993. The share apportioned to the provinces was also reduced. Remitting provinces saw their budgetary revenue share drop by more than 20 percent from 85.8 percent in 1993 to 61.8 percent in 1998. The subsidies-receiving provinces faced a similar situation: their share decreased from 112.7 percent to 86.3 percent during the same period.

While the new system strengthened the fiscal power of the central government, it drastically affected relations between different levels of government. In particular, the impact of the change was felt most at the county and township levels in two ways. First, while the new system shifted fiscal power from local governments to the center, the responsibilities did not shift to the central government accordingly. For example, the central government should be responsible for financing the cost of the nine-year compulsory education, but in reality, local governments at county and township levels still have to foot the bill, and consequently, the financial burdens on these governments increased greatly. Second, the new system provided a disincentive for local governments to promote local economic growth, and thus shrunk local tax bases.[63]

The pre-1994 fiscal decentralization was widely regarded as providing a helping hand for local governments. It gave a fair share of revenues from additional growth to local governments, which effectively turned local governments into residual claimants in their regions, and thus provided strong incentives for them to promote local economic growth.[64] These fiscal incentives were found to be associated with faster development of non-state enterprises and more reform in state-owned enterprises.[65]

As discussed in Chapter 6, the central government had to address its rapidly declining fiscal power by initiating new fiscal reforms. Nevertheless, the 1994 reform turned what was originally intended to be the helping hand into the grabbing hand. It changed the incentive structure for local governments to promote economic development and led to negative consequences such as deepening corruption, widespread unemployment and a slowing down of economic growth.[66] The worsening situation of the peasants can thus also be understood in the context of the grabbing hand. An examination of the changing fiscal situation at the county and township level after 1994 will enable us to see how the 1994 fiscal reform affected peasants.

The financing of the county government is an important part of China's fiscal system.[67] The county revenue consisted of three parts, i.e., budgetary, extra-budgetary and self-collected. Budgetary revenues include state taxes and local taxes. The former is made up of industrial value-added and consumption taxes, and the latter comprised business taxes, income taxes, agricultural taxes, tax on agricultural special products, title tax, animal slaughter tax, etc. The extra-budgetary revenue comprised various local fees, assessments, fundraising, etc. The self-collected revenue covers a wide range of illicit and illegal income. The so-called *sanluan* (three unrulies, namely illicit fees, assessments and fundraising) are in this category.

Before the 1994 fiscal reform, the revenue-sharing system was implemented nationwide, under which the center shared the total revenue with the provinces according to previously reached agreements (contracts) between the two. This same arrangement existed between the provincial government and county government, as well as between the county government and township government. It was widely believed that the revenue-sharing system in the countryside laid a sound institutional foundation for the rise of local development, which effectively improved the lives of the peasants.[68] The 1994 reform introduced a major change to this system. While the provincial government implemented the tax-sharing system with the county government, the revenue-sharing system still applied to the county–township fiscal relations. The county government was caught in an unenviable position of having to "surrender more to higher authorities" and "not able to take more (from the township government)." According to the tax-sharing arrangement, 25 percent of the total state tax revenue collected by the central government within a county is to be returned to the county government, and the county government retains all local taxes it collected. The central government shares the largest portion of the local tax source, i.e., value-added tax, with the county government. Further, this portion of the tax is guaranteed. In contrast, the county government is unable to extract more revenue from the township government according to the revenue-sharing system, and the amount of local taxes imposed depended heavily on local economic performance.

The 1994 fiscal reform drastically changed the incentive structure for local governments. Since the higher authorities shared the greatest portion of revenue from local economic growth, the local government became less motivated in promoting local investment. The slower the local growth, the smaller the local tax base. For example, in a county in Anhui province, the share of income tax from local state-owned enterprises in total local tax declined from 14 percent in 1995 to less than 3 percent in 1997. Overall, the share of local revenue collected declined from 64 percent of the total local tax in 1994 to 42 percent in 1998; since the local tax branches collected most of the county tax revenue, the amount they collected directly reflected a given county's fiscal situation.[69]

The township government faced a similar worsening of its fiscal situation. The township budget is the lowest level in China's budgetary system. The budgetary structure was similar to that of the county government, including budgetary, extra-budgetary, and self-collected revenue. In the regions with rural enterprises, township levies became the main source of the budget. The township government had to remit most budgetary revenues, i.e., formal tax revenue, to higher authorities.

Table 7.6 Average debt of townships and
villages in Anhui Province, 1998 (1,000 yuan)

Regions	Township	Village
Buyang City	4,835.0	137.0
Lu'andi Region	4,468.4	155.8
Bengbu City	4,185.3	138.7
Huainan City	4,164.0	404.8
Suzhou City	3,446.5	106.2
Qiaohu Region	3,176.3	298.5
Bozhou City	2,859.6	64.4
Tongling City	2,671.7	255.7
Huaibei City	2,555.4	341.3
Chuzhou City	1,971.8	149.6
Xuancheng Region	1,421.9	85.2

Source: Zhao Yang and Zhou Feizhou, "Nongmin fudan
he caishui tizhi" (Peasants' Burdens and Fiscal System),
Hong Kong Journal of Social Sciences, no. 17 (Autumn
2000), p. 79.

Furthermore, the central government regulated that total township and
village levies could not exceed 5 percent of net per capita annual income.
The township levies covered almost all government costs, including local
schools, militia, support for veterans, Five Guarantees (*wubaohu*), family
planning, and others. Without levies, the township government could
hardly function. Also, village levies were consumed by the village but
managed by the township government. But it was found that the management was disorganized in most places.[70] In the developed regions,
especially coastal China, the township budget revenue mainly came from
the profits submitted by rural enterprises in the 1980s. But as economic
growth slowed down in the 1990s, the township government increasingly
turned to levies to meet its fiscal needs.

The township government is the lowest level of administration but
plays an extremely important role of government in China. Its costs
come largely from three areas of expenditure: 1) administrative costs
(personnel), 2) basic construction fees (e.g., road construction, and
farmland capital construction), and 3) culture, education, and sanita-
tion (e.g., school buildings, teachers' salaries, and public health facil-
ity buildings). In many places, especially inland China, township levies
could cover only the salaries of administrative personnel and teachers.
The serious fiscal shortfall left the township budget in the red, as shown in
Table 7.6.

In 1998, many county governments began to implement the tax-sharing system with township governments in order to arrest the worsening fiscal situation. But this change led to a further deterioration in the township budget, because, as discussed above, the county government was merely taking more revenue from the township government.[71]

From the above brief discussion, we can see how the 1994 fiscal reform affected peasant burdens and thus led to the rise of rural protests. The reform enhanced the capability of the central government to extract revenue from local governments. When the central government increased its share of the revenue pie, the share for local governments declined, as did the incentive of local officials to promote local economic growth. When local growth slowed, the local tax base shrunk, and revenues from formal taxes could no longer meet the needs of local governments. Consequently, local officials turned to collect informal revenue, be it legal or illegal.

When the center grabbed wealth from local governments, the latter had to grab wealth from the peasants. Illegal and illicit grabbing drastically increased peasant burdens and pushed them to rebel against local governments.[72] An old Chinese saying goes, "Tyranny is fiercer than a tiger (*ke zheng meng yu hu*)." Nowadays, Chinese are saying, "Excessive fees are fiercer than a tiger (*ke fei meng yu hu*)." If peasant rebellions in the old days were believed to be associated with "tyranny," peasant protests today are certainly connected with "excessive fees."

Capitalism, unemployment and labor movements

Labor movements are not new in China. There were labor movements mobilized from above during the Hundred Flowers Campaign, and the Cultural Revolution,[73] and there were also labor protests from below such as the 1989 pro-democracy movement.[74] Nevertheless, the reform has contributed to the rise of new labor insurgencies especially since Deng Xiaoping's southern tour in 1992. Labor protests have become a focus of research among China scholars.[75] An official estimated that in 1995, labor-related demonstrations involved more than 1.1 million people in over 30 cities. In 1998, 3.6 million workers participated in such demonstrations.[76] Table 7.7 shows the rise in the number of labor disputes. We can see that the total number of labor disputes which occurred in the first half of 1999 was seven times that in 1994. Furthermore, collective labor disputes were also on the rise, with the number quadrupling between 1996 and 1999.

What led to the rise of labor movements in the 1990s? Like peasant protests, labor movements are also a part of state rebuilding. I have

Table 7.7 Incidence of labor disputes

Period	Total number of labor disputes	Number of collective labor disputes	Total number of workers involved in labor disputes	Number of workers involved in collective disputes
Jan.–June 1994	7,905	–	–	–
Jan.–June 1995	12,956	–	31,144	–
Jan.–June 1996	14,852	1,050	40,413	33,646
Jan.–June 1997	26,600	1,821	97,006	56,425
Jan.–June 1998	34,879	2,798	134,436	84,208
Jan.–June 1999	55,244	3,955	230,243	144,273

Sources: Complied by Shaoguang Wang based on Ru Xin, Lu Xueyi and Shan Tianlun (eds.), *Shehui lanpishu*, various issues. See, Wang, "Kaifang xing."

discussed in previous chapters how the Chinese leadership has adjusted the state structure to accommodate capitalism and the market economy. After 30 bitter years of experimentation following 1949, the leadership decided to use capitalism as a way of rebuilding the Chinese economic system. Though China's leaders do not want to give up socialism as the ultimate goal, they have recognized that learning from capitalism conforms to historical necessity. While the capitalism being practiced in advanced countries has altered its form, it still retains the popular images of nineteenth-century satanic mills that exploited workers.

In China, unemployment and managerial corruption are probably the two most important factors leading to the rise of labor movements. The official rate of unemployment is unrealistically low since it only includes those jobless persons who have bothered to register with the authorities and excludes off-post (*xia-gang*) workers and excess labor in the countryside. Chapter 6 discussed the progress of China's SOE reforms. Indeed, the off-post problem was a consequence of these SOE reforms and almost every major measure of reform exacerbated the unemployment situation.

The off-post problem surged in the early 1990s. After Deng's southern tour in 1992, various market-oriented reform measures were introduced into China's SOEs, such as "smashing the iron bowl" and "the reform of the three systems (i.e., labor, wages, pensions and insurance)."[77] These reforms immediately exacerbated the problem of off-post workers. There were only about 6 million off-post workers in 1995, but the figure rose to about 7.4 million in 1996 when a partial privatization program, i.e., *zhuada fangxiao* (Chapter 6) was implemented.[78] The situation deteriorated after 1997 when further privatization measures such as the share-holding system were implemented. By the end of 1997, off-post workers numbered about 9.4 million.[79] Although the government initiated various re-employment programs to cope with the problem, they failed to improve the situation.[80] According to official statistics, there were only 5.8 million urban residents unemployed in 1999,[81] but the figure of off-post workers reached about 10 million.[82] According to an estimate, the total number of unemployed amounted to 15–16 million in 1998 and 18–19 million in 1999.[83]

The problem of unemployment was especially difficult to deal with in the traditionally heavy industry oriented northeast provinces i.e., Liaoning, Jilin and Heilongjiang, where the real unemployment rate ranged from 12.8 percent to 15.5 percent in 1998. Unemployment was also a serious problem in interior provinces such as Hunan, Sichuan, and Shaanxi, where the unemployment rate stood above 10 percent. In contrast, the coastal provinces including Guangdong, Shandong, Zhejiang, Jiangsu, Hebei, Shanghai, and the national capital Beijing, saw low rates of unemployment.[84]

The question arises as to the need for SOEs to lay off their workers. The economic performance of SOEs improved considerably during the reform years,[85] though productivity growth was significantly lower for the state sector than for the non-state sector.[86] As shown in Table 7.8, the number of SOEs running at a loss and the amount of the losses soared in the late 1990s. In fact, the non-state sector contributed most to China's growth miracle during the reform years.[87] Among other reasons, redundant workers contributed significantly to the poor performance of China's SOEs. According to a World Bank survey of 142 SOEs in 1994, the overwhelming majority of the managers acknowledged that there were considerable numbers of redundant workers in the enterprises under their management.[88]

One major objective of the economic reform was to make enterprises legally entitled to managerial autonomy, including the power of employment and dismissal.[89] When managers had greater power to lay off workers, tension was introduced into state–labor relations. Many other factors further worsened the situation. For example, Feng Chen identified two critical factors that shaped workers' sense of injustice and drove them to protest, i.e., a subsistence crisis and managerial corruption.[90] A subsistence crisis meant a situation in which workers had income far below the local minimum wage or no income at all for a period of time. Workers facing such a situation had strong incentives to protest, and their motivation to protest increased if they believed that their economic plight was

Table 7.8 State-owned enterprises in deficit

	Amount of losses (billion yuan)	SOEs at loss/SOE total number (%)	Total losses/total pre-tax profits (%)	Total losses/total net profits (%)
1985	3.24	9.66	2.43	2.43
1986	5.45	13.07	4.06	7.90
1987	6.10	13.00	4.03	7.76
1988	8.19	10.91	4.62	9.18
1989	18.02	16.03	10.16	24.25
1990	34.88	27.55	23.20	89.86
1991	36.70	25.84	22.09	91.25
1992	36.93	23.36	18.99	69.01
1993	45.26	28.78	18.44	55.39
1994	48.26	30.89	16.78	58.21
1995	63.96	33.53	22.25	96.09
1996	79.07	37.70	28.89	191.61
1997	83.10	–	28.58	194.22

Sources: *Zhongguo tongji nianjian* (China Statistical Yearbook 1998), p. 461; Zheng Haihang, *Guoyou qiye kuisun yanjiu* (A Study of Loss-Making State-Owned Enterprises) (Beijing: Jingji guanli chubanshe, 1998), p. 33.

exacerbated by managerial corruption at the workplace – managers were enriching themselves by stripping the assets of enterprises that workers depended on for a living.[91]

In other words, market-oriented economic reform effectively eliminated the privileges that workers took for granted in the old days. Workers' standards of living declined continuously with the deepening of reform, and many workers fell into the ranks of the urban poor. Managerial reform, which granted greater autonomy to managers, subjected workers to coercive modes of labor control and arbitrary managerial power. Workers were defenseless in the face of heavy-handed enforcement of a capitalistic logic and increasingly despotic factory regimes.[92] More importantly, Chinese workers do not have the right to strike. Such rights, which had originally been granted to workers, were removed in the 1982 Constitution. The 1992 Trade Union Law also did not have such rights. The All China Federation of Trade Unions (ACFTU) failed to represent workers' interests, even though considerable changes were introduced. Indeed, for various political reasons, the ACFTU still serves the interest of the state more than that of the workers.[93] All these factors helped to create an environment conducive to the rise of labor movements.

More fundamentally, the reform changed the structure of state–labor relations and thus created opportunities for labor movements to surge. In pre-reform China, an important dimension of state–labor relations was an all-encompassing dependency of labor on the state enterprises.[94] This institutional arrangement contributed significantly to the low frequency of labor protest in the past. Workers' dependence on their enterprises was a powerful disincentive to collective action since the distribution of various benefits and services took place largely at the discretion of management and alternatives were few. Grievances were there but open confrontation could not be risked. Consequently, grievances were expressed by using what James Scott called "the weapons of the weak," i.e., by slacking off, absenteeism and sloppy work.[95] According to Chen, massive layoffs changed the form of resistance. Once removed from the workplace, workers could no longer resort to slowdown and other forms of quiet retaliation, and open confrontation outside the workplace became a feasible means to make their voices heard. Moreover, while laid-off workers were nominally still affiliated with enterprises and were entitled to minimal living allowance, many of them actually received no assistance whatsoever from their enterprises and were left to their own devices. Once the dependence of laid-off workers on enterprises was ruptured, the constraints on their collective action largely evaporated.[96]

In the state sector, labor protests rose because almost every step along the path of market reform amounted to a setback for workers' social status and livelihood.[97] The situation in the non-state sector, especially foreign investment enterprises, was not altogether rosy either. The government implemented various preferential policies towards foreign investors in order to attract foreign investment. With the surge in labor abuses in the foreign investment enterprises, the government began to emphasize labor laws in order to regulate industrial relations and protect workers. Nevertheless, the success of the labor laws and regulations depends on enforcement efforts, and major obstacles stand in the way of implementation of the law. Local protectionism is an example. Since different regions compete with each other for foreign investment, local authorities are inclined not to enforce the law in order to attract foreign capital and technology for local growth.[98]

Without effective law enforcement, labor disputes in the foreign investment enterprises surged. According to official statistics, labor disputes have occurred mostly in the non-state sector since the mid-1990s. For example, in 1999, there were 76,633 labor disputes in the non-state sector, which was 63.8 percent of the total number of labor disputes that year. Among them, 27,824 disputes or 36.3 percent of the total cases in the non-state sector took place in foreign investment enterprises. In the same year, there were 2,726 collective labor disputes, which was

30.1 percent of the total, and these involved 111,438 workers, which was 34.9 percent of the total.[99]

Conclusion

To a great extent, state rebuilding as a process of interest redistribution can be understood from two perspectives. First, state rebuilding changed the distribution of interests. Some people or groups are able to gain more or at least maintain their interests, while others have lost ground. Second, state rebuilding was aimed at promoting economic growth which has been rather impressive. Even though everyone benefited from economic reform, not everyone gained the same share from a growing economic pie. As such, state rebuilding has been associated with different forms of social movements.

State rebuilding has changed the class structure. In the pre-reform era, Mao Zedong implemented an egalitarian policy. Workers and peasants were regarded as the two leading classes in the country but the post-Mao reform dismantled this egalitarian policy, and almost all reform policies were implemented at the expense of the interests of these two classes. The leading positions of workers and peasants become only nominal. Furthermore, as discussed in Chapter 4, the state had to adjust its ruling structure in favor of new rising social classes such as the new rich and entrepreneurs. Grievances were thus prevalent among workers and peasants, and social movements became an important tool to express those grievances, since China's political process is still relatively closed to the public.

Social movements in turn affect the leadership's attempts at state rebuilding. Although social and economic interests do not directly shape policy, they infringe on the authority of the state. On occasion, when social protests succeed in exerting political pressure, the leadership has had to slow down the reform process. This is especially true for SOE reforms. Even though the state has introduced various measures of partial privatization since the mid-1990s, radical privatization never took place. Social movements also invite new policy initiatives. When the 1994 fiscal reform greatly increased peasant burdens and led to rural protests, the state initiated a new fiscal reform, i.e., the *fei gai shui* (tax-for-fee), in 2000, aimed at providing institutional constraints on local officials' arbitrary behavior in collecting illegal or illicit fees.[100] When SOE reforms led to massive unemployment, the state speeded up employment service and unemployment insurance reforms.[101] The state also put much emphasis on building new systems such as the public housing system in order to provide a better social environment for further reform measures.[102]

Social protests are often understood as a signal for the leadership to slow down reform. But this is not necessarily true. In some cases, social movements present some form of threat to the regime but in other cases, they provide new opportunities for the leadership to further the reform process. By inviting new policy initiatives, social movements indeed reinforce the efforts of state rebuilding by the leadership.

8 Contending visions of the Chinese state: New Liberalism vs. the New Left

Since state rebuilding involves interest redistribution, the affected social groups have been motivated to take part in this process. As China's political system is not open to popular participation, social groups have to find alternative ways to influence the process of state rebuilding. While underprivileged workers and peasants have resorted to "action" to achieve their goals, intellectuals have used their weapon, i.e., "knowledge", to do so.

This chapter focuses on how Chinese intellectuals have contributed to the process of state rebuilding by conjuring up and presenting different discourses on state rebuilding. Though the state still imposes tight controls on academic freedom, there is room for such discourses to take place. While everyone agrees that reform is a process of state rebuilding, most people are not sure where it is leading. Chinese intellectuals came into this void and provided some cognitive road maps for the masses. Needless to say, different intellectual groups represented different political and economic interests. They have also variously criticized the government and challenged its policies. In this sense, the rise of contending visions of the Chinese state is also a part of the social movements since the 1990s. This chapter attempts to elaborate the two most important contentious visions of the Chinese state, those of the new liberalism and the new left.

The rise of intellectual discourse in the post-Tiananmen era

The rise of the new liberal and new left intellectual discourses in the post-Tiananmen era is deeply rooted in changes in China's domestic and external affairs. In the 1980s, Chinese intellectuals expressed their strong liberal tendency in favor of economic marketization and political democratization.[1] With the implementation of the reform and open-door policy, Western ideas rapidly flowed into China and Western discourse was introduced piecemeal through translation projects, young scholars studying overseas, conferences, seminars and various publications. Many ordinary Chinese displayed their strong preference and admiration of Western cultures. As of the middle of the 1980s, Chinese intellectuals experienced a period of cultural effervescence called a new "May Fourth Movement" or "Chinese Enlightenment." Like their predecessors in the 1910s and 1920s, liberal intellectuals cast serious doubts on the old state ideology and provided various alternative models for modernization. They attempted to redefine themselves in the Chinese polity and claim a role in its evolution.[2]

Economic reforms in the 1980s led intellectuals to call for China's democratization, as they saw economic liberalization as opening up the possibility of political reforms. Even though there was no consensus on the concept of democracy, the so-called "democratic elite" insisted on a radical change in China's political system and institutions along the line of Western liberal democratic practices.[3] When the leadership failed to make such changes, intellectuals turned to attack Chinese traditional cultures. For many Chinese intellectuals, the main sources of China's difficulty in democratization lay in its traditional culture. Thus, in order to democratize China, the first priority for the intellectuals was to criticize traditional culture.[4]

But this liberal discourse was rudely interrupted by the government's crackdown on the pro-democracy movement in 1989. The immediate post-Tiananmen years (1989–92) saw the collapse of the lively and polyphonic intellectual space of the late 1980s. Conservative views on China's political and economic changes became dominant, and Chinese scholars increasingly called for political stability, central authority, tight social control, a strong role for ideology and nationalism.[5] Deng's southern tour in early 1992, while accelerating China's market reforms, brought about rather radical changes to the lives of the Chinese intellectuals. Within a few years, dozens of intellectual periodicals emerged such as *Zhanlue yu guanli* (Strategy and Management), *Dongfang* (Orient), *Xiandai yu chuantong* (Modernity and Tradition), *Zhonghua renwen* (Chinese Humanity), *Xueren* (Scholars), *Zhongguo wenhua pinglun* (Chinese Cultural Review), *Jinri xianfeng* (Today's Pioneer), and *Dongxifang wenhua pinglun* (East–West Cultural Review). Many journals in Hong Kong such as *Ershiyi shiji* (Twenty-First Century), *Zhongguo shehui kexue jikan* (Chinese Social Sciences Quarterly), and *Xianggang shehui kexue xuebao* (Hong Kong Journal of Social Sciences) also provided mainland scholars with alternative forums. Nevertheless, these thoughtful and provocative periodicals did not help revive the liberal discourse within China.

Why did Chinese intellectuals become so conservative in their orientation? There were external factors to explain this development. In 1991, while still living in the shadow of the 4 June incident, Chinese intellectuals watched on television the Russian Parliament being bombarded by the pro-Yeltsin troops. Then in 1993 came the defeat by Western governments of China's bid to host the 2000 Olympics. Although the government-sponsored application met with cynical reception among some Chinese intellectuals, more significantly, the ways in which Western countries joined hands to deny China the honor, particularly the active roles played by the US and Britain, undermined what many Chinese thought to be a very hopeful bid (Beijing eventually lost to Sydney by a mere 2 votes). This defeat shocked younger generation students, intellectuals, and urban professionals who considered hosting the Olympic game an excellent opportunity for China to march into the world on one hand, and introduce new changes into the regime on the other. Consequently, nationalistic sentiments surfaced among different social groups.

Then, in 1995–96, the first Taiwan Strait crisis broke out. The visit of Lee Teng-hui to America triggered a series of diplomatic conflicts and cross-strait tensions, and led to China "testing" missiles in the waters near the Taiwanese coast. The US government responded by deploying two aircraft carrier battle groups outside the Taiwan Strait. The US reaction somehow reopened a profound collective wound among Chinese intellectuals and the population as a whole, who recalled the humiliations of China by Western imperialism between the Opium War in 1840 and the Japanese surrender in 1945.

The Kosovo War in 1999 dampened the intellectual mood further. When NATO began air strikes against Yugoslavia, China joined Russia to oppose NATO's action. The Chinese leaders saw an eerie parallel between Taiwan and Kosovo in that the Balkans operation represented the Western alliance getting involved militarily in the internal affairs of a sovereign nation. To make matters worse, at midnight on 7 May, NATO missiles hit the Chinese Embassy in Belgrade, Yugoslavia, killing three Chinese journalists and injuring more than 20 Chinese diplomats.

The list of such unfortunate events seemed endless. These events triggered waves of Chinese nationalism from the early 1990s. More importantly, they also forced Chinese intellectuals to reflect seriously on Western liberal discourse. To be sure, many Chinese intellectuals, especially those who had been educated in the West, had begun to realize that, in the 1980s, they had been too naïve in regarding liberal ideals as universal in their application. They discovered that the Western system is not perfect and far from their original high expectations. From the annual debate in the American Congress on extending normal trade relations with China, Chinese intellectuals saw how deeply ideological the US government and media were when dealing with China. Also, American human rights rhetoric directed at China was based on their political or geopolitical concerns.

Parallel to all these developments, and throughout the 1990s, Russian economic and political liberalization was an important reference point through which Chinese intellectuals examined their own situation and weighed their options. Before the collapse of Soviet and Eastern European communist regimes, Chinese intellectuals attacked conservatism, which they regarded as a basic barrier to China's institutional reform and development. This position was highlighted in the debate about China's global citizenship in the late 1980s.[6] But events in Eastern Europe and the Soviet Union revealed the possibility that with the decline of traditional ideology and the worsening of social crises, political and social disintegration would be more dangerous than conservatism. As a result, Chinese intellectuals themselves became critics of political radicalism, and they quickly came to the conclusion that the Tiananmen "democracy" movement was but one more ill-fated mass movement propelled by an intellectual belief in radical, total social change and lofty political ideals.

The financial meltdown that swept Latin America, Eastern Europe, and East Asia between 1995 and 1998 was further proof of the debilitating effect of rapid and massive financial capital flows and the ruinous implications of excessive economic deregulation. Many of those hard-hit countries, such as South Korea, Thailand, Indonesia and Malaysia, had once been models of rapid economic growth by means of full integration into the global economic system and by attracting large amounts of foreign investment. The collapse of the national currencies in these countries and the apparent powerlessness of their national governments in the face of deliberate assault by international financial speculators on the one hand, and China's ability to defend its currency amidst the domino effect of the financial crisis on the other, led to a positive and assertive re-affirmation of the role of the nation-state in a globalized economy among Chinese intellectuals. The contrast created a deep suspicion of the neo-liberal orthodoxy and a renewed emphasis on the capacity of the state as the only mechanism to protect the fledgling national market and to fight for a just international and domestic economic and political order.

There were also various domestic factors that pushed Chinese intellectuals to rethink the liberal discourse. After two decades of phenomenal economic development, China seemed to have become a mixed economy and a divided nation. The economic growth generated enormous wealth, but it also created astounding disparities in distribution of wealth that leaves China today among the most unequal nations in the world (see Chapter 7). The social tension emanates not only from the aspiration for greater individual and political freedom, but increasingly from frustration regarding the unequal distribution of wealth and power. Underneath a mixed economy and a divided nation was the increasing incidence of corruption among party cadres and government officials, as discussed in the previous chapters. The 1990s in particular witnessed the epidemic corruption of power in the form of rent seeking, insider trading, and theft of public property.[7]

It was against such external and internal backdrops that Chinese intellectuals engaged in serious debate on how all these problems originated, how they could be dealt with, and in which direction China's development should go. After the mid-1990s, Chinese intellectuals from different fields came to associate themselves, consciously or unconsciously, with different "isms," and new liberalism and the new left stood out as the two "mainstreams" of the contesting schools.

New leftists first found their voice among overseas scholars such as Wang Shaoguang and Cui Zhiyuan. They voiced their views initially via Hong Kong journals like *Twenty-First Century*, and gradually extended their influence back home and found strong support among mainland-based scholars such as Wang Hui at the Chinese Academy of Social Sciences and Han Yuhai at Beijing University. The new left came first, since it overlapped somehow with conservatism in the argument that the state had to play an important role in China's development and that the power of the existing state had to be strengthened in order to maintain political stability. This overlap also made the new left more acceptable to the party-state than other non-governmental views.

On the other hand, new liberalism can be seen as a revival of theoretical interests in liberalism developed in the 1980s. As Geremie Barme has observed, this new body of liberal thought and theory was influenced partly by the introduction and popularization of the writings of a range of Western thinkers from Locke and Rousseau, to Popper and Hayek, and partly by the efforts of writers in Beijing, Shanghai and elsewhere to unearth and write about Chinese proponents of liberal thought from earlier in the twentieth century.[8] While liberalism never became part of the political mainstream, it nevertheless has been regarded as a main alternative to China's political regime, be it under the KMT or CCP. The pro-liberal forces were forced to "disappear" after the Tiananmen incident, but the rise of social problems provided them the opening to regain some public space among Chinese intellectuals. Liu Junning and Yu Youyu at the Chinese Academy of Social Sciences, Qin Hui at Qinghua University, and Zhu Xueqin in Shanghai, to name a few, are among the most vocal scholars among the new liberals.

The neo-liberal discourse

The so-called new liberals comprise scholars and thinkers in different fields, and they disagree with each other on certain important matters. They do not have one single philosophical origin; instead, they have drawn their thoughts from different Western thinkers. Nevertheless, there is consensus among them on some important issues. This discussion focuses on some of the major arguments of new liberalism regarding China's problems, how they have come into being, and how they can be solved.

The philosophical foundation

Among others, Liu Junning has provided the most succinct discussion of the philosophical foundation of new liberalism. The new left often criticizes liberals for ignoring the interests of the poor and the weak, and the many forms of social injustice that exist in Chinese society, and for failing to provide a solution to the problems. In response, Liu wrote a lengthy paper and, for the first time, gave the reader an overall introduction of liberal thought.[9]

Liberalism is often associated with the newly rising rich classes. But Liu disagrees with this perception, arguing that new liberalism has developed out of the Chinese context, where there is no freedom for the poor to improve their living conditions, absolutely unfair competition, close linkages between the government and business, unlimited political power, and no protection for private property. According to him, "liberalism stands in opposition to these realities, it is not for power elites and newly rising rich classes, instead, it is for the people."[10] Apparently, while the new left calls upon state power to protect the poor, new liberals argue that state power has to be constrained so that the interests of the poor can be promoted and protected. According to Liu, liberalism is universal, and it stresses universal rights and values such as representative democracy, indirect democracy, constitutionalism, rule of law, limited government, and basic human rights. While the state often deprives people of these rights, the market helps people to realize these rights. Liu contends:

liberalism believes that freedom is everyone's basic right, and everyone should equally have constitutional freedom and rights regardless of his social status, property, prestige, power, class, ethnicity, and cultural background . . . And liberalism believes that nothing else can be more efficient than a market system in improving resource allocation and economic efficiency. To establish an efficient market system is the only solution that can help the poor to improve their situation.[11]

Besides individual freedom, Liu also highlights the principle of equity: "equity means that everyone is equal before law, and everyone should be equally protected by law whose ultimate goal is to improve freedom . . . Equality enables everyone to enjoy freedom to choose and thus realize his potentials."[12] Equity does not mean absolute equality of opportunity, but equal freedom to enjoy such an opportunity. Liu argues that "equity does not mean that the government should provide the same protection to every social member, nor does it mean that everyone can equally share benefits from the government (except legal rights and equal treatments)."[13]

In the economic arena, equity means equal opportunity, that is, nobody should be constrained by the government from pursuing material welfare through his own efforts. According to liberalism, it is not the government's duty to provide individuals with economic protection, since no government is capable of achieving this goal. Once the government attempts to do that, people will be forced to give up their freedom, and consequently, while gaining economic protection, they would lose freedom.[14] New liberals also recognized China's worsening situation of income distribution, but they argued that a fair distribution of income could only be achieved by market mechanisms, not by political power. Liu argues that "justice is embedded in a market distribution of income."[15] For liberals, justice is associated with freedom.

Based on such a philosophical foundation, liberals disagree with the new left about the origins of and solutions to China's problems. According to the new left, China's problems such as income disparities are the consequence of the market-oriented reform and capitalistic economic development. By contrast, new liberals believe that such problems are the products of the old economic and political systems. If these problems are associated with reform, this is only because capitalism has not gained full development in China. Throughout the reform process, private property was not protected by the Constitution, and state ownership had enabled party cadres and government officials to "steal" state property via various forms of corruption.[16] The involvement of state power in commercial and business activities led to social injustice and unfairness. Liu argues that "the ultimate roots of unfair income distribution between the rich and poor are in China's political system, not a newly rising market economy. Consequently, without changing China's political system, it is unlikely to solve all China's problems."[17]

Globalism

While the new left regards the post-Mao market-oriented economic reform as a process of westernization, new liberals argue that liberal values associated with the market economy such as freedom and property rights are universal rather than belonging to any particular nation-state. They believe that if China wants to be modernized, it cannot and should not reject liberal globalism. As Qin Hui argues:

Liberalism is a super-national (i.e., super-civilizational) and universal value . . . Market economy is superior to a command one, democracy is superior to dictatorship, the separation of church from the state is superior to the combination of the two, religious freedom is superior to religious trial, etc.[18]

So, individual freedom resulting from market-oriented economic reforms and capitalistic development cannot be regarded as a process of "westernization." In terms of individual freedom, there is no conflict between civilizations. Human dignity and freedom are the ultimate goals of all civilizations. If China wants to be "civilized," it has to accept liberalism. Liu Xinwu, Chairman of the China Writers Association, argues that all nations have to appreciate a "shared civilization" regardless of its origin, and China, as a member of the human civilization, needs to recognize its value. According to Liu, the shared civilization may be developed by a given nation, or by several nations. But as long as it can promote other nations' productivity and improve their people's living standards, it is a shared civilization. Liu contends that "we (Chinese) have to recognize that in the past few centuries, peoples in western Europe and North America have contributed to this shared civilization more than any other peoples. We do not need to ask its origins. We have the rights to enjoy it."[19]

While the proponents of the new left are opposed to capitalism-driven globalism, new liberals identified globalism as a goal of China's modernization. The new leftists believe that the existing rules and norms have been established by the West and are not necessary in accordance with China's national interests and, therefore, China needs to reform the current distribution of power in the international system or at least modify international rules and norms in order to promote its own national interests. By contrast, new liberals argue that it is in China's interests to accept the existing international rules and norms. According to Li Shenzhi, Vice Chairman of the Chinese Academy of Social Sciences and a major proponent of liberalism, China has to abandon the old concept of geo-politics and to accept the fact that every nation can benefit from globalism and interdependence among nations. Since China was humiliated by the West throughout its modern history, it is easy for nationalism to develop into Chinese chauvinism, which in effect will constrain China from becoming a great power. So, the only way for China to become a strong nation-state and an important force promoting international peace and security is to accept the existing international rules and norms.[20]

Without doubt, the existing rules and norms of international politics, economics and diplomacy have been established under the influence of major Western powers and can be regarded as products of Western civilization. But this does not mean that China cannot benefit from accepting these rules and norms. According to Chen Shaoming in Guangdong, whether these rules and norms are fair or not cannot be judged by the actions or attitudes of the major powers toward others. He argues that "we need to see first whether these rules and norms are applicable to every country. If the answer is 'yes,' it means that Western powers also follow these rules and norms, and we cannot argue that Western powers use these rules and norms to exploit other countries."[21] Chen also contends that China cannot reject international rules and norms by claiming that China is still a developing country and these rules and norms are not applicable to China's domestic situations. This is because China can change its domestic situations by accepting these rules and norms as exemplified by other East Asian countries.[22]

Democracy

For liberals, the significance of globalism or China's integration into the world system is that it will help democratize the country's political system by bringing liberalism to China. Li Shenzhi, in his introduction to a collection of essays on pre-1949 liberalism and the history of Peking University, edited by Liu Junning and published at the time of the school's centenary in 1998, claimed that political experiments at home and abroad since the industrial revolution had proved that liberalism is the best and the most universal human value. Li believes that globalization would facilitate the development of liberalism in China.[23] Similarly, Bao Tong, a former aide to purged CCP leader Zhao Ziyang and a liberal advocate, contended that Western liberalism is more valuable and suitable to China than oriental authoritarianism, and that the Chinese Communist Party should support this imported "ism."[24] Bao Tong was jailed for his support of Zhao Ziyang during the 1989 pro-democracy movement, and to a great degree, his view is representative of the generation that experienced Maoist authoritarian rule.

While the new leftists have called for statism and argued that only a strong state can make China strong in both domestic and international affairs, new liberals contend that statism will only lead to authoritarian rule and thus call for democratization through political reforms. New liberals also see the importance of strong central power but question the existing foundation of the state. According to new liberals, throughout its modern history, a major theme of Chinese nationalism was independence and national survival. But once national liberation was achieved and national rights were realized, it was imperative to put priority on democracy to promote individual rights or civil rights.[25]

New liberals argue that a prerequisite for a strong state is democracy, and believe that without a strong internal competitive system, i.e., democracy, any political system will eventually fail to survive. According to Chen Shaoming, in order to be strong, China's political system needs to be open to its people; if individuals cannot relate their individual interests to national interests, they will naturally be indifferent to any political mobilization. Great internal dynamism depends on whether individuals can participate in the political process and have full opportunity to express their opinions.[26]

According to Shen Ruji, not only does China's economic system need to be integrated into the world system; it is also important for China to learn from the United States in constructing its political and social systems. When looking at American power, its political and social institutions have to be taken into account. The United States has been able to maintain its status as a world power because of its wealth, and because of its liberal environment and tolerant society which have successfully absorbed top talents from all over the world.[27] Shen argues that with changes in capitalist societies, capitalism and the Chinese style of socialism are increasingly convergent.[28] Therefore, China should welcome "peaceful evolution" (*heping yanbian*) since it is the natural and positive way for social progress, even though China has opposed such a strategy before.[29]

Civil society

Many new liberals emphasize the role of civil society in leading China's "peaceful" transition to democracy. According to Deng Zhenglai and Jing Yuejing, two of the most vocal scholars in this school of thought, civil society can be defined as "a private sphere of autonomous economic and social activities based on the principle of voluntary contract, and a public sphere of unofficial participation in politics."[30] Though there is disagreement on the meaning of civil society among new liberal scholars, there is consensus among them on what it refers to, that is, civil society represents a combination of economic, political, social and cultural elements such as economic freedom, property rights, contractual social relations, autonomous social organizations, individual rights and freedom, equality, and independence.[31]

For new liberals, the political significance of civil society lies in that it can help the state maintain social stability on one hand, and constrain state power on the other hand. The development of civil society has to precede the transition to democracy since the latter requires certain economic, social, and cultural preconditions that can only be generated through the creation of civil society.[32] China's reforms since the late 1970s had been caught in a vicious circle in which "decentralization leads to anarchy, anarchy leads to recentralization, and recentralization leads to overcentralization" (*yifang jiuluan, yiluan jiutong, yitong jiusi*). New liberals believe that this vicious circle is a consequence of the lack of civil society in China. When society itself does not have a system of self-management, state power becomes intrusive, and when state power is involved, this vicious circle will not go away.[33]

So, how can civil society help the state strengthen its power on one hand, and constrain state power and make the state democratic on the other hand? Deng and Jing proposed a two-stage development of civil society. In the first stage, a dualist structure in the state–society relationship should be established, that is, the state should transfer economic power to society, and civil society gains much economic freedom while remaining passive in the political realm. In the second stage, civil society is expanded from the private to the public sphere and a relationship of "positive interaction" between the state and society will be developed, in which civil society should play an active role protecting societal freedom, opposing state domination, developing social pluralism, and promoting democracy.[34]

By doing so, according to Deng and Jing, civil society can check and balance state power; more importantly, it can participate in politics. It is important to note that in Deng and Jing's view, "to check and balance" is civil society's "negative relationship" with the state, while "to participate" is its "positive relationship."[35] Other scholars in this school disagree slightly with such a definition. For example, He Zengke has argued that positive interaction only meant civil society's constructive engagement with, not antagonism to, the state. But for others, the essence of positive interaction between the state and society lay in the checks and balances between them.[36]

Constitutionalism

Many liberals, especially liberal economists and legal scholars, stress liberal constitutionalism. According to these scholars, the transition from authoritarianism to democracy depends on whether liberal constitutionalism has become the foundation of China's political structure. Constitutionalism is significant for China's peaceful and stable transition. On the one hand, the root of China's problems lies in the fact that the party-state stands above the Constitution and the law, and its behavior is not subject to any constitutional and legal constraints. On the other hand, constitutionalism means that social or non-official (governmental) forces participate in politics in legally prescribed ways, not by radical social movements and revolution.[37]

Central to the debate on constitutionalism between new liberals and new leftists is the linkage between property rights and economic reform. As will be discussed later, the new left opposes radical privatization. By contrast, new liberals regard privatization as the essence of China's economic reform. Liberal economists claim that the difficulty of China's economic reform lay in the fact that private property rights were not protected by the Constitution for a long period of time during the reform, and argue that without establishing private property rights, China's economic reform will go nowhere. According to Zhang Weiying, private property rights are a precondition to the emergence of entrepreneurs and a sufficient and necessary condition for economic efficiency.[38] Wang Ding Ding contends that to deepen the reform of China's SOEs, the first priority is "to implement constitutional reforms and establish a Constitution whose aim is to protect private property rights."[39]

Political scientist Liu Junning strongly argues that "central to individual autonomy is individuals' independent and exclusive property rights [since] without which there will be absolutely no rights to govern himself." Therefore, according to Liu, "property rights is the precursor of all political rights and the foundation of constitutional democracy."[40] Like Wang, Liu also believes that "the starting point of restructuring [China's] political system is to revise the existing Constitution and recognize that property rights is a sacred and inviolable individual right."[41] Liu concludes that only by recognizing property rights can China's political system gain political support and state power be constrained by the propertied class.

As will be discussed later, the new left emphasizes that state power, especially fiscal power, has to be highly centralized in order to strengthen the state's capacity in realizing just income distribution. New liberals see the danger of unlimited state power in dealing with income distribution, and they prefer to use constitutional means to achieve fair income distribution. According to Ji Weidong, a legal scholar, unlimited centralization, if aimed at so-called just income distribution, can only lead to Maoist absolute egalitarianism and rampant corruption among party cadres and government officials, thus undermining China's ongoing development of the market economy. Ji argues that although the state has to play an important role in reducing income disparities, "the most crucial issue is how to avoid arbitrary economic egalitarianism if the state wants to be involved in income distribution and redistribution."[42] In order to deal with the issue more effectively, China has to develop various democratic measures. According to Ji:

unfair distribution of property rights and efforts to change such a situation are the foundation and origin of [different] political parties. The pursuit of the goal of social justice has to be considered together with the establishment of a representative system in which different interests can be represented, and only by considering plural opinions and interests can social injustice be corrected.[43]

The state alone cannot dictate income distribution, and different interests have to take part in the process. Therefore, laws and regulations have to be established to limit the role of the state in (re)distributing income.[44] Overall, like new leftists, new liberals do agree that the state has to play an important role in dealing with rising social and economic issues such as income disparities. But for new liberals, in doing so, the state has to transform itself from authoritarianism to democracy.

The new left discourse

The new left stands for a number of distinct but related intellectual positions and theoretical discourse of which three general trends can be identified. First, the new left understands China's problems in the context of globalization and therefore anti-westernization is a major preoccupation for the new leftists. Second, the new left assigns a greater role to the state in dealing with China's problems and therefore its proponents have argued for strengthening the state. Third, unlike new liberals who argue for continuously learning from the West, new leftists have called for developing a Chinese alternative to Western forms of modernity.

Against globalization

While new liberals regard China's problems as resulting from the old political and economic systems, new leftists ascribe them to China's globalization. Resistance to and critique of capitalist globalization is a main theme of the new left intellectual movement.

After Deng's southern tour in 1992, China accelerated its economic development and opening to the outside world. Correspondingly, Chinese intellectuals also made great efforts to theorize the new economic phenomena. Among others, Lin Yifu, a Chicago University trained economist, and his colleagues proposed a theory of comparative advantage, and argued that the implementation of this strategy requires that the government establish various supporting institutions for a free market system.[45] The comparative advantage strategy led to enormous reaction from the new left and other proponents of anti-westernization. There are three major arguments against the theory of comparative advantage.

First of all, adopting the comparative advantage strategy implies that China's economy needs to be fully integrated into the world system. Even though China can benefit from economic integration with other countries, China's political independence and national security will be undermined. Shi Zhong, a major proponent of the new left, argues that the danger of the comparative advantage strategy is that "it will allow other countries to determine China's fate, that is, China will allow its economic future and national security to be dependent on other countries' strategic interests."[46]

According to Shi Zhong, modern Chinese history showed that dependence would eventually lead to the loss of national sovereignty. Before the Opium War, China's economy was more developed than most Western countries in many aspects. Then the West became more developed in certain key industrial technologies, which eventually led to China's defeat. Therefore, for China as a late developing country, the most urgent task for its political elites is to adopt a catching-up strategy to guarantee national survival. Mao Zedong's catching-up and surpassing strategy brought about various economic crises. But it was this strategy that made China more independent in the world of nation-states. Without a relatively independent economic system, China's sovereignty in the world system would be in jeopardy. Although China has achieved rapid economic growth since reform began in 1978, it is still backward in many key industrial technologies. Thus,

If China cannot implement a catching-up and surpassing strategy, it will again be defeated by new technological revolutions, and its fate will be even more miserable than in the last century . . . To build an independent and self-sufficient industrial system should still be China's long term development goal.[47]

Due to China's overall backwardness, the strategy of comparative advantage cannot protect national industries from intensive international competition, but will only weaken them. As a matter of fact, many ordinary Chinese believe that foreign capital is destroying China's national industries and weakening China's national power.[48] Therefore, what is needed, according to the new left, is for China to establish a solid industrial base.

Second, the proponents of the new left favor China's independence and are against an export-led development strategy. In their view, this strategy will have a negative impact on China's long-term development and national survival. One author identifies an export-led economy with a dependent one and argues that:

the most serious weakness of an export-led model is that a country's economy will be greatly influenced by international environments. Because of a great dependence on the Western (and the US) economies, a minor change in the international market will cause great fluctuation in the domestic market.[49]

This view has been confirmed by developments in other East Asian economies. The existing international economic system was established by the West, which also controlled key economic instruments and mechanisms, such as tariff, credit and loan, investment, exchange rate and so on. Almost all countries with an export-led strategy have to rely greatly on developed countries. Once their economic interests are in conflict with those of the West, they are necessarily subject to sanctions imposed by the West.[50]

According to the new left, even though China has benefited from the export-led strategy in the past decade, whether it will be successful in the long run is still doubtful. If China does not eventually subordinate its sovereignty to the West, the West will not allow China to continue its export-led development. According to Liu Liqun of the Development Research Center under the State Council, the success of the export-led development in East Asia so far depends on a number of preconditions. A political-military alliance with the West has to be formed. The West was willing to form this alliance with East Asian countries during the Cold War because it was in accordance with Western countries' national interests. Local economic activities have to be dependent on those in the West. Local socio-economic systems have to be reformed in order to fit those in the West. Apparently, if China continues to follow such a development strategy, its fate will be controlled by more advanced countries.[51]

Moreover, it is difficult for China's export-led strategy to succeed. This is because the above stated preconditions which led to the success of this strategy in other East Asian countries no longer exist. Furthermore, the West is unwilling to see China's rise. The West was previously interested in seeing China's integration into the international economic system. Now, with China's economy becoming more competitive, it is increasingly in conflict with the economic, even political and military, interests of the Western countries. The West has become determined not to let China develop into a superpower and will use all possible means to contain China's development.

An export-led development strategy is thus in conflict with China's national interest. Once China's economy is significantly integrated into the international system, the West will have more ways of containing China. It is imperative therefore to rethink China's development strategy. Even if an export-led strategy has benefited China, "China's national interests will, in the long run, be better served by independence rather than dependence."[52]

Third, the proponents of comparative advantage argue that whether China's economic reform can be deepened depends on whether the government is able to abandon the old system of planned economy and let market and economic factors play a major role in economic activities. In contrast, the new left maintains that, if China's economic reform is to succeed, government planning needs to be strengthened rather than weakened. But this does not mean that the new left proposes going back to the old planned system. Instead, its proponents stress that a new type of economic plan is necessary for China's economic growth.

The advocates of comparative advantage and those of the new left have interpreted the East Asian economic miracle differently. While the former attribute it to a comparative advantage strategy, the latter argue that East Asian economic success was because of "planned rationality" by the governments in these countries.[53] China's catching-up and surpassing development strategy during Mao's time was an example of planned rationality. One author argues that the failure of Chinese socialism was not because of its planned economic system, but because of its political system. Even during the Cultural Revolution, China's economic performance was still impressive. While the old centrally planned system rejected a market economy, a new government plan must aim at establishing a system that accommodates market forces. A market system will not come into being on its own accord but must be planned. Russia's attempt to let "market rationality" function led to economic chaos. If China wants to avoid such a misfortune, government "planned rationality" needs to be introduced and strengthened.[54]

Against institutional fetishism

Related to the new leftists' attack on globalization is their critique of the new liberals' call for learning from Western political and economic institutions. Chinese intellectuals began to reflect on this westernization-oriented reform strategy before the collapse of communist states in Europe as is shown in the debate of so-called neo-authoritarianism in the late 1980s.[55] The collapse of communism in Europe convinced Chinese intellectuals that "westernization" oriented reforms would lead to both economic and political chaos. This was one major reason why Chinese intellectuals became conservative in their orientation after the 1989 pro-democracy movement. The new left thus opposed any form of radical reform and stressed the importance of a centralized state in guiding China's development.

For new leftists, the difficulties which China's reform encountered in the 1980s resulted from radical reform policies or policy proposals raised by those who idolized Western systems. In the late 1980s, under the influence of Western liberal economists, some reformist leaders even believed in the "shock therapy" which had been used in the Soviet Union and Eastern Europe. Meanwhile, many Chinese intellectuals, backed by major reformist leaders, argued that China needed to introduce Western democracy in order to provide an institutional foundation for a free market system. It was these westernization-oriented reform measures that eventually led to China's political chaos as exemplified by the 1989 Tiananmen demonstration.[56]

Cui Zhiyuan, a vocal proponent of the new left, has developed a so-called "second thought liberation" discourse on how China can learn from the West and its own past through institutional innovations. Cui argues for dismantling the fetish with absolute market and the absolute state on the one hand, and calls for mass participation to help innovate the Chinese socio-economic and political institutions on the other hand. According to Cui, "the second thought liberation" is a dialectic transcendence of "traditional binary opposites such as private ownership and state ownership, market economy and planned economy, Chinese substance–Western function versus wholesale Westernization, and reformism and conservatism," all of which emerged during the "first intellectual liberation," namely the one waged in late 1970s against the dogmatic adherence to Maoism, which paved the way for the socialist economic reform in the 1980s. The emphasis in the second thought liberation is no longer "the negation of [socialist]conservatism, but the expansion of a new space for institutional innovation; instead of sticking with an either/or division, it searches for new opportunities for institutional innovation under the guiding principle of economic and political democracy."[57]

How can institutional innovation take place in the Chinese context of reforms? Based on a dynamic practice of dialectical thinking which comprises deconstructive and constructive elements, Cui examines a whole range of historical or contemporary cases from the writings of Rousseau and Mill to post-Fordist production, and from the Chinese village election to the Russian "shock therapy." He perceives contemporary capitalism as an ongoing process on a historical continuum. He therefore calls for a continuing effort at understanding the historical complexity and socio-political contradictions of capitalism so as to pick out those democratic, liberating elements which have moved capitalism forward over its long history. However, he also acknowledges that capitalism has been constrained, repressed, and distorted by its reified institutions and ideologies.

Institutional innovation, and in particular intellectual innovation, can occur in various fields of economic reform. Cui defines the notion of property rights as a "bundle of rights," rather than a unified and mythologized entity, and shows how power, privileges, immunities, and sub-categories such as the right to control residues, the right of residual claimant, etc., could be brought into new configurations so as to address the interests of both stockholders and stakeholders, and to open new theoretical space for economic democracy under both private and public ownership. Cui dispels the myth of the "invisible hand" by referring to concrete cases of recent institutional and intellectual changes in the US (such as the corporate laws passed in 29 states in the 1980s) to shed light on reforms in the Chinese context. In Cui's view, the contemporary capitalist system is a result of its reaction to, compromise with, and management of the socialist challenges and working class movements over a long period of time; and that even the US economy has a socialist component much more significant than admitted by its Chinese or Russian critics and admirers.

Cui explains why it is important to have institutional innovation. According to him, while the new social elite and their intellectual spokesmen in Eastern Europe, Russia, and China regard private ownership as the new Bible, corporate law in America has undergone profound changes in the opposite direction. In the West, private ownership has long been represented in corporate law in the structure of corporate governance: The shareholders are owners, to whom and only to whom the management must be held accountable in its efforts to maximize profit. However, since the 1980s, more than half of the states in the US (29 in total so far) have modified their corporate laws. Their new laws require management to serve not only the shareholders, but the stakeholders as well. Such reform in American corporate law breaks through the seemingly axiomatic logic of private ownership, thus becoming the most significant event in recent US politics and economy.[58]

Similarly, Cui also sees the possibility of institutional innovation from China's own past. For instance, in analyzing the phenomenal growth of Chinese rural industry in the past two decades, Cui traces its origin in Mao's failed idea of rural industrialization during the disastrous "Great Leap Forward" movement in the late 1950s, and its not so spectacular prehistory of infrastructure building under the People's Commune system. According to him, the success of Chinese village and township industry after 1978 shows that "the failure of previous practice does not prevent its positive elements from being absorbed and transformed under new circumstance."[59]

From this point of view, Cui seems to be dissatisfied with the new Chinese corporate law. In order to build modern enterprise institutions, the new Chinese corporate law downgraded the three old *hui*s, i.e., *dang-weihui* (party committee), *zhigong daibiao dahui* (the workers' congress), and *gonghui* (trade union), and institutionalized three new *hui*s, i.e., *dongshihui* (board of directors), *gudong dahui* (meetings of shareholders), and *jianshihui* (board of supervisors). Cui contends that in aiming to observe "international convention," the new law fails to follow the progressive trend to institutionalize workers' participation in corporate decision-making, allowing workers' representation in the board of trustees only in state enterprises, thus cutting the ties between the workers' congress and the board of trustees. Cui rejects the uniformity of obsolete ideas related to the capitalist corporate system and calls for innovative explorations of a Chinese model appropriate to modern enterprises.[60]

New leftists like Cui Zhiyuan thus argue that China should not follow any Western model if it wants to further its industrial reform and improve the economic performance of enterprises in the state sector and the collectives as well. Institutional fetishism (westernization) led Russia and many former East European socialist countries to political and economic chaos. If China wants to avoid such a misfortune, it should not appeal to any Western ideas to guide its reform. Private ownership, privatization and other capitalistic means are the products of the Western civilization and are unlikely to bring favorable results to China.[61] What is important for China is that it have its own non-Western theories to guide its development. What has been wrong with China's industrial reform is that many leaders are too westernized in their economic decision-making. Various Maoist legacies, with their positive elements, were thus neglected. According to Cui, while looking at the West for its industrial management and reform, China also needs to look for lessons of experience in Mao Zedong's industrial practice since, to a great degree, it provided the most important modern form of industrial management, i.e., management through workers' participation.[62]

Statism

For new leftists, the collapse of East European communism and consequent economic chaos highlighted the significance of a centralized regime. Once the regime collapsed, the nation-state *per se* would be in crisis. According to the proponents of the new left, a "wrong" perception that became prevalent among Chinese intellectuals and political leaders in the 1980s was that economic and political reforms needed to go together. Therefore, with the introduction of a free market system, the regime itself had to be liberalized. In effect, a centralized regime is necessary for China's economic reforms. Without such a regime, it will be hard to cope with various unexpected consequences resulting from rapid economic growth. If the regime is weakened, economic modernization will lead to a crisis of national survival rather than political democracy.

Wang Shaoguang and Hu Angang have developed a theory of state capacity in this regard. They argue that the state has to play an important role not only in regulating the market, but also in curbing its tendency toward regional protectionism and fragmentation, and toward monopoly and unequal competition. More importantly, a capable state has to maintain a credible national defense, a socially just distribution of wealth, and uphold the morality and political unity of the nation. Central to the state capacity theory is the necessity for the state to retain a powerful capacity in extracting taxes in order to fulfill its vital and indispensable role in fostering a meaningful and creative national life.[63]

Wang and Hu's argument can be regarded as one of the earliest discourses on the relationship between the state and market within the Chinese context and one of the early responses to the economic collapse, political failure, and social tragedy of those transitional societies in Eastern Europe, especially the former Soviet Union and Yugoslavia. The imperative of taxation in their thesis was made vis-à-vis both the ruinous consequences of neo-liberal theory in Russia and with reference to the relatively primitive mechanisms of the Chinese socialist state to secure tax revenues in an emergent market environment. Though theirs is not an argument against the market, they do not believe in the sanctity of the market as the new liberals do. The state capacity theory stresses the imperative to explore ways to an economically successful, socially just, and politically stable transition to the "socialist market economy." According to them, the market economy that China strives to build has to be based on a modern institution of enterprise, finance, and taxation, not one based on petit agrarian production. The Chinese market must be a unified domestic market free from local and regional division and protectionism; this market has to operate on the principle of equal competition guaranteed by taxation policies and government services; and such a modern, equal, and unified market has to be regulated and protected by a legal structure based on a social contract.[64]

According to Wang and Hu, China's transition from a planned to a market economy depends on certain conditions. First, the function of central power has to be transformed and reconfigured to give rise to a new, efficient macro-administrative framework. Second, the government has to eradicate systematic corruption which inevitably leads to massive social instability and makes the establishment of a socially just economic order impossible. And third, the government has to allow free debate between different quarters and make the policy-making processes more democratic.[65]

The "state capacity" thesis led to a heated debate among Chinese intellectuals in the middle 1990s. Not surprisingly, the most vocal reactions came from the new liberals. To buttress their theory of state capacity, Wang responded with a book review article on Holmes and Sunstein's new book, *The Cost of Rights*,[66] in which the authors argued that all rights, including the so-called "negative rights," depend on the state and its taxation capacity; that all rights are public goods whose protection requires the government to make socially responsible and morally satisfying choices; and that, in view of the sorry reality in "free" Russia, "statelessness spells rightlessness." Wang points out that the Chinese "liberals" would be considered right-wingers and libertarians in the Western social-political spectrum whereas liberal economists like Holmes and Sunstein would be "sharing the same trench with the Chinese new left."[67]

New collectivism

The first aim of the proponents of the new left is to show why China's reform cannot be guided by any Western models, and second, provide an alternative explanation of China's rapid economic growth, i.e., a Chinese discourse on economic reform. Neo-classical economists attribute China's success to its Western style of economic reform, and argue that further economic growth depends on China achieving privatization and establishing a free market system. By contrast, the new left argues that it was Maoist legacies rather than westernization-oriented economic reform that promoted China's rapid economic growth. While neo-classical economists are interested in how the dynamism of economic development can be created, the new left sees the impact of rapid economic growth on social and political stability and national integration, and emphasizes social justice.

According to the new left, Maoism's contribution to China's economic growth lies in its practice of collectivism. This is especially true in rural development. In rural areas, growth gained momentum during Deng's era. But rural growth did not begin with Deng's reform. In many parts of China, especially in coastal provinces, rapid rural development occurred long before Deng's reform, even during the Cultural Revolution. Also important is that even in Deng's era, it was within the Maoist collectivism that rural economic development occurred.[68] In other words, Deng Xiaoping's reform only provided a political condition for Maoist collectivism to promote rural growth. Deng's reform did not lead to a Western-style individualism in rural areas. Privatization did not spread in rural China. Even after more than a decade of reform, private ownership did not become dominant. The main economic players are not individuals, but local communities. For the new left, all these factors contributed to rapid rural growth.[69]

Since the reform began in the late 1970s, Maoist ideology has increasingly become a target for social and intellectual criticism. But for the new left, Maoist ideology cannot be rejected altogether. In many areas, it is still capable of providing individuals, especially lower level government officials, with "spiritual" motivation to lead local development. In many localities, it is Maoist "good" leadership that provides economic dynamism. The proponents of the new left firmly believe that Maoist ideology plays an important role in strengthening rural collectivism, reducing income disparities among farmers and thus maintaining rural stability. So, a precondition for China's further rural reform is not to abandon Maoist ideology. Instead, it needs to be developed in accordance with existing conditions in China.[70]

From his reading of rural development in post-Mao China, Gan Yang seems to suggest that he has found a Chinese way of building a new state. In Gan's view, the rise of the village and township enterprise is not only an economic phenomenon; it is also politically significant, and it signifies that China has developed a way of development different from the classical model of Western modernity.[71] The profound historic significance of the rise of Chinese rural industry, according to Gan, is that it provides the Chinese industrial transformation with a dependable foundation of micro-social organization. In other words, the development of Chinese rural industry is not achieved at the expense of weakening, undermining, and eventually destroying existing rural communities, but rather it thrives on the basis of its close ties to and mutual dependency on the rural community. Its prosperity reinforces the reconstruction of the communities in rural China. If use of such historical experience proves feasible, its meaning to the continuation of a Chinese way of life will be unlimited; and its contribution to the history of civilization invaluable.[72]

Political and economic democracy

The new left calls for China's economic democratization. While new liberals emphasize various forms of freedom, political rights and a multi-party system, the proponents of the new left argue that democratization is not westernization, i.e., following the Western models of democracy. Instead, they believe that Maoist practice contained various important elements of democracy. If these elements can be developed properly, they will contribute to China's democratization.[73]

According to Cui Zhiyuan, there are two forms of democracy: procedural and deliberative. The former regards democracy as a political method in which political elites "buy" votes from people and thus emphasizes formal elections. The latter emphasizes the substance of democracy and various forms of popular participation. It seems to the proponents of the new left that because too much attention has been paid to procedural democracy, deliberative democracy is neglected among Chinese intellectuals. It was Mao Zedong who, during his long political career, especially during the Cultural Revolution, developed a theory of deliberative democracy, although it was not systematic. For the new left, Mao's deliberative democracy was the origin of rapid economic growth in the post-Mao era. China's deliberative democracy was characterized mainly by decentralization. During Mao's time, both China's economic and its political systems were highly decentralized. This made it possible for local communities and individuals to participate in the process of development. China's township and village enterprises developed as a direct result of Maoist development strategy, i.e., mobilizing mass participation into the production process. Similarly, the Constitution of the Anshan Steel Mill also provided workers with an institutional framework to participate in the production process.[74] Deliberate democracy also made it possible for local governments at different levels to play an important role in China's economic affairs. It is this Maoist legacy that makes it possible for China to avoid the misfortune of the former Soviet Union. For the new left, deliberative or economic democracy rather than private property rights and individualism should guide China in its further economic reform.[75]

Politically, the proponents of the new left have also proposed to draw lessons from the Maoist theory of "mass democracy" which was developed during the Cultural Revolution. In fact, re-evaluating the Cultural Revolution has been a major theme of the new left. According to the new left, Mao Zedong's main purpose of "mass democracy" was not political struggle, but constituted real democracy based on mass participation. Maoist mass democracy was a reflection of the crisis of Western modernity, and aimed to provide an alternative to Western democracy. What Mao wanted was to create opportunities for people to be a part of Chinese political and economic development. But for various reasons, Mao's mass democracy was "distorted" during the Cultural Revolution. The new left thus calls for a transformation and institutionalization of Mao's mass democracy. China needs democratization, but it does not mean that China should follow any single Western model of political democracy. The institutionalization of Mao's mass democracy will make it possible for China to re-structure Western modernity based on its own political practice, to establish a democracy with Chinese characteristics, and thus to become a strong nation-state in world affairs.[76]

Conclusion

We can see from the above discussion that new liberalism and the new left strongly disagree over a number of important issues. To a large extent, the ideological conflict between them reflects their different visions of the Chinese state. Nevertheless, both schools are concerned with what kind of state the country should build and what role the state should play in shaping China's socio-economic development.

The new left discourse criticizes capitalism-driven globalization and its proponents believe that all the problems that China faces today are the result of globalization. Therefore, they call for a strengthening of state power in order to resist globalization and to cope with the problems related to globalization. In contrast, the new liberal discourse identifies with globalism and its proponents believe that China's problems are related to the fact that the country has not yet been fully integrated into the world community. New liberals generally tend to favor the neo-classical economic orthodoxy, namely the primacy of market and private ownership. According to them, the making of an autonomous Chinese middle class or a proto-bourgeoisie can stimulate and stabilize a growth-oriented society, just as it has in many Western societies; therefore, joining the mainstream of world civilizations can help China's transition towards a market economy and democracy.

New liberals also believe that market-oriented reforms are the only way for China to establish an effective economic system. Thus they call for developing private property rights and letting people have equal opportunities to share the public properties that were taken by party cadres and government officials. Moreover, according to new liberals, the state is a necessary evil and in order to let the state play this role and yet limit its evilness, state power has to be constrained by various means such as developing civil society and implementing constitutional reforms.

By contrast, the new left can be seen as responding to the disastrous Russian experiment after the Cold War, and its proponents oppose privatization on the economic side and unlimited liberalization on the political side. New leftists do not believe that the market alone will achieve just income distribution, and thus stress the central role of the state in this process. Furthermore, the new left attempts to develop a systematic discourse on the limit of bourgeois democracy and capitalist development. Unlike the liberals, the new left does not see joining the mainstream of world civilization as offering a resolution to China's current difficulties.

In fighting for legitimacy in building a future Chinese state, new liberals and new leftists have attempted to highlight each other's association with the existing state in a negative light. New leftists regard new liberals as having adopted the mainstream discourse of the Chinese state, that is, the ideology of modernization and universal progress. While the Chinese state has implemented various market-oriented reform measures, new liberalism has been accused of justifying the development course led by the government. On the other hand, new liberals have repeatedly accused new leftists of rejecting the idea of the free market, the discourse of "classical social sciences;" the universality of the liberal discourse; and the universal values and institutions represented by the West, such as liberal democracy. According to new liberals, the new left demonstrates an affinity with traditional socialism, a nostalgia for Mao's China, a positive attitude toward direct democracy, the centrality of politics, and public passion, a longing for a poetic and romantic idealism, and discontentment with a social transition of a practical nature in contemporary China.

The political significance of both new liberalism and the new left lies in the fact that both can draw support from different social and economic forces. As discussed in the previous chapter, market-oriented economic reform has enabled the rise of a new middle class while causing a weakening of the socio-economic position of workers in the state sector and farmers in rural areas. To a great degree, new liberals represent the interest of newly rising rich class, while the new left represents the interest of workers and farmers. However, in reality, neither new liberals nor new leftists want to associate themselves with any social forces fully. Nevertheless, drastic socio-economic changes are rapidly pushing intellectuals to associate themselves distinctly with their corresponding social forces. Once such a connection is established, they will become politically powerful, whether they are new liberals or new leftists.

9 Globalization and towards a rule-based state governance?

Globalization, as defined by Badie, is a process of establishing an international system which tends towards unification of its rules, values, and objectives.[1] Will globalization cause China's state governance to converge towards the international norm? I have so far discussed how globalization has led to the transformation of the Chinese state. State transformation is the result of the country's integration into the world market and global capitalism. Despite difficulties, the Chinese state has made enormous efforts to adjust the governance structure to accommodate globalization on the one hand, and facilitate the process of China's integration into the global system on the other. The Chinese leadership has developed a new mindset of globalism which perceives the integration of China into global capitalism as an inevitable process for the country to be a strong nation-state (Chapter 3). Therefore, the leadership has adjusted China's political order to accommodate a rising interest-based social order (Chapter 4), rebuild the state bureaucratic system and economic institutions to promote capitalistic economic development and nurture a nascent market economy (Chapters 5 and 6). All these reform measures appear to have moved China closer towards internationally accepted norms of the modern state.

Will capitalistic economic development in China lead the country down the road of democracy as has occurred in many countries? Will the Chinese leadership be able to internationalize its political system as it has done with its economic system? Some scholars and policy-makers believe so. Such an optimistic perspective stems from their belief that global capitalism would induce democratization. It is widely considered that capitalism and democracy are inseparable twins; that capitalism and economic wealth are conducive to the formation of a democratic government, and that democracy as a form of government is likely only in market or capitalist economies. This argument has been very popular since Seymour Lipset conceptualized the linkage between economic development and democracy in 1959 and is reflected in many works by contemporary scholars such as Charles Lindblom, Samuel Huntington, and

Barrington Moore.[2] All of these authors saw the historical and logical connections between capitalism and democracy.

The reasoning goes like this. Based on the experience of political development in East Asia, promoting capitalist economic growth while monopolizing political power is an almost impossible balancing act in the long term, especially in a world that is increasingly linked by communications and trade. As people's incomes rise and their horizons broaden, they are more likely to demand the right to participate in government and to enjoy full protection under the rule of law. So, in the first news conference of his second term, US President Clinton said that "the impulses of the society and the nature of the economic change will work together, along with the availability of information from the outside world, to increase the spirit of liberty over time;" that China could not hold back democracy, just as eventually the Berlin Wall fell.[3]

Nevertheless, as I have shown so far, despite its efforts to promote globalization, the Chinese leadership has been unwilling to convert China's political system towards international rules and norms. Although capitalist development has resulted in a marked improvement in the living standards of ordinary Chinese, the workers and farmers in China are still not granted any institutional and legal tools to voice their interests, nor can Chinese religious believers express their beliefs (Chapter 7). Chinese intellectuals, both new liberals and new leftists, have been quite vocal in propounding their own visions of the future Chinese state, but the CCP continues to make decisions rather independently of these social influences (Chapter 8).

Why is capitalistic economic development not able to democratize China? Apparently, the CCP has engaged in state transformation in order to benefit from globalization with no intention of giving up its monopoly of power. How does the monopoly of power by the CCP affect China's move towards a rule-based state governance? As outlined in Chapter 1, this study has so far focused more on the Chinese state than the CCP. In doing so, I have not addressed another important issue: the tension between state-building and the monopoly of power wielded by the CCP. While globalization has pushed the Chinese state to build a governance structure, to a great degree, in accordance with international rule and norms, this is not the case when we look at the CCP and its relationship with the state. While the CCP still stands above the state, and party policies rather than professional norms govern decision-making, China's state-building will be retarded. This final chapter focuses on the contradictions between the monopoly of power by the CCP and a rule-based governance structure. It shows that while Chinese leaders have made efforts to rebuild the state, there are also disintegrating factors which threaten the survival of the CCP; and therefore while the party has tried to build a system of the rule of law, it is reluctant to give up its monopoly on power, which in turn has obstructed China's move towards a rule-based state governance. Whether China will be able to establish a rule-based state governance can be measured in various ways since the term "rule" covers many types of directives including both formal and informal rules, norms, compliance procedures, and other institutionalized operating practices.

Rule of law or rule by law

In the Western context, according to *Black's Dictionary of Law*, "the rule of law" refers to:

a legal principle, of general application, sanctioned by the recognition of authorities, and usually expressed in the form of a maxim or logical proposition. The rule of law, sometimes called 'the supremacy of law', provides that decisions should be made by the application of known principles or laws without the intervention of discretion in their application.[4]

The rule of law was developed in the context of Western liberalism as a means of restraining the arbitrary actions of power-holders. According to Hayek, the rule of law means that:

government in all its actions is bound by rules fixed and announced beforehand – rules which make it possible to foresee with fair certainty how the authority will use its coercive powers in given circumstances and to plan one's individual affairs on the basis of this knowledge.[5]

More concretely, the rule of law means, first, that laws must be applicable to every individual in a given society; second, the rulers must follow the laws as the ruled do, and third, the rulers' behavior is predictable.[6]

Nevertheless, in Chinese tradition, law was an instrument of state power; and the basic unit of society was the family, clan and guilds, not individuals. This tradition enabled the state to rely on the gentry, family heads, and village elders to enforce local customs, while in the West, these tasks were transferred to the courts applying rules of civil law.[7] Richard Baum thus distinguishes "the rule of law" from "the rule by law." According to Baum, the concept of the rule of law belongs to the West and connotes a pluralistic law reflecting a delicate balance of social forces, acting as a shield to protect various socio-economic classes and strata against the arbitrary tutelage of government. On the other hand, the concept of the rule by law in China means "statist instrumentalism and invokes both the doctrines of traditional Chinese legalism" and the "bureaucratic ethos of Soviet socialist legality."[8] In the same vein, Edward Epstein has pointed out that law in China is "still conceived and operates as an instrument with which to uphold the socialist political order and perpetuate party domination," and "used to carry out and consolidate institutional, primarily economic, changes according to predetermined policy."[9]

Although China does not have a tradition of the rule of law, it has become a, if not *the*, major aim of Chinese political and legal development since economic reform began in the late 1970s. "The rule of law" is clearly expressed in the sixteen-word formula proposed by the Third Plenum of the Eleventh Party Congress convened in 1978, that is, *"you fa ke yi, you fa bi yi, zhi fa bi yan, wei fa bi jiu"* (literally, there must be laws for people to follow, these laws must be observed, their enforcement must be strict, and law-breakers must be dealt with). In this context, the terms such as "equality before the laws," "the supremacy of the law," "the rule-of-law-state," and "legalization" have become some of the popular terms in the Chinese discourse of building a legal state.

In the West, the rule of law was discussed in the context of democracy. As a matter of fact, *"minzhu"* (democracy) and *"fazhi"* (legal system) are often two interchangeable terms in China. The Communiqué of the Third Plenum of the Eleventh Party Congress stated:

To safeguard people's democracy, it is imperative to strengthen the socialist legal system so that democracy is systematized and written into law in such a way as to ensure the stability, continuity and full authority of this democratic system and laws.[10]

One of the aims of the rule of law is to protect the ruled from arbitrary rule. Deng Xiaoping once argued that "Democracy has to be institutionalized and written into law so as to make sure that institutions and laws do not change whenever the leadership changes or whenever the leaders change their views."[11]

With rapid socio-economic changes, the Chinese leadership has vigorously pursued, using a process of trial and error, a legal state as a new and effective way of governance. In the 1980s and early 1990s, the highest priority was given to building a legal system and ending an era without law. The leadership called for ruling the country by law. After the mid-1990s, the leadership made efforts to establish a system of the rule of law, which was set up as the goal of China's political development by the Fifteenth Congress of the CCP in 1997. To be sure, legal development in terms of introducing laws and regulations has been rather impressive, and the growth rate of laws has been much higher than the economic growth rate. For example, while 514 laws and regulations were made from 1949 to 1978, 16,493 were made between 1979 and 1997.[12] The National People's Congress made 7 laws from 1966 to 1978, and 327 laws from 1979 to 1998.[13]

Embedded in the leadership's efforts to promote legal development was the recognition that laws have to be used to strengthen the capability of the state to govern a country in which the socio-economic complexity is rapidly increasing. In other words, any new governing system needs to be based on the rule by law.

In a sense, the rule by law became imperative because of economic necessity. The aim of economic reform was to replace the old planned economy with a market-oriented one. In the process, laws came to regulate China's economic activities, and gradually replaced plans to manage economic relations among different actors and govern people's economic behavior. For example, the number of economic cases heard in the people's courts grew from 226,600 in 1985 to 1,483,356 in 1997.[14] It is understandable that most of the laws made since 1978 are related to economic and commercial activities, and foreign investment.

As discussed in Chapter 4, in the pre-reform China, the state exercised tight control over its citizens through the "unit" system and household registration system. With the development of a market system, laws became more important in governing people's social activities. Economic liberalization led to the rise of various non-state sectors which employed a large part of the population. Conflicts of interest between different sectors of the economy could no longer be coordinated or resolved simply by political means as before. Moreover, economic liberalization rendered the household registration system ineffective. When money instead of political fiat became important in regulating human behavior, and when people were able to obtain a better life by participating actively in the free market, they are prepared to venture further. Today, millions of people in China, especially rural workers, are migrating from one place to another. Large-scale migration of the population has complicated human interaction in China.[15] The rural migrant population, together with the urban unemployed such as "off-post workers," posed a serious threat to public order.[16] Laws undoubtedly are becoming increasingly important in coping with public order crisis, even though different administrative measures are still used to counter public violence.

A more important driving force behind China's rapid development of a legal system is related to the political legitimacy of the leadership. With the passing of the old generation of revolutionaries, the new generation of leadership had to create a new base of political legitimacy. Laws, rules, norms and other forms of institutions obviously could be used to consolidate and strengthen their hold on power.[17] In order to increase and strengthen its political legitimacy, the leadership had, first, to establish public order, and second, to reduce official arbitrariness. Without doubt, maintaining public order is the most basic function of modern states, and laws were made to guarantee such an order. Chinese leaders also realized that official arbitrariness could cause people to rebel against the rule of the CCP. During Mao's time, the CCP initiated waves of popular movements against officials' arbitrariness. But this strategy was no longer feasible because popular mobilization could lead to social chaos, and also because stability was the highest priority for the new leadership. Therefore, laws became important in regulating officials' behavior. In 1989, China passed the administrative litigation law, which created the basis for seeking a judicial review of the acts of state agents.[18] In 1994, the State Compensation Law established guidelines for seeking compensation for damages resulting from illegal state actions. The 1996 Administrative Penalties Law guaranteed protection for people subject to non-criminal, administrative sanctions. The 1996 revision of the Criminal Procedure Code introduced reforms in pre-trial detention, the right to counsel, prosecutorial determination of guilt, and the conduct of trials. Most significantly, China has signed the International Covenant on Economic, Social and Cultural Rights, and the International Covenant on Civil and Political Rights. All these laws are far from perfect, but they are an institutional means of constraining officials' arbitrary behavior and they thus help to increase the state's political legitimacy.

The party vs. the rule of law

Despite all these efforts in building a legal state, China has not yet achieved the rule of law. Chinese leaders appreciate the importance of laws because they recognize that laws are an effective means of governing or regulating people's activities as well as constraining and coping with socio-economic chaos. But as yet, laws have not been made to govern the party itself. That the party itself is still not subject to laws casts serious doubts on whether a rule-based state governance can be built in China.

In building a rule-based state governance, China encounters seemingly intractable difficulties related to the monopoly of power by the CCP. The rule by law means that the CCP continues to stand above the laws. From the perspective of the CCP, building a legal state does not involve surrendering the party's monopoly on power. Some scholars have found that post-Mao reforms have led to the erosion of the CCP's control over law-making. For example, according to Murray Scot Tanner, the law-making process has become so complex that the CCP officials have tended to become less involved in the details of drafting laws and regulations, and the Political Bureau can neither diminish confusion on policy nor monopolize law-making as other institutions come to play an increasingly important role in law-making. The NPC has begun to exercise something more than a "rubber-stamp" function and its reviews of proposed legislation are no longer perfunctory or simply a public show of socialist democracy.[19] While it is certainly true that power over law-making is more pluralized, the weakening of the CCP's power over law-making does not necessarily mean that the CCP is under the control of law. The CCP continues to dominate the political scene and what it says or does still counts.

According to Jiang Ping, former Vice-President of the Law Committee of the National People's Congress, law-makers still live under the shadow of the CCP, and a major difficulty facing Chinese legal reform is "the contradiction between the country's legal and political structures." For example:

under the Constitution, budgets drafted by the State Council are to be approved by the NPC, but in reality the State Council has frequently broken ceilings imposed on the budget without obtaining prior consent from the NPC. In a draft law called the supervision law, the powers of the NPC would have been shored up against the executive organs. This law would have given the NPC power to review the performance of China's executive organs. However, it never progressed beyond the status of a draft.[20]

The CCP's power is also dominant in other areas such as making laws for freedom of speech and the press, and determining the role of the judiciary, and the representation of the CCP in the Chinese economy.[21] Although Jiang made these observations based on his own experience in the NPC in the 1980s and early 1990s, they are still relevant today.

The dominion of the CCP over the law is reinforced by the CCP's role in promoting China's economic development. As a "stationary bandit," the CCP has been responsible for providing political order and facilitating socio-economic development from above. This has resulted in party domination of society, which in turn retards the development of the rule of law. To a large extent, what is being practiced by the party is contradictory to the rule of law. The rule of law requires the party to obey the law just as society does, but what the party advocates is actually the rule by law so that it can impose its own "rational order" on society. The party's domination of society also constrains the rise of civil society, i.e., of forces independent of the party. As discussed in Chapter 4, the CCP has allowed capitalists to strengthen its social base while remaining intolerant of any independent social forces that might challenge its monopoly on power. Without strong pressure from society, the Party and in particular its leaders will be unwilling to make laws to constrain itself.[22]

Furthermore, there are cultural obstacles inhibiting China's move towards the rule of law. The rule of law is a foreign concept in the Chinese tradition, in both the "big" tradition (Confucianism and Legalist), and the "small" tradition (communism). Confucianism assumes that the rule by law would not be a "good" way to govern people, and that political elites should not be constrained by any institutional forces like law.[23] Even though Confucius put much emphasis on the role of rites (*li*) in governance, with their established processes, his emphasis was on individual virtue and public morality. Since rulers or political elites are a symbol of virtue and morality and are superior to ordinary people from whatever perspective, ordinary people should be ready to surrender their own decision-making power to government officials. This cultural perspective coincided with the Chinese interpretation of the modern concept of democracy. Democracy or popular sovereignty, as a Western concept, was derived by the Chinese from a Japanese translation. Chinese interpreted "democracy" as "to make decisions for people" (*weimin zuozhu*). Obviously, "to make decisions for people" is in accordance with Confucian elitism.

The rule of law is also contradictory to China's Legalist tradition. According to the Legalist, laws were made for governing people, not for checking the rulers' behavior. Also, laws must be sufficiently draconian in order to deter the people. As de Bary pointed out:

law, as developed by the Legalists, was perceived as an instrument of state power, imposed on the people for their own good but not ratified by any consensual process. Law and the state were absolute in their authority. There was no sense of a need for countervailing powers, or checks and balances, such as modern constitutionalism has most often attempted to provide.[24]

The rule of law is also foreign to the Chinese small tradition of communist ideology. As Epstein pointed out, "following the Leninist interpretation of law and state, Chinese communists have taken an instrumentalist approach to law."[25] Law and the state are nothing but the coercive expression of economic power enjoyed by the ruling class. In the Chinese socialist state, as long as classes exist, law could only reflect the will of the CCP, the vanguard class. Within this small tradition, law is taken as a tool of state administration. Even though Chinese leaders have put much emphasis on the rule of law, the law as a tool continues to dominate their mindset. For example, it is still a wonder to some in the party that the CCP should be subordinated to constitutional supervision because in their view,

> the CCP is the state's leading political party, and it exercises control over the NPC in many ways. Its activities extend beyond the realm of the state system, and its authority is therefore greater than that of the NPC. The NPC is simply unable to conduct constitutional supervision over the CCP.[26]

As discussed in Chapter 4, during the Sixteenth Congress of the CCP in 2002, the leadership stated that the party no longer represents the interests of only workers and farmers, but also of other newly rising social classes such as capitalists and private entrepreneurs. The party constitution now states that the party is the vanguard not only of workers, but also of the Chinese nation and the people. As long as the party regards itself as the vanguard of the Chinese people and Chinese nation, it is unlikely to subject itself to the rule of law.

The party and governance crisis

The most serious hurdle China faces in its attempt to move towards a rule-based state governance is the concern of the leadership for the party's survival. While the leadership has made tremendous efforts to build a rule-based state governance, this process has ironically resulted in the rise of forces that threaten the very survival of the party. The CCP leadership has had great difficulty in adjusting the party to global capitalism. The leadership believes that the rule of law has to be the pillar of the state governance in the long run, but it also realizes that the rule of law cannot guarantee the survival of the party. The leadership's effort to engender capitalistic transformation in China has created a multifaceted crisis of governance for the CCP.

The most obvious crisis is the decline of party ideology. This development became inevitable after Deng Xiaoping came back to power in the late 1970s. The Deng leadership downplayed the role of ideology, weakened the ideological controls of Maoism and orthodox Marxism, and encouraged officials and the people to experiment with reform initiatives. In 1978, he oversaw an ideological movement that refuted Maoism. Also, in 1989, in response to the rise of conservatism in the aftermath of the crackdown on the pro-democracy movement, Deng initiated what came to known as the "second thought liberation" in China that ended the long-lasting debate on whether China's economic development should be socialistic or capitalistic.

De-ideologization fostered an atmosphere conducive for capitalistic economic development. It, however, affected the people, especially the party, badly. When Deng provided opportunities to the people to make profits, he did not expect excessive and unfettered capitalism and money worship. When people got rich, they found that they were living in a moral vacuum. Spiritually, they did not know where they were or where to head.

With the erosion of the primacy of ideology, many party cadres began to embrace a variety of alternative mindsets, including materialism, old and new leftism, Western liberalism, nationalism, and even religion. The party's control over its members weakened considerably. For example, despite the party's prohibiting party members from believing in religion, which it views as an opiate of the masses, 7 percent of regular members and 46 percent of the leading organizers of the Falun Gong movement in Shandong Province in the 1990s were party members.[27]

More serious is corruption among party cadres and government officials. Corruption was the main factor that led to the 1989 pro-democracy movement. It continues to be the major factor driving popular discontent in the 1990s, as discussed in Chapter 7. Corruption is a result of the lack of law enforcement among leading cadres and officials on the one hand, and it makes law enforcement even more difficult on the other. In 1995, the procuratorial organ investigated 2,153 officials at the county level and above for possible corruption crimes. This was up 27 percent from the previous year, and constituted the largest increase since the CCP came to power.[28] In that year, Chen Xitong and Wang Baosen, the Mayor and Vice Mayor of Beijing, were investigated for corruption. Wang committed suicide, and Chen was jailed. Between 1993 and 2000, the number of cases investigated and handled by the discipline inspection and procuratorial organs throughout the country increased 9 percent annually, and the number of officials given party and administrative disciplinary punishments went up 12 percent. Between 1990 and 1998, procuratorial organs nationwide accepted and handled more than 1.1 million corruption cases, of which over 500,000 cases were placed on file for investigation and prosecution. More than 600,000 offenders were involved.[29] From January to August 2000 alone, the procuratorates throughout the country prosecuted 23,464 criminal cases involving graft and embezzlement.[30] According to the latest report by the Central Discipline Inspection Commission during the Sixteenth Congress of the CCP in 2002, from October 1997 to September 2002, the procuratorial organs nationwide accepted 861,917 corruption cases, and 846,150 party cadres were punished, among them, 28,996 were cadres at the *chu* (county) level, and 2,422 were at the *ju* (bureau) level, and 98 were at the *sheng* (province or ministry) level.[31]

Three main trends of corruption can be discerned. First, there is increasing involvement of high-ranking government officials such as Hu Changqing, Vice-Governor of the Jiangxi provincial government, and Cheng Kejie, Vice-Chairman of the Standing Committee of the NPC.[32] This is a nationwide phenomenon called "first-in-command-corruption" (*diyi bashou fubai*), i.e., corruption among leading cadres and officials. Apparently, when power is still monopolized by the party, nothing, not even the law, can constrain the behavior of leading cadres and officials. Second, there is an increase in group or collective corruption involving officials in a department or local government. Corruption has rapidly become an organized crime, particularly in smuggling cases, such as the widely publicized Zhanjiang and Yuanhua cases. Third, the amount of bribes and embezzled funds has ballooned. For instance, between 1990 and 2000, 77 of the 589 cases of corruption investigated by the Beijing procuratorate involved 1 million yuan each, and Cheng Kejie alone solicited and accepted 41 million yuan in bribes.[33]

From the perspective of the Chinese leaders, it is imperative to cure all these social ills that erode the legitimacy of the party and government. Since the early 1990s, Chinese leaders have initiated waves of anti-corruption campaigns. Nevertheless, corruption is still rampant. Premier Zhu Rongji had to admit, in his Work Report to the NPC in March 2000, that "the emergence and spread of corruption and undesirable practices have not been brought under control."[34] More recently Jiang Zemin also recognized that serious corruption undermines the leadership of the party.[35] The leadership also initiated political campaigns to crack down on the Falun Gong religious movement, with many cadres and government officials among its followers. Apparently, when legal measures failed, the leadership resorted to political campaigns, and this undermined all efforts that the leadership had made to build a legal state.

Return to tradition?

When Jiang Zemin, in his report to the Sixteenth Congress of the CCP in November 2002, declared that China is not going to and should not learn from democracy of the multiparty type in the West,[36] he meant that the party would not give up its monopoly on power. When the leadership refuses to import some of the most important political products of the modern Western state, such as democracy and the rule of law, it ironically looks back to Chinese traditions, both the big tradition of Confucianism and Legalist and the small tradition of communism, to find solutions to the problems plaguing the party in order to maintain its monopoly on power. The call for a return to virtue and moral values in recent years has become one of the most important avenues for the leadership to revive the party.

In 1995, the Jiang leadership initiated a political campaign called "*jiang zhengzhi*" (literally, talking about politics). Leading cadres and officials were exhorted to be serious about the political direction they espoused and to exercise political discipline, discretion, and sensitivity, and not to deviate from the party's aim of serving the people.[37] In March 1996, Jiang initiated another political campaign called the "three talks" (*san jiang*) and urged leading party cadres to stress politics, virtue, and studies. By launching the "talk about politics" and "three talks" campaigns, Jiang tried to re-orient party development. Nevertheless, these campaigns were widely regarded as outdated Mao-style slogans and were not popular among party cadres and government officials. So, on his tour to Guangdong in February 2000, Jiang began to assert that the rule by virtue and the rule of law should be promoted hand-in-hand in reaffirming the party's ethos. Jiang believed that moral education could improve the quality and spirit of the cadres and reduce violation of laws and party discipline.[38]

Increasingly, Jiang shifted his focus from the rule of law to the rule by virtue. At a talk with the heads of the country's propaganda departments in January 2001, Jiang reaffirmed and explained his notion of the rule both by virtue and of law. He stressed that the party, in the course of building a socialist market economy, should strengthen the construction of both a socialist legal system and a socialist morality. He argued that the rule of law and the rule by virtue should complement each other, receive equal attention, and be ultimately integrated.[39] Jiang apparently wanted the CCP to govern the country by combining the rule of law (*yifa zhiguo*) with the rule by virtue (*yide zhiguo*). While the CCP should make establishing the rule of law its priority, promoting the rule by virtue, he stated, could greatly enhance the rule of law.[40]

The so-called "rule by virtue" campaign attracted a great deal of attention. Many speculated that the leadership was trying to revive old Confucian teachings in order to unify a populace that had become disillusioned with communism and was indulging in Western individualism. The CCP propaganda machinery went into overdrive to extol the concept of the rule by virtue among party cadres and government officials. On February 1, 2001, *People's Daily* published an editorial, pointing out that in order to build a market economy, it was necessary to promote the rule by virtue while developing the rule of law.[41]

What does the rule by virtue mean? Jiang did not explain it clearly. But his loyal theoretical thinkers have shed some light on Jiang's thinking. According to a group of scholars in the Shanghai Academy of Social Sciences, this concept, although it originated in ancient China, needs to be redefined in China's new context. They argued that while rule by virtue usually refers to the role of morality in governing the country, today, it "means not only morality, but also ideal (*lixiang*) and believing (*xinnian*)."[42] More concretely, rule by virtue implies:

1) building a socialist moral thought system compatible with the socialist legal system and Marxism-Leninism, Mao Zedong Thought and Deng Xiaoping theory as its bases;
2) serving the people as its core activity, collectivism as its principle, "to love the country, people, work, science and socialism" as its basic requirements;
3) constructing professional ethics, public morality and family virtue as a basic starting point;
4) that, when party cadres and government officials are selected and promoted, their moral standards are assessed;
5) that leading party cadres are a role model for the people;
6) that, most significantly, the recognition of the importance of the rule of law underpins rule by virtue.[43]

Certainly, rule by virtue has to be set in the modern context. Its traditional meanings no longer fit modern needs, and it has to be based on modernity, rationality, and advancement. What is the modern context of rule by virtue? According to these scholars, its modern context lies in China's practice of the rule of law. The rule by virtue "is required not only by the need for spiritual development, but also by the need of the rule of law per se."[44]

Thus, what is important is the relation between the rule of law and rule by virtue. For those who support the concept, rule of law and rule by virtue are not in conflict, but are mutually complementary. First of all, both are aimed at developing the good and discarding the evil, purifying the social atmosphere, lifting the quality of citizens, and facilitating social progress. Second, when law-makers make law and law implementers enforce the law, they must have a sense of morality. Third, without the support of rule by virtue, the system of the rule of law itself will not work effectively. Since the implementation of reform and open-door policy, China has made numerous laws and regulations but they have not been enforced. One major problem is that many law enforcers are not morally qualified. Moreover, there is also a large gap between people's moral quality and their demands for law. To a great degree, the problem associated with law enforcement is that the moral basis of the enforcers is under-developed. Although socio-economic development has facilitated legal development, people's moral progress lags behind. Surely, when much progress in legal development has been achieved, it becomes politically significant to realize moral progress.[45]

How can rule by virtue play an important role in educating party cadres and government officials? According to these proponents, the leadership has to 1) emphasize the moral dimension of administrative and social justice; 2) cultivate (*jiaohua*) party cadres and government officials – the most important function of rule by virtue; 3) set examples as moral rulers; and 4) balance law and morality in drafting legislation and administrating justice.

There is also an institutional side to rule by virtue. Without certain institutions, rule by virtue will not reach its fullest potential in government. As Jiang's supporters alleged, the realization of virtue in government can be assured by developing a set of institutions, including: 1) a system of moral evaluation and moral supervision; 2) ethical codes in different areas of administration, and political, economic and religious activities; and 3) individual professional ethical codes.[46]

Even though Jiang Zemin showed his enthusiasm and even passion for the rule by virtue, and despite mobilizing the party's machinery to drum up support for the concept, the movement received a very cold reception. The movement provided political conservatives with an opportunity to lay claim to the moral superiority of the party and justify its existing monopoly on power. Naturally, the propaganda movement is extremely unpopular among Chinese liberal-minded intellectuals and serious criticisms followed even with tight political control over the print and media. For the liberal-minded, the campaign was highly hypocritical. It not only reminded them of the quasi-fascist nature of the New Life Movement under Chiang Kai-shek, but also, more importantly, it was a stark reminder of how Mao's personal dictatorship was justified by the "Learning from Lei Feng" movement, and how this movement pushed Mao's personal cult during the Cultural Revolution.[47] Indeed, it was difficult for many Chinese to understand that a leadership tainted with corruption could initiate such a campaign.

Despite its unpopularity, Jiang formally claimed in his report to the party congress in 2002 that the party would continue to emphasize both the rule of law and rule by virtue.[48] Earlier, Liu Ji, a senior aide to Jiang and former Deputy Chairman of the Chinese Academy of Social Sciences, argued that in building a modern state, China should draw on its 5,000-year civilization to guide its use of moral values to complement the legal system. A country that is governed solely by law can be unhealthy. Law must be complemented by moral values, human feelings and family concerns. Liu believed that if individualism, albeit permitted by law, went too far, it would become a cancer in society; and that China should not repeat the mistakes made by the West. Hence, collectivism, not individualism, is more suitable for China.[49] Needless to say, in order to justify the monopoly of power by the CCP, the most convenient way is for the party to appeal to traditional values. Apparently, the modern concept of the rule of law is incompatible with the party's monopoly of power.

Conclusion

Will Chinese leaders be able to build a rule-based state governance in an age of globalization? Compared to Mao's time, China is increasingly becoming a country ruled by law. But in terms of instituting the rule of law, many obstacles stand in the way. The law is used by the party as an instrument for its authoritarian rule. While the party promotes legal development on the one hand, it hinders the country's process towards the rule of law on the other.

The existing state governance is still not rule-based. Nevertheless, rapid socio-economic progress is likely to generate its own dynamics for political change in China. We have seen in European history how the rule-based governing structure was gradually developed. The development of the rule of law occurred in tandem with the development of democracy. Central to the rule of law is how state power can be tamed. The historical analysis of European democracies suggests the importance of a vibrant bourgeoisie. The rising business class successfully tamed the monarchical state, challenging the aristocratic claim of government as a prerogative of birth and slowly replacing it by the principle of government as a natural domain of wealthy "commoners." Later, a rising and organized working class came to challenge the power of the bourgeois state and established the notion of equal citizenship before the law.

China is unlikely to repeat what happened in Europe, but rapid socio-economic transformation has produced enormous pressure on the CCP. Party power is still pre-eminent in society. However, with the rise of social forces, the party will have to adjust its own power structure to gradually accommodate social reality. In rural areas, with the establishment of the rural election system, positive changes have occurred to the rural power structure. The leadership's decision to allow capitalists to join the party is also likely to have a major impact on party transformation and possibly even lead to party pluralism.

The Chinese leadership has succeeded, to a degree, in importing Western state products to rebuild the country's economic institutions.

However, it has rejected any Western political products to rebuild the political system. While leaders like Jiang Zemin have appealed to Chinese traditions to revive the party, nothing concrete has been achieved so far. With China becoming rapidly globalized and its socio-economic system being increasingly integrated into the international community, the party leadership has opted not to transform its political system. As long as the party stands above the state or for that matter the law, China's state-building will remain unfinished, and rule-based state governance an impossibility.

Notes

1 Globalization: State decline or state rebuilding?

1 Elizabeth Economy and Michel Oksenberg (eds.), *China Joins the World: Progress and Prospects* (New York: Council On Foreign Relations Press, 1999), p. v.
2 Zalmay M. Khalilzad, et al., *The United States and a Rising China: Strategic and Military Implications* (Santa Monica, CA: Rand, 1999); Ezra F. Vogel (ed.), *Living with China: U. S. – China Relations in the Twenty-First Century* (New York: W. W. Norton & Company, 1997); Richard Bernstein and Ross H. Munro, *The Coming Conflict with China* (New York: A. A. Knopf, 1997); James Shinn (ed.), *Weaving the Net: Conditional Engagement with China* (New York: Council On Foreign Relations Press, 1996); Stuart Harris and Gary Klintworth (eds.), *China as a Great Power, Myths, Realities and Challenges in the Asia-Pacific Region* (New York: St. Martin's Press, 1995); and Michael D. Swaine, *China: Domestic Change and Foreign Policy* (Santa Monica, CA: Rand, 1995).
3 On the impact of China's increasing interaction with the world on its domestic economic reforms, see Thomas G. Moore, *China in the World Market: Chinese Industry and International Sources of Reform in the Post-Mao Era* (Cambridge: Cambridge University Press, 2002).
4 On how China's domestic interests pursued globalization, see David Zweig, *Internationalizing China: Domestic Interests and Global Linkages* (Ithaca, NY: Cornell University Press, 2002).
5 This is especially true in the case of China's WTO agreement with the USA, see Harry Hongyi Lai, "Behind China's World Trade Organization Agreement with the USA," *Third World Quarterly*, 22: 2 (2001), pp. 237–55.
6 For the origins and development of township and village enterprises, see William A. Byrd and Lin Qingsong (eds.), *China's Rural Industry: Structure, Development, and Reform* (Oxford: Oxford University Press, 1990); Martin L. Weizman and Chenggang Xu, *Chinese Township Village Enterprises as Vaguely Defined Cooperatives* (London: Development Economics Research Program, 1992); Christopher Findlay, Andrew Watson, and Harry X. Wu (eds.), *Rural Enterprises in China* (New York, NY: St. Martin's Press, 1994); John Wong, Rong Ma and Mu Yang (eds.), *China's Rural Entrepreneurs: Ten Case Studies* (Singapore, Times Academic Press, 1995); Chen Hongyi, *The Institutional Transition of China's Township and Village Enterprises: Market Liberalization, Contractual Form Innovation and Privatization* (Aldershot: Ashgate, 2000).

7 George T. Crane, *The Political Economy of China's Special Economic Zones* (Armonk: M. E. Sharpe, 1990).

8 For the impact of the southern tour on China's development, see John Wong and Zheng Yongnian (eds.), *The Nanxun Legacy and China's Development* (Singapore and London: Singapore University Press and World Scientific, 2001).

9 *China Economic News* (Hong Kong), no. 39, October 11, 1999, p. 1.

10 *China Economic News* (Hong Kong), no. 33, August 30, 1999, pp. 2–3.

11 *China Economic News* (HK), no. 38, October 4, 1999, p. 6.

12 John Wong and Sarah Chan, "China's Rapidly Changing Export Structure," *EAI Background Brief* no. 85, East Asian Institute, National University of Singapore, April 9, 2001, p. 1.

13 Ibid.

14 Lu Ding, "China's Institution Development for a Market Economy since Deng Xiaoping's 1992 Nanxun," in Wong and Zheng (eds.), *The Nanxun Legacy*, pp. 51–76.

15 "Don't Stifle China's IT Revolution," *Asian Wall Street Journal*, February 28, 2000; and "China Succeeds Japan As Largest Cellphone Market in Asia-Pacific Region," *China News Service*, August 22, 2000. Also see, *China Daily*, August 10, 2000.

16 *China Daily*, July 22, 1999.

17 Y. J. Mo, "The Current Status and Future Prospects of China's Mobile Telecommunication," paper presented at the Conference on China's WTO Accession and Its Impact on Northeast Asia, Seoul, Korea, June 28–29, 2000.

18 "China IT Industry Sales Reached US$ 21 Billion in 1999," *Chinaonline*, February 1, 2000, http://www.chinaonline.com.

19 "War on Net Hots Up," *South China Morning Post*, July 12, 2000; and "E-Commerce in China: The CCIDnet Survey," *CCIDnet.com*, April 27, 2000, http://www.ccidnet.com.

20 "China's Information Industry Booming in 1999," *Chinaonline*, February 1, 2000. http://www.chinaonline.com.

21 Shaoguang Wang, "The Social and Political Implications of China's WTO Membership," *Journal of Contemporary China*, 9: 25 (2000), pp. 373–405.

22 An overview of China's corruption, see Hu Angang (ed.), *Zhongguo tiaozhan fubai* (China: Fighting Against Corruption) (Hanzhou: Zhejiang renmin chubanshe, 2001).

23 *China Daily*, October 26, 1998.

24 Zheng Yongnian and Zou Keyuan, *Toward More Effective Governance: China's Politics in 1998* (London and Singapore: World Scientific and Singapore University Press, 1999).

25 *Ming Pao*, Hong Kong, January 8, 1998.

26 Chen Zhongdong (ed.), *Shehui tuanti zuzhi daquan* (Almanac of Social Organizations in China), 3 volumes (Beijing: Zhuanli wenxian chubanshe, 1998).

27 "What Future for the State?" was the title of a special issue of *Daedalus*, 124: 2 (Spring 1995).

28 Peter Evans, "The Eclipse of the State? Reflection on Stateness in an Era of Globalization," *World Politics*, 50 (October 1997), pp. 62–82.

29 Michael Mann, "Has Globalization Ended the Rise and Rise of the Nation-State?" in T. V. Paul and John A. Hall (eds.), *International Order and the Future of World Politics* (Cambridge: Cambridge University Press, 1999), p. 237.

30 Karl Marx and F. Engels, "Manifesto of the Communist Party," in Robert C. Tucker (ed.), *The Marx–Engels Reader* (New York: W. W. Norton & Company, Inc., 1978), pp. 469–500.

31 Eric J. Hobsbawn, *The Age of Capital 1848–1875* (London: Weidenfeld and Nicolson, 1975).

32 Immanuel Wallerstein, *The Capitalist World-Economy* (Cambridge: Cambridge University Press, 1979).

33 Kenichi Ohmae, *The End of the Nation State* (New York: HarperCollins, 1995), p. 75.

34 Ibid., p. 5. Also see Ohmae, *The Borderless World* (London: Collins, 1990); Water B. Wriston, *The Twilight of Sovereignty* (New York: Charles Scribners Sons, 1992).

35 Mathew Horsman and Andrew Marshall, *After the Nation-State* (New York: HarperCollins, 1994), p. 235.

36 Susan Strange, "The Defective State," *Daedalus*, special issue "What Future for the State?" 124: 2 (Spring 1995), p. 56.

37 David Held and Anthony McGrew, David Goldblatt and Jonathan Perraton, *Global Transformations: Politics, Economics and Culture* (Stanford, CA: Stanford University Press, 1999), p. 3.

38 Vicent Cable, "The Diminished Nation-State: A Study in the Loss of Economic Power," *Daedalus*, special issue, "What Future for the State?" 124: 2 (Spring 1995), pp. 23–53.

39 Ibid., pp. 27–8.

40 Evans, "The Eclipse of the State?", p. 65.

41 The OECD Public Management Service, *Globalization: What Challenges and Opportunities for Government?* (Paris: OECD, 1996).

42 Ibid. Also see Susan Strange, *The Retreat of the State: The Diffusion of Power in the World Economy* (Cambridge: Cambridge University Press, 1996).

43 Robert Keohane and Joseph Nye, *Power and Interdependence: World Politics in Transition* (New York: Longman, 2000).

44 James N. Rosenau, *Turbulence in World Politic: A Theory of Change and Continuity* (Princeton, NJ: Princeton University Press, 1990).

45 Held and McGrew, et al., *Global Transformations*, p. 8.

46 Evans, "The Eclipse of the State?", p. 72.

47 The term "Washington Consensus" was given by economist John Williamson in 1989 to a list of ten policy recommendations for countries willing to reform their economies. See John Williamson (ed.), *Latin American Adjustment: How Much Has Happened?* (Washington, DC: Institute for International Economics, 1990).

48 Dani Rodrik, *Has Globalization Gone Too Far?* (Washington, DC: Institute for International Economics, 1997).

49 For a review of the development of international nongovernmental organizations, see John Boli and George M. Thomas (eds.), *Constructing World Culture: International Nongovernmental Organizations since 1875* (Stanford, CA: Stanford University Press, 1999).

50 Evans, "The Eclipse of the State?", pp. 78–9.
51 For example, Shiping Zheng, *Party vs. State in Post-1949 China: The Institutional Dilemma* (Cambridge: Cambridge University Press, 1997).
52 For an analysis, see Yongnian Zheng, "Political Incrementalism: Political Lessons from China's 20 Years of Reform," *Third World Quarterly*, 20: 6 (1999), pp. 1157–77.
53 Following Bertrand Badie, I use "state products" instead of "ideas on state-building." See, Badie, *The Imported State: The Westernization of the Political Order* (Stanford, CA: Stanford University Press, 1992).

2 The state, leadership and globalization

1 Michael Mann, "Has Globalization Ended the Rise and Rise of the Nation-State?" In T. V. Paul and John A. Hall (eds), *International Order and the Future of World Politics* (Cambridge: Cambridge University Press), p. 259.
2 Ibid.
3 Peter Evans, "The Eclipse of the State? Reflection on Stateness in an Era of Globalization," *World Politics*, 50 (October 1997)," p. 70.
4 Ibid., p. 64.
5 Vicent Cable, "The Diminished Nation-State: A Study in the Loss of Economic Power," *Daedalus*, special issue, "What Future for the State", 124: 2 (Spring 1995), p. 24.
6 P. Hirst and G. Thompson, *Globalization in Question: The International Economy and the Possibilities of Governance* (Cambridge: Polity Press, 1996).
7 Linda Weiss, *The Myth of the Powerless State: Governing the Economy in a Global Era* (Cambridge: Polity, 1998).
8 Robert Wade, "Globalization and Its Limits: Reports of the Death of the National Economy Are Greatly Exaggerated," in Suzanne Berger and Ronald Dore (eds.), *National Diversity and Global Capitalism* (Ithaca, NY: Cornell University Press, 1996), pp. 60–88.
9 Robert Gilpin, *The Political Economy of International Relations* (Princeton, NJ: Princeton University Press, 1987); and *The Challenge of Global Capitalism: The World Economy in the 21st Century* (Princeton, NJ: Princeton University Press, 2000).
10 For example, W. Ruigrok and R. van Tulder, *The Logic of International Restructuring* (London: Routledge, 1995), and R. Boyer and D. Drache (eds.), *States Against Markets* (London: Routledge, 1996).
11 David Held, Anthony McGrew, David Glodblatt and Jonathon Perraton, *Global Transformations: Politics, Economics and Culture* (Stanford, CA: Stanford University press, 1999), p. 6.
12 Samuel Huntington, *The Clash of Civilizations and the Remaking of World Order* (New York: Simon and Schuster, 1996).
13 Stephen Krasner, "Economic Interdependence and Independent Statehood," in R. H. Jackson and A. James (eds.), *States in a Changing World* (Oxford: Oxford University Press, 1993), pp. 301–21.
14 Bertrand Badie, *The Imported State: The Westernization of the Political Order*, translated by Claudia Royal (Stanford, CA: Stanford University Press, 2000), pp. 1–2.

15 Joel S. Migdal, *Strong Societies and Weak States: State–Society Relations and State Capabilities in the Third World* (Princeton, NJ: Princeton University Press, 1988), p. 19. For Weber's original definition, see Max Weber, *The Theory of Social and Economic Organization* (ed.), Talcott Parsons (New York: Free Press, 1964), p. 156.

16 Q. Skinner, *The Foundations of Modern Political Thought* (Cambridge: Cambridge University Press, 1978), vol. 2; and D. Held, *Democracy and the Global Order: From the Modern State to Cosmopolitan Governance* (Cambridge: Polity Press, 1995), chapter 2.

17 Held, McGrew, Glodblatt and Perraton, *Global Transformations*, chapter 1.

18 Robert Dahl, *Democracy and Its Critics* (New Haven: Yale University Press, 1989), pp. 221, 223.

19 G. Poggi, *The Development of the Modern State* (Stanford, CA: Stanford University Press, 1978), pp. 60–1. Also see Held, McGrew, Glodblatt and Perraton, *Global Transformations*, p. 36.

20 Barrington Moore, Jr., *Social Origins of Dictatorship and Democracy: Lord and Peasant in the Making of the Modern World* (Boston, MA: Beacon Press, 1966); Reinhard Bendix, *Nation Building and Citizenship* (Berkeley, CA: University of California Press, 1977); and T. H. Marshall, *Class Citizenship and Social Development* (New York: Doubleday and Co., 1964).

21 This discussion is based on Held, McGrew, Glodblatt and Perraton, *Global Transformations*, chapter 1.

22 P. Anderson, *Lineages of the Absolutist State* (London: New Left Books, 1974), pp. 15–41; Michael Mann, *The Source of Social Power*, vol. 1: *A History of Power from the Beginning to AD 1760* (Cambridge: Cambridge University Press, 1986), chapters 12–15.

23 Charles Tilly (ed.), *The Formation of National States in Western Europe* (Princeton, NJ: Princeton University Press, 1975), p. 19.

24 Stephen Krasner, *Sovereignty: Organized Hypocrisy* (Princeton, NJ: Princeton University Press, 1999).

25 For example, Suzanne Berger and Ronald Dore (eds.), *National Diversity and Global Capitalism* (Ithaca, NY: Cornell University Press, 1996).

26 John W. Meyer, John Boli, George M. Thomas, and Franciso O. Ramirez, "World Society and the Nation-State," in Frank J. Lechner and John Boli (eds.), *The Globalization Reader* (Blackwell Publishers, 2000), pp. 84–92.

27 Ibid.

28 Samuel S. Huntington, *The Third Wave: Democratization in the Late Twentieth Century* (Norman: University of Oklahoma Press, 1991).

29 D. Potter, et al. (eds.), *Democratization* (Cambridge: Polity Press, 1997), p. 9.

30 Francis Fukuyama, *The End of History and the Last Man* (New York: The Free Press, 1992).

31 Francis Fukuyama, *Trust* (New York: Free Press, 1995), p. 4

32 Huntington, *The Clash of Civilizations*.

33 Francis Fukuyama, "Confucianism and Democracy", *Journal of Democracy*, 6:2 (1995), p. 33.

34 For example, Charles A. Myers, *Industrialism and Industrial Man* (Cambridge, MA: Harvard University Press, 1960); and Daniel Bell, *The Coming of Post-Industrial Society* (New York: Basic Books, 1973).

35 Berger and Dore (eds.), *National Diversity and Global Capitalism*, p. 5.

36 Ibid., p. 1.

37 Ibid.

38 Ibid., p. 23.

39 Badie, *The Imported State*, p. 7.

40 Kjeld Eric Brodsgaard and Susan Young, "Introduction: State Capacity in East Asia," in Brodsgaard and Young (eds.), *State Capacity in East Asia: Japan, Taiwan, China, and Vietnam* (Oxford: Oxford University Press, 2000), p. 7. Also see Peter Dauvergne (ed.), *Weak and Strong States in Asia-Pacific Societies* (Sydney: Allen & Unwin, 1988), p. 16.

41 For a comprehensive review, see Merilee S. Grindle and John W. Thomas, *Public Choices and Policy Change: The Political Economy of Reform in Developing Countries* (Baltimore: The Johns Hopkins University Press, 1991), chapter 1.

42 Peter B. Evans, D. Rueschmeyer, and T. Skocpol (eds.), *Bringing the State Back In* (Cambridge: Cambridge University Press, 1985); and Andrew Vincent, *Theories of the State* (Oxford: Basil Blackwell, 1987).

43 Brodsgaard and Young, "Introduction," p. 3.

44 Joel S. Migdal, Atul Kohli, and Vivienne Shue (eds.), *State Power and Social Forces: Domination and Transformation in the Third World* (Cambridge: 0 Cambridge University Press, 1994).

45 Peter Evans, *Embedded Autonomy: States and Industrial Transformation* (Princeton: Princeton University Press, 1995).

46 Gerald M. Meier, "Policy Lessons and Policy Formation," in Meier (ed.), *Politics and Policy Making in Developing Countries: Perspectives on the New Political Economy* (San Francisco, CA: ICS Press, 1991), p. 8.

47 Grindle and Thomas, *Public Choices and Policy Change*, Chapter 1.

48 Ibid., p. 19.

49 David Shambaugh (ed.), *The Modern Chinese State* (Cambridge: Cambridge University Press, 2000); Vivienne Shue, *The Reach of the State: Sketches of the Chinese Body Politic* (Stanford, CA: Stanford University Press, 1988); and Kenneth Lieberthal and Michel Oksenberg, *Policy Making In China: Leaders, Structures, and Processes* (Princeton, NJ: Princeton University Press, 1988).

50 For discussions of the technocrat nature of the Chinese leadership in the post-Mao era, see Hong Yong Lee, *From Revolutionary Cadres to Party Technocrats in Socialist China* (Berkeley, CA: University of California Press, 1991); and Cheng Li, *China's Leaders: The New Generation* (Lanham: Rowman & Littlefield Publishers, Inc., 2001).

51 Li Cheng and Lynn White, "The Fifteenth Central Committee of the Chinese Communist Party: Full-Fledged Technocratic Leadership with Partial Control by Jiang Zemin," *Asian Survey*, xxxviii: 3 (March 1998), pp. 231–64.

52 Ezra Suleiman, *Politics, Power and Bureaucracy in France: The Administrative Elite* (Princeton, NJ: Princeton University Press, 1974), p. 374.

53 Ernst B. Hass, *Beyond the Nation-State: Functionalism and International Organization* (Stanford, CA: Stanford University Press, 1964).

54 Suleiman, *Politics, Power, and Bureaucracy*, p. 380.

55 Lee, *From Revolutionary Cadres to Party Technocrats*, p. 404.

56 For a discussion of the concept "encompassing interest," see Mancur Olson, *The Rise and Decline of Nations* (New Haven: Yale University Press, 1982).

57 See Olson, *Power and Prosperity: Outgrowing Communist and Capitalist Dictatorship* (New York: Basic Books, 2000); also see, Olson, "Big Bills Left on the Sidewalk: Why Some Nations Are Rich, and Others Poor," and "Dictatorship, Democracy, and Development," in Olson and Satu Kahkonen (eds.), *A Not-So-Dismal Science: A Broader View of Economics and Societies* (New York: Oxford University Press, 2000), pp. 37–60, 119–37, respectively.

3 Globalism, nationalism and selective importation

1 For example, Nicholas R. Lardy, *Integrating China into Global Economy* (Washington, DC: Brookings Institution Press, 2002); Thomas G. Moore, *China in the World Market: Chinese Industry and International Sources of Reform in the Post-Mao Era* (Cambridge: Cambridge University Press, 2002); and David Zweig, *Internationalizing China: Domestic Interests and Global Linkages* (Ithaca, NY: Cornell University Press, 2002).

2 For discussions on foreign investment and trade, see, for example, Nicholas R. Lardy, *China in the World Economy* (Washington, DC: Institute for International Economics, 1994); Lardy, *Foreign Trade and Economic Reform in China, 1978–1990* (Cambridge: Cambridge University Press, 1992); Lardy, *China's Entry Into the World Economy: Implications for Northeast Asia and the United States* (Lanham, MD: University Press of America, 1987); George T. Crane, *The Political Economy of China's Special Economic Zones* (Armonk, NY: M. E. Sharpe, 1990). For discussions on institutional integration, see, for example, Elizabeth Economy and Michael Oksenberg (eds.), *China Joins the World: Progress and Prospects* (New York: Council on Foreign Relations Press, 1999); and Harold K. Jacobson and Michel Oksenberg, *China's Participation in the IMF, the World Bank, and GATT: Toward a Global Economic Order* (Ann Arbor: University of Michigan Press, 1990).

3 Robert O. Keohane and Joseph S. Nye, "Globalization: What's New? What's Not? (And So What?)," *Foreign Affairs*, no. 118 (Spring 2000), p. 105. Also, see, Keohane and Nye, *Power and Interdependence: World Politics in Transition*, third edition (New York: Longman, 2000).

4 Keohane and Nye, "Globalization," p. 107.

5 Carlton J. H. Hayes, *The Historical Evolution of Modern Nationalism* (New York: Macmillan, 1948); Hans Kohn, *The Idea of Nationalism* (New York: Collier, 1944), and Hans Kohn, *The Age of Nationalism: The First Era of Global History* (New York: Harper, 1962); Anthony. D. Smith, *Theories of Nationalism* (London: Duckworth, 1971), and Anthony D. Smith, *Nations and Nationalism in a Global Era* (Cambridge: Polity Press, 1995).

6 For examples, Lowell Dittmer and Samuel S. Kim (eds.), *China's Quest for National Identity* (Ithaca, NY: Cornell University Press, 1993); Jonathan Unger (ed.), *Chinese Nationalism* (Armonk, NY: M. E. Sharpe, 1996); Wang Gungwu, *The Revival of Chinese Nationalism* (Leiden, International Institute for Asian Studies, 1996), Wang, *The Chinese Way: China's Position in International Relations* (Oslo, Scandinavian University Press, 1995);

Suisheng Zhao, "Chinese Nationalism and Its International Orientations," *Political Science Quarterly*, 115 (Spring 2000), pp. 1–33; Zhao, "Chinese Intellectuals' Quest for National Greatness and Nationalistic Writing in the 1990s," *The China Quarterly*, no. 152 (December 1997), pp. 725–45; and Yongnian Zheng, *Discovering Chinese Nationalism in China: Modernization, Identity, and International Relations* (Cambridge: Cambridge University Press, 1999).

7 Cited in Wang Gungwu, *The Revival of Chinese Nationalism* (Leiden, International Institute for Asian Studies, 1996), p. 10.

8 Kuang-sheng Liao, *Antiforeignism and Modernization in China, 1860–1980: Linkage Between Domestic Politics and Foreign Policy* (New York: St. Martin's Press, 1984).

9 Wang, *The Revival of Chinese Nationalism*, p. 8.

10 Zheng, *Discovering Chinese Nationalism*, p. x.

11 Joseph L. Levenson, *Liang Ch'i Ch'ao and the Mind of Modern China* (Berkeley, CA: University of California Press, 1970).

12 Horold Z. Schiffrin, *Sun Yat-sen and the Origins of the Chinese Revolution* (Berkeley, CA: University of California Press, 1968), pp. 287–88.

13 Ibid.

14 Sun Yat-sen, *San min zhu yi* (Three People's Principles) (Taipei, China Publishing Co., 1974), p. 29. Cited in Liao, *Antiforeignism and Modernization in China*, p. 89.

15 Cited in Liao, *Antiforeignism and Modernization in China*, p. 14.

16 Milton J. T. Shieh, *The Kuomintang: Selected Historical Documents, 1894–1969* (New York: St. John's University Press, 1970), p. 69.

17 Tyau Min-Shien (ed.), *Two Years of Nationalist China* (Shanghai: Kelly and Walsh, 1930), p. 29. Cited in Liao, *Antiforeignism and Modernization in China*, p. 83.

18 Liao, *Antiforeignism and Modernization in China*, p. 83.

19 Mao Zedong, "The Chinese Revolution and the Chinese Communist Party," in *Selected Works of Mao Zedong*, vol. II (Beijing: Foreign Language Press, 1967), pp. 311–14.

20 Ibid., p. 313.

21 Wang, *The Revival of Chinese Nationalism*, p. 15.

22 For a brief discussion, see Benjamin I. Schwartz, "Themes in Intellectual History: May Fourth and After," in John K. Fairbank (ed.), *The Cambridge History of China*, vol. 12 (Cambridge: Cambridge University Press, 1983), pp. 406–50.

23 Citied in Wang, *The Revival of Chinese Nationalism*, p. 8.

24 Wang Gungwu, *Joining the Modern World: Inside and Outside China* (Singapore and London: Singapore University Press & World Scientific, 2000), p. 4.

25 Mao Zedong, "The Role of the Chinese Communist Party in the National War," in Mao, *Selected Works of Mao Zedong*, vol. 2 (Beijing: Foreign Languages Press, 1975), pp. 209–10.

26 Wang, *Nationalism and Confucianism* (Singapore: Unipress, 1996), pp. 7–8.

27 Wang, *The Revival of Chinese Nationalism*, p. 19.

28 For a discussion on China's strong-state-complex, see Zheng, *Discovering Chinese Nationalism*, chapter 2.

29 Paul Kennedy, *The Rise and Fall of the Great Powers: Economic Change and Military Conflict from 1500 to 2000* (New York: Random House, 1987).

30 I have elsewhere discussed perceptional changes among Chinese intellectuals and leaders on modern nation-states. See Zheng, *Discovering Chinese Nationalism*, chapter 1.

31 Sun Yat-sen, *Sun Zhongshan quanji* (Collected Works of Sun Zhongshan), vol. 8 (Beijing: Zhonghua shuju, 1986), p. 281.

32 Michael H. Hunt, "Chinese National Identity and the Strong State: The Late Qing-Republic Crisis," in Dittmer and Kim (eds.), *China's Quest for National Identity*, p. 68.

33 Sun Yat-sen, *Sun Zhongshan quanji*, vol. 9 (Beijing: Zhonghua shuju, 1986), pp. 103–4.

34 Ssu-yu Teng and John King Fairbank, *China's Response to the West: A Documentary Survey, 1839–1923* (Cambridge, MA: Harvard University Press, 1979), p. 265.

35 Arif Dirlik, "The Ideological Foundation of the New Life Movement: A Study in Counterrevolution," *Journal of Asian Study*, 34: 4 (August 1975), pp. 945–80.

36 Joseph B. R. Whitney, *China: Area, Administration, and Nation Building* (Chicago, Department of Geography, University of Chicago, 1970), p. 71.

37 Chalmers A. Johnson, *Peasant Nationalism and Communist Power: The Emergence of Revolutionary China, 1937–1945* (Stanford, CA.: Stanford University Press, 1962).

38 Wang, *Joining the Modern World.*

39 Deng Xiaoping, "Women ba gaige dangzuo yizhong geming" (We Regard the Reform as A Revolution) (October 10, 1984), and "Gaige shi Zhongguo de di'erci geming" (The Reform Is China's Second Revolution) (March 28, 1985), in Deng, *Deng Xiaoping wenxuan* (Selected Works of Deng Xiaoping), vol. 3 (Beijing: Renmin chubanshe, 1993), pp. 81–2 and 113–14.

40 Merle Goldman, *Sowing the Seeds of Democracy in China: Political Reform in the Deng Xiaoping Era* (Cambridge, MA: Harvard University Press, 1994); Andrew J. Nathan, *China's Transition* (New York: Columbia University Press, 1997); Nathan, *China's Crisis: Dilemma of Reform and Prospects for Democracy* (New York: Columbia University Press, 1990); Nathan, *Chinese Democracy* (New York: Knopf, 1985).

41 Deng Xiaoping, "On the Reform of the System of Party and State Leadership," in Deng, *Selected Works of Deng Xiaoping* (1975–1982) (Beijing: Foreign Languages Press, 1984), p. 316.

42 Many of Deng's speeches touched on the issue of political reform and democratization. For examples see Deng Xiaoping, "Zhengzhi shang fazhan minzhu, jingji shang shixing gaige" (To Develop Democracy in Politics, and To Implement Reform in Economics) (April 15, 1985); "Guanyu zhengzhi tizhi gaige wenti" (On the Problems of Reforming the Political System) (September–November 1986), and "Zenyang pingjia yige guojia de zhengzhi tizhi" (How A Country's Political System Should Be Evaluated) (March 27, 1987). All in Deng, *Deng Xiaoping wenxuan* (Selected Works of Deng Xiaoping), vol. 3 (Beijing: Renmin chubanshe, 1993), pp. 115–18, 176–80, and 213–14, respectively.

43 This period of history is detailed by Wu Guoguang, who served Zhao Ziyang during that period. See Wu Guoguang, *Zhao Ziyang yu zhengzhi gaige* (Political Reform under Zhao Ziyang) (Hong Kong: The Institute of Pacific Century, 1997).
44 Goldman, *Sowing the Seeds of Democracy*.
45 Susan Shirk, *The Political Logic of Economic Reform in China* (Berkeley, CA: University of California Press, 1993).
46 See Zheng, *Discovering Chinese Nationalism in China*.
47 Wang, *The Chinese Way*.
48 See Zheng Yongnian, "Zhongguo xinyibo minzu zhuyi: genyuan, guocheng he qianjing" (A New Wave of Chinese Nationalism: Origins, Processes, and Prospects), in Lin Chia-lung and Zheng Yongnian (eds.), *Minzu zhuyi yu liang'an guanxi* (Nationalism and Cross-Strait Relations) (Taipei: Xinziran zhuyi gufen chuban youxian gongsi, 2001), pp. 21–40.
49 Wang, *The Revival of Chinese Nationalism*, p. 20.
50 Wang, *The Chinese Way*, p. 36.
51 Ibid., p. 21.

4 Power, interests, and the justification of capitalism

1 Karl Marx and F. Engels, "Manifesto of the Communist Party," in Robert C. Tucker (ed.), *The Marx–Engels Reader* (New York: W. W. Norton, 1978), pp. 476–77.
2 By "government-scholars," I refer to those who hold positions in the government and work for the government.
3 Gu Yuanyang, "Dangdai shijie jingji quanqiuhua: shijie jingji fazhan zong qushi" (Economic Globalization in Contemporary World: Grand Trend of World Economy) in The Department of Educational Administration (ed.), *Wuge dangdai jianggao xuanbian* (Five Selected Contemporary Lectures) (Beijing: Zhonggong zhongyang dangxiao chubanshe, 2000), p. 17.
4 Deng Xiaoping, "Zai Wuchang, shenzhen, Zhuhai, Shanghai dengdi de tanhua yaodian" (Main points of the talks made in Wuchang, Shenzhen, Zhuhai, and Shanghai) (January 18 – February 21, 1992), in Deng, *Deng Xiaoping wenxuan* (Selected Works of Deng Xiaoping), vol. 3 (Beijing: Renmin chubanshe, 1993), p. 373.
5 Albert O. Hirschman, *Shifting Involvements: Private Interest and Public Action* (Princeton, NJ: Princeton University Press, 1982).
6 This section focuses on primarily Hirschman, *The Passions and the Interests: Political Arguments for Capitalism before its Triumph* (Princeton, NJ: Princeton University Press, 1977), and Hirschman, "The Concept of Interest: From Euphemism to Tautology," and "Rival Views of Market Society," in Hirschman, *Rival Views of Market Society and Other Recent Essays* (Cambridge, MA: Harvard University Press, 1992), pp. 35–55, and pp. 105–41, respectively.
7 Hirschman, "The Concept of Interest," p. 35.
8 Ibid., p. 43.
9 Ibid., p. 36.
10 Ibid., p. 42.

11 Ibid., p. 43.

12 Cited in Hirschman, "Rival Views of Market Society," p. 107. For a discussion of Montesquieu's ideas, also see Stephen Rosow, "Commerce, Power and Justice: Montesquieu on International Politics," *Review of Politics*, 46: 3 (1984), pp. 346–67.

13 Hirschman, "Rival Views of Market Society," pp. 89–93.

14 Adam Smith, *Wealth of Nations* (Oxford University Press, 1976), pp. 443, 456.

15 Similar ideas are also expressed by Milton Friedman, *Capitalism and Freedom* (Chicago: University of Chicago Press, 1982).

16 Franz Schurmann, *Ideology and Organization in Communist China* (Berkeley, CA: University of California Press, 1968), p. 1.

17 Tang Tsou, *The Cultural Revolution and Post-Mao Reforms: A Historical Perspective* (Chicago: University of Chicago Press, 1986).

18 For a discussion of the household registration system, see, Tiejun Cheng and Mark Selden, "The Construction of Spatial Hierarchies: China's Hukou and Danwei System," in Timothy Cheek and Tony Saich (eds.), *New Perspectives on State Socialism in China* (Armonk, NY: M. E. Sharpe, 1977), pp. 23–50. All organizations in urban China where people worked such as enterprises, retail shops, hospitals, schools, civil associations, government organs, were called "*danwei.*" Broadly speaking, three types of *danwei* can be identified: 1) enterprise units, including all units engaged in making profit; 2) non-profit units, including scientific, educational, professional, cultural, athletic, and healthcare organizations; and 3) administrative units or governmental organs. For a discussion of the *danwei* system, see Xiaobo Lü and Elizabeth J. Perry (eds.), *Danwei: The Changing Chinese Workplace in Historical and Comparative Perspective* (Armonk, NY: M. E. Sharpe, 1997), pp. 3–7.

For a discussion of "conscription society," see Gregory J. Kasza, *The Conscription Society: Administered Mass Organization* (New Haven: Yale University Press, 1995).

19 Vivienne Shue, "State Power and Social Organization in China," in Joel S. Migdal, Atul Kohli, and Vivienne Shue (eds.), *State Power and Social Forces: Domination and Transformation in the Third World* (Cambridge: Cambridge University Press, 1994), pp. 65–88.

20 On December 18, 1978, the Chinese Communist Party held the historic Third Plenum of the Eleventh Party Congress in Beijing. The Third Plenum shifted the party's priority from the Maoist class struggle to economic modernization. Officially, the Third Plenum marks the beginning of China's market-style economic reform and the open-door policy.

21 For a discussion of China's economic reform and development in the 1980s see, Barry Naughton, *Growing Out of the Plan: Chinese Economic Reform 1978–1993* (New York: Cambridge University Press, 1996).

22 Wang Gungwu, *The Chinese Way: China's Position in International Relations* (Oslo: Scandinavian University Press, 1995).

23 For a discussion of different perceptions on socialism and capitalism, see Yan Sun, *The Chinese Reassessment of Socialism, 1976–1992* (Princeton, NJ: Princeton University Press, 1995).

24 Wang Gungwu discussed why the leadership used the term "socialist market economy" rather than capitalism, see Wang, *The Chinese Way*, part I.

25 Sun, *The Chinese Reassessment of Socialism*.

26 John Wong, "*Xiao-kang*: Deng Xiaoping's Socio-Economic Development Target for China," in Wang Gungwu and John Wong (eds.), *China's Political Economy* (Singapore and London: Singapore University Press and World Scientific, 1998), pp. 211–26.

27 Deng, "Zai Wuchang, Shenzhen, Zhuhai, Shanghai dengdi de tanhua yaodian," p. 379.

28 This is not the place for a full discussion of this rising interest-based social order. But it is worth noting that terms associated with economic interests such as "interest" (or "interests") and "class" have been increasingly used by scholars in China to analyze the Chinese society since Deng's southern tour. See Zhu Guanglei, *Dangdai Zhongguo shehui ge jieceng fenxi* (An Analysis of Social Strata in Contemporary China) (Tianjin: Tianjin renmin chubanshe, 1998); Lu Xueyi and Jing Tiankuai (eds.), *Zhuanxing zhong de Zhongguo shehui* (Chinese Society in Transition) (Ha'erbin: Helongjiang renmin chubanshe, 1994); Qin Shaoxiang and Jia Ting, *Shehui xin qunti tanmi: Zhongguo siying qiyezhu jieceng* (A Study of A New Social Group: China's Private Entrepreneurial Class) (Beijing: Zhongguo fazhan chubanshe, 1993).

29 For discussions of increasing autonomy of social groups, see Wang Ying, *Shehui zhongjian ceng: gaige yu Zhongguo de shetuan zuzhi* (Intermediate Social Strata: the Reform and Social Groups in China) (Beijing: Zhongguo fazhan chubanshe, 1993); Deborah S. Davis, Richard Kraus, Barry Naughton, and Elizabeth J. Perry (eds.), *Urban Spaces in Contemporary China: the Potential for Autonomy and Community in post-Mao China* (Washington, DC, and New York: Woodrow Wilson Center Press and Cambridge University Press, 1995; Timothy Brook and B. Michael Frolic (eds.), *Civil Society in China* (Armonk, NY: M. E. Sharpe), 1997; Gordon White, Jude Howell, and Shang Xiaoyuan, *In Search of Civil Society: Market Reform and Social Change in Contemporary China*, Oxford: Oxford University Press, 1996.

30 Li Qiang, "Guanyu siyingjingji de ruogan ziliao" (Some Data on the Private Economy), *Zhenli de zhuiqiu* (The Seeking of Truth), no. 5 (2001), pp. 18–19.

31 Ibid.

32 Ibid., p. 19.

33 Hu Angang (ed.), *Zhongguo tiaozhan fubai* (China: Fighting Against Corruption) (Hanzhou: Zhejiang renmin chubanshe, 2001), p. 49.

34 Hein Mallee, "China's Household Registration System under Reform," in Alan Hunter and Kim-kwong Chan (eds.), *Protestantism in Contemporary China* (Cambridge: Cambridge University Press, 1993), pp. 10–16.

35 John Wong, "The *Xia Hai* Phenomenon in China," *Ritsumeikan Journal of International Relations and Area Studies*, 6 (March 1994), pp. 1–10.

36 Li Qiang, "Guanyu siyingjingji," p. 23.

37 Cited in Li Qiang, "Guanyu siyingjingji," pp. 23–4.

38 Ibid., p. 27.

39 Ibid., p. 26.

40 Jiang Nanyang, "Lun siying qiyezhu de zhengzhi canyu" (Political Participation by the Owners of Private Businesses), in Zhang Houyi and Ming Zhili (eds.), *Zhongguo siying qiye fazhan baogao 1978–1998* (A Report of the

Development of Private Enterprises in China, 1978–1998) (Beijing: Shehui kexue wenxuan chubanshe, 1999), pp. 103–17.

41 Keyuan Zou and Yongnian Zheng, "China's Third Constitutional Amendment: An Assessment," in A. J. De Roo and R. W. Jagtenberg (eds.), *Yearbook Law and Legal Practice in East Asia*, vol. 4, 1999 (The Hague, London and Boston: Kluwer Law International, 2000), pp. 29–42.

42 See *Wan Yan Shu*, "Some Elements that Influence Our National Security," *Yazhou Zhoukan* (Asiaweek), Hong Kong, January 14, 1996, p. 23.

43 Lin Yanzhi, "Gongchandang yao lingdao he jiayu xin zichan jieji (The CCP Must Lead and Control the New Bourgeoisie), *Zhenli de zhuiqiu* (The Seeking of Truth), no. 5 (2001), pp. 2–11.

44 The figure excluded these private enterprises with fewer than 8 employees. Ibid., p. 3.

45 Ibid., p. 3.

46 Ibid., pp. 5–6.

47 Ibid., p. 5.

48 Ibid., p. 7.

49 Ibid.

50 Ibid.

51 Ibid., p. 8.

52 Ibid., p. 9.

53 Ibid.

54 Zhang Dejiang, "Yao mingque siying qiyezhu buneng rudang" (To Make Clear that Private Entrepreneurs Cannot Join the Party), *Zhenli de zhuiqiu*, no. 5 (2001), p. 28. Zhang's original paper was published in *Dang de jianshe* (Party Constructing), no. 4 (2000). Zhang Dejiang was promoted to the Political Bureau during the Sixteenth Congress of the CCP in 2002.

55 This is especially true in the case of Wan Runnan, the former head of the Stone Group. See, Merle Goldman, *Sowing the Seeds of Democracy: Political Reform in the Deng Xiaoping Era* (Cambridge, MA: Harvard University Press, 1994).

56 The Office of the Documentary Research of the Central Committee of the CCP (ed.), *Xinshiqi dang de jianshe wenjian xuanbian* (Selected Documents of Party Building in the New Era) (Beijing: Renmin chubanshe, 1991), p. 456.

57 Ibid., p. 442.

58 Cited in *Zhenli de zhuiqiu*, no. 5 (2001), pp. 35–9.

59 Ibid., pp. 29–31.

60 John Pomfret, "Why 'Beijing Spring' Cooled: Dissidents Overstepped," *International Herald Tribune*, 4 January 1999, pp. 1, 7. At the beginning, some local government organizations permitted Democratic Party members to submit their applications. The Democracy Party was consequently banned by the central government, and the key party members were arrested and sentenced to prison for a long period ranging from 10 to 13 years. For a case study of this event, see Xiao Gongqing, "Cong 'Zhongguo minzhu dang' zudang shijian kan hou Deng shidai Zhongguo de zhengzhi zouxiang" (The "China Democratic Party" Event and the Political Trends in Post-Deng China), *EAI Working Paper*, East Asian Institute, National University of Singapore, 21 January 2002.

61 Zou and Zheng, "China's Third Constitutional Amendment: An Assessment."
62 The Xinhua News Agency, "Jiang Zemin tongzhi zai quanguo dangxiao gongzuo huiyi shang de jianghua," 9 June 2000) (Comrade Jiang Zemin's Talk in National Party Schools Working Conference), *People's Daily*, July 17, 2000.
63 Jiang Zemin, "Jiang Zemin zai qingzhu Zhongguo gongchandang chengli bashi zhounian dahui shang de jianghua" (Jiang Zemin's Speech at the Conference Celebrating the Eightieth Anniversary of the Chinese Communist Party, 1 July 2001), *People's Daily*, July 2, 2001.
64 The Xinhua News Agency, November 18, 2002.

5 Bureaucratic reform and market accommodation

1 Barry Naughton, *Growing Out of the Plan: Chinese Economic Reform 1978–1993* (New York: Cambridge University Press, 1996), and Susan Shirk, *The Political Logic of Economic Reform in China* (Berkeley, CA: University of California Press, 1993).
2 John P. Burns, "Reforming China's Bureaucracy, 1979–82," *Asian Survey*, xxiii: 6 (June 1983), pp. 692–722.
3 In China, constitutionally, Premier is nominated by the State President and approved by National People's Congress. But in reality, the CCP leadership selects the Premier and the National People's Congress only confirms the CCP's decision.
4 Burns, "Reforming China's Bureaucracy, 1979–82."
5 Su Shangxiao and Han Wenwei, *Zhonghua renmin gongheguo zhongyang zhengfu jigou* (Central Government Organizations of the People's Republic of China), (Beijing: Jingji kexue chubanshe, 1993), p. 92.
6 Cited in Jiang Zemin, "Jiang Zemin tongzhi zai quanguo dangxiao huiyi shang de jianghua" (Comrade Jiang Zemin's Speech at the National Conference for Party Schools, 9 June 2000), *People's Daily*, July 7, 2000.
7 Zhang Zhenlong (ed.), *Jundui shengchan jingying guanli* (Management of Military Production) (Beijing: Jiefangjun chubanshe, 1989), pp. 15–16.
8 For more detailed analysis of budget problems and the PLA's enterprises, see Thomas J. Bickford, "The Chinese Military and Its Business Operations: The PLA as Entrepreneur," *Asian Survey*, xxxiv: 5 (May 1994), pp. 460–76.
9 John Pomfret, "Jiang Orders Military to Go Out of Business: in an effort to end rampant smuggling, army must close commercial empire," *International Herald Tribune*, July 23, 1998.
10 "PLA Told to Close Down All Its Firms," *China Daily*, July 23, 1998.
11 "PLA to Get $28b for Businesses," *South China Morning Post*, August 3, 1998; "PLA Chief Accepts & a 47b Payout," *South China Morning Post*, October 9, 1998.
12 *Ming Pao*, Hong Kong, December 15, 1998.
13 The State Council, *Zhongyang zhengfu zuzhi jigou* (The Organizational Structure of the Central Government) (Beijing: Zhongguo fazhan chubanshe, 1995), pp. 58–60.

14 Luo Gan, "Guanyu guowuyuan jigou gaige fang'an de jidian shuoming" (Some Explanations to the Plan of Organizational Reform of the State Council), *Wen Hui Bao* (Hong Kong), March 7, 1998, A7.

15 "Off-post" workers refer to those who were allowed to leave their original companies with partial payment while taking a second, even a third job in other companies. For a discussion of "xia gang," see Qiu Zeqi and Zheng Yongnian, "Xia-Gang and Its Sociological Implications of Reducing Labor Redundancy in China's SOEs," in Wang Gungwu and John Wong (eds.), *China's Political Economy*, London and Singapore: World Scientific and Singapore University Press, 1998, pp. 211–26.

16 Xin Xiangyang, "Zhongguo zhengfu jigou gaige: sannian jincheng yu weilai zoushi" (The Reform of Government Organizations in China: Progress in the Past Three Years and Future Trends), in Ru Xin, Lu Xueyi and Shan Tianlun (eds.), *Shehui lanpishu: Zhongguo shehui xingshi fenxi yu yuce* (Social Bluebook: Analysis and Forecast of Social Situation in China) (Beijing: Shehui kexue wenxian chubanshe, 2001), p. 114.

6 Building a modern economic state

1 Cheng Rulong (ed.), *Dangdai Zhongguo de caizheng* (China Today: Finance) (Beijing: Zhongguo shehui kexue chubanshe, 1988), vol. 1, p. 277; Xu Yi and Xiang Jinquan, *Diliuge wunian jihua shiqi de guojia caizheng (1981–1985)* (State Finance During the Sixth Five Year Plan) (Beijing: Zhongguo caizheng jingji chubanshe, 1987), p. 42.

2 He Shengming, *Zhongguo caizheng gaige ershi nian* (Twenty Years of Fiscal Reform in China) (Zhengzhou: Zhonggu chubanshe, 1998), p. 96. Also see, Chong Pengrong, *Shinian jingji gaige: licheng, xianzhuang, wenti, chulu* (Ten Years of Economic Reforms: Process, Current Situation, Problems and Prospects) (Zhengzhou: Henan renmin chubanshe, 1990), pp. 183–4.

3 The World Bank, *China: Revenue Mobilization and Tax Policy* (Washington, DC: World Bank, 1990), p. 2.

4 The Study Group on the Proportion of Financial Revenue in the National Income, "Jizhong caili rugai wenti de lilun pouxi" (Some Theoretical Analysis on Resource Concentration), *Caimao jingji* (Finance and Trade Economics), no. 4 (April 1991), pp. 23–32; Chong, *Shinian jingji*, p. 89.

5 Ibid.

6 For a discussion of the institutional aspects of China's taxation system before fiscal federalism was implemented in 1994, see The World Bank, *China: Revenue Mobilization and Tax Policy*, annex 3.

7 See Cheng Rulong (ed.), *Dangdai Zhongguo de caizheng*.

8 Ibid., vol. 1, p. 322.

9 Wang Shaofei, "Caizheng zhuangkuang guanxi shehuizhuyi jingji gaige qiantu" (The Vital Importance of Fiscal Status to the Fate of Socialist Economic Reform), *Caimao jingji* (Finance and Trade Economics), no. 4 (1990), p. 23.

10 Cheng Rulong (ed.), *Dangdai Zhongguo de caizheng*, vol. 1.

11 Shaoguang Wang, "The Rise of the Regions: Fiscal Reform and the Decline of Central State Capacity in China," in Andrew Walder (ed.), *The Waning*

of the Communist State (Berkeley, CA: University of California Press, 1995), pp. 87–113; Wang Shaoguang and Hu Angang, *Zhongguo guojia nengli baogao* (A Study of China State Capacity) (Shengyang: Liaoning renmin chubanshe, 1993).

12 The World Bank, *China: Revenue Mobilization and Tax Policy*, p. 2.

13 Ibid., p. 147.

14 Ibid.

15 Ibid., p. 296.

16 The State Tax Bureau, *Zhongguo shuizhi gaige shinian (1978–1988)* (China's Ten Years of Taxation Reform) (Dalian: Dongbei caijing chubanshe, 1988), pp. 160–1.

17 Yu Xiaoping, "Zai woguo shixing fenshuizhi de jiben gouxiang" (Basic Ideas On Implementing the Revenue-Division System in China), *Caimao jingji*, no. 2. (1990), p. 62.

18 Nicholas Lardy, "China and the Asian Contagion," *Foreign Affairs* (July/August), 1998, p. 79.

19 Liu Zhiqiang, "Pregress in China's Banking Sector Reform," *EAI Background Brief* No. 62 (East Asian Institute, National University of Singapore, 9 May 2000), p. 2.

20 John Wong and Liu Zhiqiang, "China's Progress in Banking Reform and Financial Liberalization," *EAI Working Paper* No. 52 (East Asian Institute, National University of Singapore, 23 August 2000), p. 3.

21 Nicholas Lardy, *China's Unfinished Economic Revolution* (Washington, DC: Brookings Institution Press, 1998), pp. 63–4.

22 The Finance Study Team of the State Planning Commission, *Jinrong tizhi gaige yu hongguan jingji guanli* (Financial System Reform and Macro-Economic Management) (Beijing: Jingji kexue chubanshe, 1988), p. 48.

23 John Burns (ed.), *The Chinese Communist Party's Nomenklatura System* (Armonk, NY: M. E. Sharpe, 1989), p. xviii.

24 Lardy, *China's Unfinished Economic Revolution*, pp. 174–5.

25 Wong and Liu, "China's Progress in Banking Reform and Financial Liberalization;" and Wang Hongying, "The Asian Financial Crisis as Impetus for Financial Reforms in China," *EAI Working Paper* No. 27, East Asian Institute, National University of Singapore, 18 June 1999.

26 Lardy, *China's Unfinished Economic Revolution*, pp. 202–9.

27 For the first argument, see Pang Zhongying, "Guoji jinrong tixi yunniang gaige" (International Financial System Considers Reform), *People's Daily*, April 9, 1998; Guan Chajia, "Jingji quanqiuhua huhuan jinrong anquan" (Economic Globalization Calls for Financial Security), *People's Daily*, overseas edition, October 22, 1998. For the second argument, see Ding Jianming and Li Jianxin, "Dongnanya jinrong weiji de qishi" (Lessons of the Southeast Asian Financial Crisis), *People's Daily*, January 5, 1998; Cao Jianming, "Jinrong anquan yu fazhi jianshe" (Financial Securities and Legal Construction), *People's Daily*, June 16, 1998; and Zhu Min, "Dongya jinrong dongdang yinfa de sikao" (Thoughts Provoked by the East Asian Financial Upheaval), *People's Daily*, January 26, 1998.

28 For example, Lin Zhiyuan, "Shangye yinhang yao yingjie jinrong quanqiuhua de tiaozhan" (Commercial Banks Should Meet the Challenge of Financial Globalization), *Financial News*, May 15, 1999.

29 "China's Central Bank Tightens Oversight," *Asian Wall Street Journal*, November 17, 1998.

30 *Business Times*, Singapore, October 30, 1998.

31 "ITICs Faces Shakeup," *China Daily*, August 8, 2000.

32 Wang Hongying, "The Asian Financial Crisis as Impetus for Financial Reforms in China."

33 Lardy, *China's Unfinished Economic Revolution*, pp. 175–6.

34 Ibid., p. 172.

35 See Premier Li Peng's "Government Work Report" presented at the National People's Congress in March 1997, in *Zhongguo gongshang shibao* (The China Commercial and Industrial Times), March 2, 1997.

36 The State Statistical Bureau, *China Statistical Yearbook, 1996* (Beijing: Zhongguo tongji chubanshe, 1997).

37 The State Statistical Bureau, *The Statistical Survey of China 1997* (Beijing: Zhongguo tongji chubanshe, 1997).

38 This employment figure refers to the end of June 1997. See China Economic Information Service of the Xinhua News Agency, August 6, 1997.

39 For instance, in 1994, the "Top Three," in terms of profits and taxes, were the three largest iron and steel corporation of Baoshan, Shougang and Anshan. *China Daily*, August 25, 1994. In 1995, the Daqing Petroleum ranked first. The Xinhua News Agency, English Service, April 11, 1995.

40 "Triangular debt" refers to a situation whereby Firm A owes Firm B, Firm B owes Firm C, Firm C owes Firm D, and the chain runs on.

41 The World Bank, *China: Reform of State-Owned Enterprises* (Washington, DC: The World Bank, 1996).

42 "The 6-Measure of Promoting SOE Reform," *The China Industrial and Commercial Times*, Beijing, March 2, 1997.

43 "Workers Daily says that State-Owned Firms are Bottomless Pits," *South China Morning Post*, August 30, 1997.

44 Jiang Zemin's Report to the 15th Party Congress on September 21, 1997 entitled "Hold High the Great Banner of Deng Xiaoping Theory for an All-round Advancement of the Cause of Building Socialism with Chinese Characteristics to the 21st Century."

45 "Asian Crisis 'No Deterrent' to Reforms," *South China Morning Post*, March 12, 1998.

46 Wang Shaoguang, *Jianli yi ge qiang you li de minzhu guojia* (Building a Strong Democratic State: On Regime Type and State Capacity), Papers of the Center for Modern China, 4 (February 1991).

47 Wang Huning, "Zhongguo gaige nanti de fei jingji sikao" (Non-Economic Causes of Difficulties in China's Reform), in *Shijie jingji daobao* (World Economic Herald), August 29, 1988. The essay was republished in the organ journal of the CCP, *Qiushi* (Seeking Truth), 35: 7 (1988), pp. 35–6.

48 David Bachman, *Chen Yun and the Chinese Political System* (Berkeley: University of California Press, 1985); and N. Lardy and K. Lieberthal (eds.), *Chen Yun's Strategy for China's Development* (Armonk, NY: M. E. Sharpe, 1983).

49 Chen Yuan, "Woguo jingji de shenceng wenti he xuanze: guanyu woguo jingji fazhan geju he yunxing jizhi de ruogan wenti" (Deep Problems of Our Economy and Choice: On Some Problems on the Situation of Our Economic Development and Operating Mechanism), internal circulation, March 1991.

50 Ibid.
51 *People's Daily* (overseas edition), March 10, 1994.

7 State rebuilding, popular protest and collective action

1 For a comprehensive overview of social movements in post-Mao China, see Elizabeth J. Perry and Mark Selden (eds.), *Chinese Society: Change, Conflict and Resistance* (New York: Routledge, 2000).
2 Doug McAdam, John D. McCarthy, Mayer N. Zald (eds.), *Comparative Perspectives on Social Movements: Political Opportunities, Mobilizing Structures, and Cultural Framings* (New York: Cambridge University Press, 1996), Introduction.
3 Sidney Tarrow, *Power in Movement: Social Movements, Collective Action and Politics* (New York: Cambridge University Press, 1994), pp. 3–4.
4 For example, Charles Bright and Susan Harding (eds.), *Statemaking and Social Movements: Essays in History and Theory* (Ann Arbor: University of Michigan Press, 1984).
5 Tarrow, *Power in Movement*, p. 62.
6 Charles Tilly, *From Mobilization to Revolution* (Reading, MA: Addison-Wesley Publishing Co., 1978); and Doug McAdam, *Political Process and the Development of Black Insurgence, 1930–1970* (Chicago: University of Chicago Press, 1982).
7 See Tarrow's discussion, *Power in Movement*, chapter 4.
8 Ibid., p. 62.
9 Bright and Harding, "Processes of Statemaking and Popular Protest," in Bright and Harding (eds.), *Statemaking and Social Movements*, p. 3.
10 Ibid., pp. 3–4. Also see a more recent study, Joel S. Migdal, Atul Kohli and Vivienne Shue (eds.), *State Power and Social Forces: Domination and Transformation in the Third World* (New York: Cambridge University Press, 1994).
11 Bright and Harding, "Processes of Statemaking and Popular Protest," p. 10.
12 Ibid., p. 4.
13 Ibid., p. 10.
14 Tarrow, "States and Opportunities: The Political Structuring of Social Movement," in McAdam, McCarthy, Zald (eds.), *Comparative Perspectives on Social Movements*, pp. 48–9.
15 Ibid., p. 49.
16 Tarrow, *Power in Movement*, p. 66.
17 Charles Tilly, "Social Movements and National Politics," in Bright and Harding (eds.), *Statemaking and Social Movements*, pp. 297–317; Tilly, *From Mobilization to Revolution*; and Tilly, *Coercion, Capital, and European States, A. D. 990–1990* (Cambridge, MA: Basil Blackwell, 1990).
18 For example, Perry and Selden (eds.), *Chinese Society*.
19 Robert D. Putman, *Making Democracy Work: Civic Traditions in Modern Italy* (Princeton, NJ: Princeton University Press, 1993).
20 Kevin A. Hill and John E. Hughes, *Cyberpolitics: Citizen Activism in the Age of the Internet* (Lanham: Rowman & Littlefield, 1998); David Holmes (ed.), *Virtual Politics: Identity and Community in Cyberspace* (London: Sage, 1997); Howard Rheingold, *The Virtual Community: Homesteading on the*

Electronic Frontier (New York: Harper & Row, 1994); and R. Tsagarousianou, D. Tambini and C. Bryan (eds.), *Cyberdemocracy: Technology, Cities, and Civic Networks* (London: Routledge, 1998).

21 Jürgen Habermas, *The Structural Transformation of the Public Sphere* (Cambridge: Polity Press, 1989), and C. Calhoun (ed.), *Habermas and the Public Sphere* (Cambridge, MA: The MIT Press, 1992).

22 P. Dahlgren, *Television and the Public Sphere: Citizenship, Democracy and the Media* (London: Sage, 1995), and D. Schuler, *New Community Networks: Wired for a Change* (New York: ACM Press, 1996).

23 L. K. Gorssman, *The Electronic Republic: Reshaping Democracy in the Information Age* (New York: Viking, 1995).

24 K. W. Grewlich and F. H. Pederson (eds.), *Power and Participation in an Information Society* (Brussels: Europe Commission, 1994).

25 John Wong and William T. Liu, *The Mystery of China's Falun Gong: Its Rise and Its Sociological Implications* (London & Singapore: World Scientific & Singapore University Press, 1999).

26 "Fear of Non-Party Faithful," *South China Morning Post*, April 29, 1999.

27 "China Exposes *Falun Gong* Structure," *Straits Times*, Singapore, July 31, 1999.

28 Associated Press, August 8, 2000.

29 *People's Daily*, August 9, 2000. Cited in *The Straits Times*, Singapore, August 10, 2000.

30 The State Council, *Hulianwang xinxi fuwu guanli banfa* (Methods for Management of Internet Information), The Xinhua News Agency, October 1, 2000.

31 *The Straits Times*, Singapore, August 10, 2000.

32 The World Bank, *China 2020: Sharing Rising Incomes* (Washington, DC: The World Bank, 1997), p. 7.

33 Wang, "The Social and Political Implications of China's WTO Membership," *Journal of Contemporary China*, 9: 25 (2000), pp. 379–80.

34 The World Bank, *China 2020: Sharing Rising Incomes*, p. 17.

35 Hu Angang, "Kuaru xin shiji de zuida tiaozhan: woguo jinru gaoshiye jieduan" (The Biggest Challenge in Entering a New Century: China Enters a Period of High Unemployment) (unpublished manuscript, Beijing: Chinese Academy of Science, 1999).

36 The State Statistical Bureau, *Zhongguo tongji nianjian 1999* (China Statistical Yearbook, 1999) (Beijing: Zhongguo tongji chubanshe, 1999), p. 388.

37 The World Bank, *China 2020: Sharing Rising Incomes*, p. 17.

38 The State Statistical Bureau, *Annual Prices and Family Incomes and Expenditures in Chinese Cities, 1998* (Beijing: Zhongguo tongji chubanshe, 1998), p. 9.

39 Wang, "The Social and Political Implications of China's WTO Membership," p. 385.

40 Ibid., p. 386.

41 The World Bank, *Sharing Rising Incomes: Disparities in China*, p. 16.

42 The State Statistical Bureau, *Zhongguo tongji nianjian 1999*, pp. 133, 161.

43 The World Bank, *China 2020: Sharing Rising Incomes*, p. 22.

44 Shaoguang Wang and Hu Angang, *The Political Economy of Uneven Development: The Case of China* (Armonk, NY: M. E Sharpe, 1999).

45 Ibid., pp. 56–7.
46 The annual survey reports are organized by the Institute of Sociology of the Chinese Academy of Social Sciences, see its annual report, Ru Xin, Lu Xueyi and Shan Tianlun (eds.), *Shehui lanpishu: Zhongguo shehui xingshi fenxi yu yuce* (Social Bluebook: Analysis and Forecast of Social Situation in China) (Beijing: Shehui kexue wenxian chubanshe), various issues.
47 Wang Chunguang, "1997–1998 nian: Zhongguo shehui wending zhuangkuang de diaocha" ("A Survey on Social Stability in 1997–1998"), in Ru Xin, Lu Xueyi and Shan Tianlun (eds.), *Shehui lanpishu 1998* (Social Bluebook) (Beijing: Shehui kexue wenxian chubanshe, 1998), p. 127.
48 Borge Bakken, "State Control and Social Control in China," in Brodsgaard and Young (eds.), *State Capacity in Japan, Taiwan, China and Vietnam* (Oxford: Oxford University Press, 2000), pp. 185–202.
49 Ibid., p. 129.
50 The Research Group of the Department of Organization, the CCP Central Committee (ed.), *2000–2001 Zhongguo diaocha baogao: xin xingshi xia renmin neibu maodun yanjiu* (China Investigation Report, 2000–2001: Studies of Contradictions Within the People under New Conditions) (Beijing: Zhongyang bianyi chubanshe, 2001). Also see, Erik Eckholm, "China Party Says Unrest Is Spreading in Country: Frank Official Report Calls Relations With the Masses 'Tense'," *International Herald Tribune*, June 2–3, 2001.
51 The Development Research Center of the State Council and the Editorial Office of *Peasants Daily*, "Maodun, yindao he lishi de qiji – guanyu 196 feng nongmin laixin de chubu fenxi" (Contradictions, Proper Guidance, and Historical Opportunities – A Primary Analysis of the 196 Letters from Peasants), *Peasants Daily*, December 8, 1998.
52 Lu Xueyi, "Zhongguo nongcun zhuangkuang ji cunzai wenti de genyuan" (China's Rural Situation, Problems and their Origins), in Ru Xin, Lu Xueyi and Shan Tianlun (eds.), *Shehui lanpishu 2001* (Social Bluebook) (Beijing: Shehui kexue wenxian chubanshe, 2001), p. 159.
53 Ibid.; and Zhao Yang and Zhou Feizhou, "Nongmin fudan he caishui tizhi" (Peasants' Burdens and Fiscal System), *Hong Kong Journal of Social Sciences*, no. 17 (Autumn 2000), pp. 67–85.
54 Thomas P. Bernstein and Xiaobo Lü, "Taxation without Representation: Peasants, the Central and the Local States in Reform China," *The China Quarterly*, 163 (September 2000), p. 744. A 'scissors differential' is where the government kept the prices of agricultural products low in order to benefit urban residents.
55 Cheng Baisong and Zhang Bing, "Nongmin fudan xianzhuang, chengyin ji duice" (The Current Situation of Peasant Burdens, its Origins, and Policy Choice), *Nongye jingji wenti* (Agricultural Economy Studies), no. 3 (1993), pp. 4–11.
56 Liao Jinjing, "Nongmin fudan guozhong de diaocha yu sikao" (An Investigation to Peasant Burdens and Some Thoughts), *Zhongguo nongcun jingji* (Agricultural Economy in China), no. 6 (1993), pp. 54–6.
57 Li Xiangang, "Guanyu nongcun feishui zhidu gaige de diaocha yu sikao" (An Investigation of the Reform of the Rural Tax-for-Fee System and Some Thoughts), *Nongcun diaocha* (Rural Investigation), no. 7 (1995), cited in Zhao and Zhou, "Nongmin fudan he caishui tizhi," p. 70.

58 The Research Team of the Suzhou University, "Dangqian nongcun luan shoufei xianxiang chengyin fenxi ji duice" (An Analysis of the Origins of Illegal Levies in Rural Areas and Policy Choices), *Zhongguo nongcun jingji*, no. 3 (1997), cited in Zhao and Zhou, "Nongmin fudan he caishui tizhi," p. 70.

59 For example, Lü Xiaobo, "The Politics of Peasant Burdens in Reform China," *Journal of Peasant Studies*, 25: 1 (1997), pp. 113–38.

60 For example, The Research Team of the Suzhou University, "Dangqian nongcun luan shoufei;" and Huang Yanxin, "Nongmin fudan guozhong de zhidu xing genyuan yu duice" (The Institutional Origins of Peasant Burdens and Policy Choices), *Zhongguo nongcun jingji*, no. 5 (1994), pp. 38–42.

61 For example, Albert Park, Scott Rozelle, Christine Wong, and Changqing Ren, "Distributional Consequences of Reforming Local Public Finance in China," *The China Quarterly*, 147 (1996), pp. 751–79.

62 Zhao and Zhou, "Nongmin fudan he caishui tizhi," pp. 73–4.

63 Lu Xueyi, "Zhongguo nongcun zhuangkuang," p. 163.

64 Yingyi Qian and Barry R. Weigast, "China's Transition to Market: Market-Preserving Federalism, Chinese Style," *Journal of Policy Reform*, 1 (1996), pp. 149–85, and, Qian and Weigast, "Federalism as a Commitment to Market Incentives," *Journal of Economic Perspective*, 11 (1997), pp. 83–92.

65 Hehui Jin, Yingyi Qian and Barry R. Weigast, "Regional Decentralization and Fiscal Incentives: Federalism, Chinese Style," *Stanford University Working Paper*, SWP-99-013, 1999.

66 Kang Chen, Arye L. Millman and Qingyang Gu, "From the Helping Hand to the Grabbing Hand: Fiscal Federalism and Corruption in China," *EAI Working Paper* No. 67, East Asian Institute, National University of Singapore, February 2001.

67 See, for example, Christine P. W. Wong (ed.), *Financing Local Government in the People's Republic of China* (Hong Kong: Oxford University Press, 1997), chapter 5.

68 See, for example, Jean Oi, *Rural China Takes Off* (Berkeley, CA: University of California Press, 1999); and Andrew Walder (ed.), *Zouping in Transition: The Process of Reform in Rural North China* (Cambridge, MA: Harvard University Press, 1998).

69 Zhao and Zhou, "Nongmin fudan he caishui tizhi," p. 76.

70 Liao Jinjing, "Nongmin fudan guozhong;" and Zhang Yuanhong, "Lun Zhongguo nongye shuizhi gaige" (Reforming China's Agricultural Tax System), *Zhongguo nongcun jingji*, no. 12, 1997, pp. 4–11.

71 Zhao and Zhou, "Nongmin fudan he caishui tizhi," p. 79.

72 See, for example, Bernstein and Lü, "Taxation without Representation."

73 Elizabeth Perry, "Shanghai's Strike Wave of 1957," *The China Quarterly*, no. 137 (March 1994), pp. 1–27; Elizabeth Perry and Li Xun, *Proletarian Power: Shanghai in the Cultural Revolution* (Boulder: Westview, 1997).

74 Andrew Walder, "Workers, Managers and the State: The Reform Era and the Political Crisis of 1989," *The China Quarterly*, no. 127 (September 1991), pp. 467–92.

75 For example, Feng Chen, "Subsistence Crisis, Managerial Corruption and Labor Protests in China," *The China Journal*, 44 (July 2000), pp. 41–63;

and Ching Kwan Lee, "Pathways of Labor Insurgency," in Perry and Selden (eds.), *Chinese Society*, pp. 41–61.

76 Chen, "Subsistence Crisis, Managerial Corruption and Labor Protests in China," p. 41.

77 For a discussion of some immediate reaction to these policies, see, Yang Aihua and Lu Sishan, *Zapo "santie" hou de Zhongguo ren* (Chinese After the Smashing of the "Three Irons") (Beijing: Beijing ligong daxue chubanshe, 1992).

78 *Zhongguo laodong nianjian* (China Labor Statistical Yearbook, 1996) (Beijing: Zhongguo nianjian chubanshe), p. 409.

79 *China Daily*, February 28, 1998.

80 Edward X. Gu, "From Permanent Employment to Massive Lay-Offs: The Political Economy of 'Transitional Unemployment' in urban China (1993–8)," *Economy and Society*, 28: 2 (May 1999), pp. 281–99.

81 Yang Yiyong, "2000 nian zhongguo jiuye xinshi jiqi zhengce xuanze," (Employment in 2000 and Policy Options), in Liu Guoguang (ed.) *Jinji lanpishu 2000* (Economic Bluebook 2000) (Beijing: Shehui wenxian chubanshe, 2000), p. 151.

82 Ibid., 150.

83 Hu Angang, "Kuaru xin shiji de zuida tiaozhan: woguo jinru gaoshiye jieduan," in Hu Angang (ed.), *Zhongguo zouxiang* (Prospects of China) (Hangzhou: Zhejiang renmin chubanshe, 2000), pp. 49–77.

84 Hu Angang, "High Unemployment in China: Estimates and Policies," a paper presented at International Conference "Center-Periphery Relations in China: Integration, Disintegration or Reshaping of An Empire?" The French Center for Contemporary China and the Chinese University of Hong Kong, Hong Kong, March 25, 2000.

85 Theodore Groves, Yongmiao Hong, John McMillan, and Barry Naughton, "Autonomy and Incentives in Chinese State Enterprises," *Quarterly Journal of Economics*, 109: 1 (1994), pp. 183–209; Wei Li, "The Impact of Economic Reform on the Performance of Chinese State Enterprises 1980–1989," *Journal of Political Economy*, 105: 5 (1997), pp. 1080–106; Bai Chong-en, David D. Li and Yijiang Wang, "Enterprise Productivity and Efficiency: When is up really down," *Journal of Comparative Economics*, 24: 3 (1997), pp. 265–80.

86 F. C. Perkins, "Productivity Performance and Priorities for the Reform of China's State-Owned Enterprises," *Journal of Developmental Studies*, 32: 3 (1996), pp. 414–44.

87 Xiaowen Tian, "The Rise of Non-State Owned Enterprises in China," *Communist Economies and Economic Transformation*, 9: 2 (1997), pp. 219–31.

88 The World Bank, *China: Reform of State-Owned Enterprises* (Washington, DC: The World Bank, 1996).

89 Barry Naughton, *Growing Out of the Plan: Chinese Economic Reform 1978–1993* (New York: Cambridge University Press, 1996), pp. 294–5.

90 Feng Chen, "Subsistence Crisis," p. 42.

91 For example, X. L. Ding, "The Illicit Asset Stripping of Chinese State Firms," *The China Journal*, no. 43 (January 2000), pp. 1–28.

92 Ching Kwan Lee, "From Organized Dependence to Disorganized Despotism: Changing Labor Regimes in Chinese Factories," *The China Quarterly*, no. 157 (March 1999), pp. 44–71.

93 Elizabeth Perry, "Labor's Battle for Political Space: the Role of Worker Associations in Contemporary China," in Deborah S. Davis, Richard Kraus, Barry Naughton, and Elizabeth J. Perry (eds.), *Urban Spaces in Contemporary China: the Potential for Autonomy and Community in Post-Mao China* (Washington, DC and New York: Woodrow Wilson Center Press and Cambridge University Press, 1995), pp. 302–25.

94 Andrew Walder, *Communist Neo-Traditionalism* (Berkeley, CA: University of California Press, 1986).

95 James Scott, *Weapons of the Weak: Everyday Forms of Peasant Resistance* (New Haven: Yale University Press, 1985). For a discussion of everyday resistance in urban China, see, Ching Kwan Lee, "The Labor Politics of Market Socialism-Collective Inaction and Class Experience Among State Workers in Guangzhou," *Modern China*, 24: 1 (1998), pp. 3–33.

96 Feng Chen, "Subsistence Crisis," p. 60.

97 Ching Kwan Lee, "Pathways of Labor Insurgency."

98 Lo Vai Io, "Labor Law for Foreign Investment Enterprises in China," in Wang Gungwu and Zheng Yongnian (eds.), *Reform, Legitimacy and Dilemmas: China's Politics and Society* (Singapore and London: Singapore University Press and World Scientific, 2000), pp. 167–95.

99 Ru Xin, Lu Xueyi and Shan Tianlun (eds.), *Shehui lanpishu: Zhongguo shehui xingshi fenxi yu yuce* (Social Bluebook: Analysis and Forecast of Social Situation in China) (Beijing: Shehui kexue wenxian chubanshe, 2001), p. 320.

100 Lu Xueyi, "Zhongguo nongcun zhuangkuang," pp. 165–6.

101 Gu Xin, "Employment Service and Unemployment Insurance," in John Wong and Zheng Yongnian (eds.), *The Nanxun Legacy and China's Development in the Post-Deng Era* (Singapore and London: Singapore University Press and World Scientific, 2001), pp. 143–69.

102 For example, Edward X. Gu, "The Political Economy of Public Housing Reform," in Wang and Zheng (eds.), *Reform, Legitimacy, and Dilemmas*, pp. 195–230.

8 Contending visions of the Chinese state

1 For a discussion on intellectual life in the 1980s, see Edward X. Gu, "Plural Institutionalism and the Emergence of Intellectual Public Spaces in China: A Case Study of Four Intellectual Groups," in Suisheng Zhao (ed.), *China and Democracy: Reconsidering the Prospects for a Democratic China* (New York: Routledge, 2000), pp. 141–72; and "Cultural Intellectuals and the Politics of Cultural Public Space in Communist China (1979–1989): A Case Study of Three Intellectual Groups," *The Journal of Asian Studies*, 58: 2 (May 1999), pp. 389–431.

2 Xu Jilin, "Qimeng de mingyun: Ershi nianlai de Zhongguo sixiangjie"(The Fate of the Enlightenment: China's Intellectual Realm in the Past Twenty Years), *Ershiyi shiji* (The Twenty-First Century), Hong Kong, no. 50 (1998), pp. 4–13. Also see Geremie R. Barme, "The Revolution of Resistance," in Elizabeth J. Perry and Mark Selden (eds.), *Chinese Society: Change, Conflict and Resistance* (New York: Routledge, 2000), pp. 198–220.

3 Merle Goldman, *Sowing the Seeds of Democracy in China: Political Reform in the Deng Xiaoping Era* (Cambridge, MA: Harvard University Press, 1994).

4 Su Xiaokang, Yuan Zhiming and Wang Luxiang, *Heshang* (River Elegy) (Beijing: Xiandai chubanshe, 1988).

5 Feng Chen, "Order and Stability in Social Transition: Neoconservative Political Thought in Post-1989 China," *The China Quarterly*, 151 (September 1997), pp. 593–613.

6 In the debate of China's global citizenship (*qiuji*), many people, including reformist leaders, argued that if China was not able to reform its economic and political system, China's survival as a nation-state would be problematic.

7 He Qinglian, *Xiandaihua de xianjing: dangdai Zhongguo de jingji shehui wenti* (The Perils of Chinese Modernization: Economic and Social Problems in Contemporary China) (Beijing: Jinri Zhongguo chubanshe, 1998).

8 Barme, "The Revolution of Resistance," p. 210.

9 Liu Junning, "Ziyou zhuyi yu gongzheng: dui ruogan jienan de huida" (Liberalism and Justice: Responses to Some Major Criticisms), *Dangdai Zhongguo yanjiu* (Modern China Studies), no. 4 (2000), pp. 50–67. Liu was a fellow at the Institute of Political Science of the Chinese Academy of Social Sciences, but was expelled from the institute for his liberal ideas.

10 Ibid., p. 51.

11 Ibid.

12 Ibid., p. 52.

13 Ibid.

14 Ibid., pp. 51–2.

15 Ibid., p. 57.

16 Ibid., pp. 58–62.

17 Ibid., p. 60.

18 Qin Hui, "Ziyou zhuyi yu minzu zhuyi de jiehedian zai nali" (Where Is the Meeting Point of Liberalism and Nationalism), *Dong Fang*, 3 (1996), p. 45.

19 Liu Xinwu, "Queli renlei gongxiang wenmin guannian" (To Establish the Concept of Shared Human Civilization), an interview by Qiu Huadong, *Dong Fang*, 6 (1996), p. 25.

20 Li Shenzhi, "Cong quanqiuhua shidian kan Zhongguo de xiandaihua wenti" (Understanding the Problems of China's Modernization from the Perspective of Globalization), *Zhan lue yu guanli*, 1 (1994), p. 6. Also see Li, "Quanqiuhua shidai zhongguoren de shiming" (The Chinese Mission in an Age of Globalization), *Dong Fang*, 5 (1994), pp. 13–18.

21 Chen Shaoming, "Minzu zhuyi: fuxing zhidao?" (Nationalism: A Way of Revival?), *Dong Fang*, 2 (1996), p. 75.

22 Ibid.

23 Liu Junning (ed.), *Ziyouzhuyi de xiansheng: Beida chuantong yu jindai Zhongguo* (The Onset of Liberalism: The Tradition of Beijing University and Modern China) (Beijing: Zhongguo renshi chubanshe, 1998).

24 Bao Tong, "Toushi zhonggong" (See through the Essence of the Chinese Communist Party), *Xinbao* (Hong Kong Economic Journal), June 29, 2001, p. 32.

25 Luo Rongqu, "Zouxiang xiandaihua de Zhongguo daolu" (Chinese Way to Modernization), *Zhongguo shehui kexue jikan*, 17 (Winter 1996), pp. 43–53.

26 Chen Shaoming, "Minzu zhuyi: fuxing zhidao?" p. 75.
27 Shen Ruji, *Zhongguo bu dang "Bu Xiansheng"* (China Does not Want to Be "Mr No") (Beijing: Jinri Zhongguo chubanshe, 1998), p. 351.
28 Ibid., pp. 36–42.
29 Ibid, pp. 42–6.
30 Deng Zhenglai and Jing Yuejing, "Jian'gou Zhongguo de shimin shehui" (Building Civil Society in China), in Luo Gang and Ni Wenjian (eds.), *Jiushi niandai sixiang wenxuan* (Selected Papers of Thoughts in the 1990) (Nanning: Guangxi renmin chubanshe, 2000), vol. 2, p. 8.
31 Yijiang Ding, "The Conceptual Evolution of Democracy in Intellectual Circles' Rethinking of State and Society," in Zhao (ed.), *China and Democracy*, pp. 111–40.
32 Guo Dingping, "Woguo shimin shehui de fazhan yu zhengzhi zhuanxing" (Development of Civil Society and Political Transition in China), *Shehui kexue* (Social Sciences), no. 12 (1994), pp. 52–5.
33 Lu Pinyue, "Zhongguo lishi jincheng yu shimin shehui jian'gou" (China's Historical Progress and the Development of Civil Society), *Zhongguo shehui kexue jikan*, 8 (1994), pp. 173–8.
34 Deng and Jing, "Jian'gou Zhongguo," pp. 3–22.
35 Ibid.
36 Ding, "The Conceptual Evolution of Democracy," p. 128.
37 For example, Ji Weidong, "Xianzheng de fuquan" (Return Power to Constitutional Arrangement), in Luo and Ni (eds.), *Jiushi niandai sixiang wenxuan*, vol. 2, pp. 386–400.
38 Zhang Weiying, *Qiye de qiyejia: qiyue lilun* (Entrepreneurs in Enterprises: The Contract Theory) (Shanghai: Sanlian shudian, 1995), chapter 3.
39 Wang Ding Ding, "Zhongguo guoyou zichan guanli tizhi gaige de kunjing" (The Dilemma of Reforming the Management of China's State-Owned Assets), *Ershiyi shiji* (The Twenty-First Century), Hong Kong, no. 6 (1995), p. 17.
40 Liu Junning, "Feng neng jin, yu neng jin, guowang buneng jin: zhengzhi lilun shiye zhong de caichanquan yu renlei wenming" (Wind Can Enter, Rain Can Enter, but Not King: Property Rights and Human Civilization from the Perspective of Political Theory), in Luo and Ni (eds.), *Jiushi niandai sixiang wenxuan*, p. 340.
41 Liu Junning, "Chanquan baohu yu youxian zhengfu" (Property Rights Protection and Limited Government), in Dong Xuyu and Shi Binhai (eds.), *Zhengzhi Zhongguo: Mianxiang xintizhi xuanzede shidai* (Political China: An Age Facing New Institutional Choices) (Beijing: Jinri Zhongguo chubanshe, 1998), p. 47.
42 Ji Weidong, "Zhongguo xianfa gaige de tujing yu caichanquan wenti" (The Path of China's Constitutional Reforms and the Problem of Property Rights), *Dangdai Zhongguo yanjiu* (Modern China Studies), no. 3 (1999), p. 50.
43 Ibid., p. 50.
44 Ibid.
45 Lin Yifu, Cai Fang and Li Zhou, *Zhongguo de qiji: fazhan zhanlue he jingji gaige* (China's Miracle: Development Strategy and Economic Reform) (Shanghai: Sanlian shudian, 1994); and "Ziyuan jiegou shengji: ganchao zhanlue de

wuqu – dui 'bijiao youshi zhanlue' piping de jidian huiying" (Upgrading the Resource Structure: Misunderstanding the Catching-Up and Surpassing Strategy – Some Responses to Criticism on the 'Comparative Advantage Strategy'), *Zhanlue yu guanli*, 1 (1996), pp. 35–45.

46 Shi Zhong, "Bu ying ba bijiao youshi de luoji tuixiang jiduan" (The Logic of Comparative Advantages Should not Be Pushed to Extremes), *Zhanlue yu guanli* (Strategy and Management), 3 (1995), p. 11.

47 Ibid., p. 14.

48 Wu Yuetao and Zhang Haitao, *Waizi nengfou tunbing Zhongguo- Zhongguo minzu chanye xiang he chu qu* (Can Foreign Capital Swallow up China: Whither China's National Industries) (Beijing: Qiye guanli chubanshe, 1997).

49 Liu Liqun, "Chukou daoxiang xing jingji fazhan moshi bu shihe Zhongguo guoqing" (An Export-Led Model of Economic Development Is not Suitable for China's National Conditions), *Zhanlue yu guanli*, 2 (1994), p. 44.

50 Ibid.

51 Ibid., pp. 44–5.

52 Ibid., p. 46.

53 Cheng Ming, "Dongya moshi de meili" (The Glamour of the East Asian Model), *Zhanlue yu guanli*, 2 (1994), pp. 18–27; Yin Baoyun, "Jiquan guan-liaozhi de xiandaihua daolu: Hanguo fazhan jingyan tansuo" (The Centralist-Bureaucratic Model of Modernization: An Exploration of the Experiences of Development in South Korea), *Zhanlue yu guanli*, 2 (1994), pp. 35–42; Jiang Shixue, "Lamei, dongya fazhan moshi de bijiao yu qishi" (A Comparison of the Development Models in Latin America and East Asia and Its Implica-tions), *Zhanlue yu guanli*, 5 (1995), pp. 58–68; Hu Wei, "Zhongguo fazhan de 'bijiao youshi' hezai? – chaoyue chun jingji guandian de fenxi" (Where Does China's Comparative Advantage Lie for Its Development? – An Analysis beyond a Mere Economic Point of View), *Zhanlue yu guanli*, 5 (1995), pp. 69–78; and Cheng Fengjun, "Lun dongya chenggong de zonghe yaosu: dongya jingji minzu zhuyi" (A Comprehensive Factor of East Asian Miracle: East Asian Economic Nationalism*)*, *Zhongguo shehui kexue jikan*, 15 (Summer 1996), pp. 88–99. It is worth noting that all these authors cannot simply be regarded as the supporters of the New Left even though they all believe in the saliency of economic planning by the government.

54 Hu Wei, "Zhongguo fazhan," pp. 75–6.

55 For a collection of articles published during the debate, see Liu Jun and Li Lin (eds.), *Xin quanwei zhuyi: dui gaige lilun gangling de lunzheng* (Neo-Authoritarianism: A Debate on the Theories of China's Reform) (Beijing: jingji xueyuan chubanshe, 1989). For a discussion of this debate, see Mark P. Petracca and Mong Xiong, "The Concept of Chinese Neo-Authoritarianism: An Exploration and Democratic Critique," *Asian Survey*, xxx: 11 (November 1990), pp. 1099–117.

56 The Department of Thought and Theory of *China's Youth*, "Sulian jubian zhihou Zhongguo de xianshi yingdui yu zhanlue xuanze" (China's Practical Countermeasures and Strategic Choice after Dramatic Changes in the Soviet Union), internal circulation, September 9, 1991.

57 Cui Zhiyuan, *Di'erci sixiang jiefang yu zhidu chuangxin* (The Second thought Liberation and Institutional Innovation) (Hong Kong: Oxford University Press, 1997), p. 13.

58 Ibid, pp. 197–8.
59 Ibid., p. 5.
60 Ibid, pp. 212–13.
61 Cui Zhiyuan, "Zhongguo shijian dui xingudian zhuyi jingjixue de tiaozhan" (China's Practice and Its Challenges to Neo-Classical Economics), *Xianggang shehui kexue xuebao*, Special Issue (July 1995), pp. 1–33.
62 Cui Zhiyuan, "Angang xianfa yu hou fute zhuyi" (The Angang Constitution and Post-Fordism), *Dushu*, 3 (1996), pp. 11–21. Cui argued that Maoist industrial management as shown in the Constitution of the Anshan Steel Company is equivalent to post-Fordism in the West.
63 Wang Shaoguang and Hu Angang, *Zhongguo guojia nengli baogao* (A Study of China State Capacity) (Shengyang: Liaoning renmin chubanshe, 1993).
64 Ibid., p. 159.
65 Ibid.
66 Stephen Holmes and Cass Sunstein, *The Cost of Rights: Why Liberty Depends on Taxation* (New York: Norton, 1999).
67 Wang Shaoguang, "Quanli de daijia yu gaige de lujing yilai" (The Cost of Liberty and the Path-Dependence of the Reform), *Zhanlue yu guanli*, no. 5 (2000), pp. 112–15.
68 Cui Zhiyuan, "Zhidu chuangxin yu di'erci sixiang jiefang" (Institutional Innovation and A Second Liberation of Thoughts), *Ershiyi shiji*, 24 (1994), pp. 5–15.
69 Wang Ying, "Xin jiti zhuyi yu Zhongguo tese de shichang jingji" (New Collectivism and A Market Economy with Chinese Charteristics), *Ershiyi shiji*, 25 (1994), pp. 11–14.
70 According to a case study of Nanjie Village, Maoist ideology and its collective institutions played an important role in leading the village's successful economic growth. See Deng Yingtao, Miao zhuang, and Cui Zhiyuan, "Nanjie cun jingyan de sikao" (Reflection on the Experience of Nanjie Village), *Zhanlue yu guanli*, 3 (1996), pp. 14–24.
71 Gan Yang, "Wenhua zhongguo yu xiangtu zhongguo" (Cultural China and Rural China), in *Jiangcuo jiucuo* (Leave the Mistake Uncorrected and Make the Best of It) (Hong Kong: Oxford University Press, 2000), p. 186.
72 Ibid, pp. 186–7.
73 Cui Zhiyuan, "Mao Zedong 'wenge' lilun de deshi yu 'xiandaixing' de chongjian" (Mao Zedong's Idea of Cultural Revolution and the Restructuring of Chinese Modernity), *Xianggang shehui kexue xuebao*, 7 (Spring 1996), pp. 49–74.
74 Cui, "Zhidu chuangxin."
75 Cui, "Mao Zedong 'wenge' lilun," pp. 70–1.
76 Ibid., pp. 67–72.

9 Globalization and towards a rule-based state governance?

1 Bertrand Badie, *The Imported State: The Westernization of the Political Order* (Stanford, CA: Stanford University Press, 2000), p. 1.

2 Seymour. M. Lipset, "Some Social Requisites of Democracy: Economic Development and Political Legitimacy," *American Political Science Review*, 53 (1959), pp. 69–105, and Lipset, *Political Man: The Social Base of Politics* (New York: Doubleday & Company, Inc., 1963); Charles Lindblom, *Politics and Markets: The World's Political-Economic Systems* (New York: Basic Books, 1977); Samuel Huntington, "Will More Countries Become Democratic?" *Political Science Quarterly*, 99 (Summer 1984), pp. 193–218; Moore," *The Social Origins of Dictatorship and Democracy*. For a comprehensive review of this argument, see, Dietrich Rueschemeyer, Evelyne H. Stephens, and John D. Stephens, *Capitalist Development and Democracy* (Chicago: Chicago University Press, 1992).

3 Lee Siew Hua, "China will be 'more democratic over time'," *The Straits Times*, Singapore, January 30, 1997, p. 1.

4 Henry Campbell Black, et al., *Black's Law Dictionary* (St. Paul, Minn.: West Publishing Co., 1990), p. 1332.

5 F. A. Hayek, *The Road to Serfdom* (Chicago: University of Chicago Press, 1994), p. 80.

6 Ibid., chapter 6.

7 Stanley Lubman, *Bird in a Cage: Legal Reform in China After Mao* (Stanford, CA: Stanford University Press, 1999).

8 Richard Baum, "'Modernization' and Legal Reform in Post-Mao China: the Rebirth of Socialist Legality," *Studies in Comparative Communism*, xix: 2 (Summer 1986), pp. 70–2.

9 Edward J. Epstein, "Law and Legitimation in Post-Mao China," in Pitman B. Potter (ed.), *Domestic Law Reforms in Post-Mao China* (Armonk, NY: M. E. Sharpe, 1994), p. 19.

10 "The Communiqué of the Third Plenum of the Eleventh Central Committee of the Communist Party of China," December 22, 1978, *Peking Review*, no. 52 (December 29, 1978), p. 14.

11 Deng Xiaoping, "Emancipate the Mind; Seek Truth from Facts and Unite as One in Looking to the Future," December 13, 1978, in Deng, *Selected Works of Deng Xiaoping (1975–1982)* (Beijing: Foreign Language Press, 1984), p. 158.

12 The Center of Legal Information at Beijing University and Beijing Zhongtian Software Company (eds.), *Zhongguo falu fagui guizhang daquan* (Complete Collection of Laws, Regulations and Rules in China) (Beijing: Beijing University Press, 1997).

13 Yongnian Zheng, "From Rule by Law to Rule of Law: A Realistic View of China's Legal Development," *China Perspective*, 25 (1999), p. 35.

14 The Editorial Office of the Law Year Book of China (ed.), *Zhongguo falu nianjian* (The Law Year Book of China) (Beijing: Zhongguo falu nianjian chubanshe, 1985–98), various issues.

15 Lincoln H. Day and Ma Xia (eds.), *Migration and Urbanization in China* (Armonk, NY: M. E. Sharpe, 1994); and Cheng Li, "Surplus Rural Laborers and Internal Migration in China: Current Status and Future Prospects," *Asian Survey*, xxxvi: 11 (November 1996), pp. 1122–45.

16 Qiu Zeqi and Zheng Yongnian, "*Xia-Gang* and Its Sociological Implications of Reducing Labor Redundancy in China's SOEs," in Wang Gungwu and John Wong (eds.), *China's Political Economy*, (London and Singapore:

World Scientific and Singapore University Press, 1998), pp. 211–26; and Greg Austin, "The Strategic Implications of China's Public Order Crisis," *Survival*, 37: 2 (Summer 1995), pp. 7–23.

17 This coincided with various debates in the Chinese legal circles on Weberian distinction between personal authority and legal-rational authority. Since the early 1980s, Max Weber's discussion of modernization and law, especially the transition from personality-based authority to legal authority, has become increasingly attractive to the Chinese.

18 *People's Daily*, "Zhonghua renmin gongheguo xingzheng susong fa" (Administrative Litigation Law of the PRC), April 10, 1989, p. 2. For a discussion, see Pitman B. Potter, "The Administrative Litigation Law of the PRC: Judicial Review and Bureaucratic Reform," in Potter (ed.), *Domestic Law Reforms*, pp. 270–304.

19 Murray Scot Tanner, *The Politics of Lawmaking in Post-Mao China: Institutions, Processes, and Democratic Perspectives* (New York: Oxford University Press, 1998).

20 Jiang Ping, "Chinese Legal Reform: Achievements, Problems and Prospects," *Journal of Chinese Law*, 9: 1 (Spring 1995), p. 72.

21 Ibid.

22 For discussions of this line of thinking, see Atul Kohli, "Democracy and Development," in John P. Lewis and Valeriana Kallab (eds.), *Development Strategies Reconsidered* (New Brunswick: Transaction, 1986), pp. 153–82; and Yongnian Zheng, "Development and Democracy: Are They Compatible in China?" *Political Science Quarterly*, 109: 2 (Summer 1994),; pp. 235–59.

23 Confucius, *Analects*, 2: 3. For the translation quoted here see Wm. Theodore De Bary, "The 'Constitutional Tradition' in China," *Journal of Chinese Law*, 9: 1 (Spring 1995), p. 8.

24 Ibid., p. 11.

25 Epstein, "Law and Legitimation in Post-Mao China," p. 22.

26 Cai Dingjian, "Constitutional Supervision and Interpretation in the People's Republic of China," *Journal of Chinese Law*, 9: 2 (Fall 1995), p. 228. Cai discussed the different viewpoints on constitutional supervision over the Chinese Communist Party.

27 Wu Guoguang, "The Return of Ideology? Struggling to Organize Politics During Socio-Economic Transitions," in John Wong and Zheng Yongnian (eds.), *The Nanxun Legacy and China's Post-Deng Development* (Singapore and London: Singapore University Press and World Scientific, 2001), pp. 221–46.

28 Mirror Post Editorial Department (ed.), *Jiang Zemin yunchou weiwo* (Jiang Zemin Devises Strategies within a Command Tent) (Hong Kong, 1999), p. 54.

29 "Major Corruption Cases," *Beijing Review*, 22 May 2000, p. 14.

30 *People's Daily*, September 15, 2000, p. 1.

31 The Xinhua News Agency, December 19, 2002.

32 Hu was sentenced to death on February 15, 2000 and was executed on March 18, 2000 for soliciting and accepting large bribes. Cheng was sentenced on July 31, 2000 for accepting bribes and executed on September 14, 2000, and he was the first highest ranking official who was punished for corruption in the history of the People's Republic of China.

33 Li Ming, "City Beefs up Anti-Graft Drive," *China Daily*, April 22, 2000. It is worth pointing out that one million yuan in China is a huge amount given the low salaries of civil servants, normally around two thousand yuan a month.

34 *China Daily*, March 6, 2000.

35 *People's Daily*, November 9, 2002.

36 Ibid.

37 Jiang Zemin, "Leading Cadres Must Talk Politics," *Lilun Tansuo* (Theoretical Exploration) (special edition, 1996), pp. 2–3.

38 "Jiang Zemin Stresses to Strengthen Party Building and Steadfastly Lead the People to Facilitate the Development of Productive Force in Light of New Historical Conditions," *People's Daily*, May 18, 2000.

39 "Jiang Zemin Stresses It Is Necessary to Rule the Country Both by Law and by Virtue," Zhongguo xinwen she (China News Service), January 10, 2001.

40 *People's Daily*, January 11, 2001.

41 *People's Daily*, February 1, 2001.

42 Zhang Qian and Ji Haiqing, "Fade jianzhi, jianshe you Zhongguo tese she-huizhuyi fazhi guojia" (Rule of Law cum Rule by Virtue: Building a Socialist State of Rule of Law with Chinese Characteristics), *Shanghai shehui kexueyuan jikan* (Quarterly Journal of the Shanghai Academy of Social Sciences), no. 2 (2001), p. 189. This paper is a summary of a conference on Jiang's concept of rule by virtue, held in the Academy.

43 Ibid.

44 Ibid., pp. 189–90.

45 Ibid., 190.

46 Ibid., p. 191.

47 For a serious criticism, see Wei Yi, "Zhongguo xin dezhi lunxi: gaige qian Zhongguo daode hua zhengzhi de lishi fenxi" (An Analysis of New Theory of Rule by Virtue in China: A Historical Reflection of Chinese Moralized Politics in Pre-Reform China), *Zhanlue yu guanli*, no. 2 (2001), pp. 25–38.

48 *People's Daily*, November 9, 2002.

49 Clara Li, "Culture as Vital as Law, says Jiang aide," *South China Morning Post*, February 13, 2001. On Confucian communitarianism, see David L. Hall and Roger T. Ames, *The Democracy of the Desad: Dewey, Confucius, and the Hope for Democracy in China* (Chicago: Open Court, 1999).

Bibliography

Anderson, P., *Lineages of the Absolutist State*, London: New Left Books, 1974.

Asian Wall Street Journal, February 28, 2000.

Asian Wall Street Journal, November 17, 1998.

The Associated Press, August 8, 2000.

Austin, Greg, "The Strategic Implications of China's Public Order Crisis," Survival, 37: 2 (Summer 1995), pp. 7–23.

Bachman, David, *Chen Yun and the Chinese Political System*, Berkeley, CA: East Asian Studies, University of California, 1985.

Badie, Bertrand, *The Imported State: The Westernization of the Political Order*, translated by Claudia Royal, Stanford, CA: Stanford University Press, 2000.

Bai Chong-en, David D. Li and Yijiang Wang, "Enterprise Productivity and Efficiency: When is up really down," *Journal of Comparative Economics*, 24: 3 (1997), pp. 265–80.

Bakken, Borge, "State Control and Social Control in China," in Kjeld Erik Brodsgaard and Susan Young (eds.), *State Capacity in Japan, Taiwan, China and Vietnam*, Oxford: Oxford University Press, 2000, pp. 185–202.

Bao Tong, "Toushi zhonggong" (See through the Essence of the Chinese Communist Party), *Xinbao* (Hong Kong Economic Journal), June 29, 2001.

Barme, Geremie R., "The Revolution of Resistance," in Elizabeth J. Perry and Mark Selden (eds.), *Chinese Society: Change, Conflict and Resistance*, New York: Routledge, 2000, pp. 198–220.

Baum, Richard, " 'Modernization' and Legal Reform in Post-Mao China: The Rebirth of Socialist Legality," *Studies in Comparative Communism*, xix: 2 (Summer 1986), pp. 69–103.

Bell, Daniel, *The Coming of Post-Industrial Society*, New York: Basic Books, 1973.

Bendix, Reinhard, *Nation-Building and Citizenship*, Berkeley, CA: University of California Press, 1977.

Berger, Suzanne, and Ronald Dore (eds.), *National Diversity and Global Capitalism*, Ithaca, NY: Cornell University Press, 1996.

Bernstein, Richard and Ross H. Munro, *The Coming Conflict with China*, New York: A. A. Knopf, 1997.

Bernstein, Thomas P., and Xiaobo Lü, "Taxation without Representation: Peasants, the Central and the Local States in Reform China," *The China Quarterly*, 163 (September 2000), pp. 742–63.

Bickford, Thomas J., "The Chinese Military and Its Business Operations: The PLA as Entrepreneur," *Asian Survey*, xxxiv: 5 (May 1994), pp. 460–76.

Black, Henry Campbell, *Black's Law Dictionary*, St. Paul, Minn.: West Publishing Co., 1990.

Boli, John, and Geoge M. Thomas (eds.), *Constructing World Culture: International Nongovernmental Organizations since 1875*, Stanford, CA: Stanford University Press, 1999.

Boyer, R., and D. Drache (eds.), *States Against Markets*, London: Routledge, 1996.

Bright, Charles, and Susan Harding (eds.), *Statemaking and Social Movements: Essays in History and Theory*, Ann Arbor: University of Michigan Press, 1984.

Brodsgaard, Kjeld Eric, and Susan Young, "Introduction: State Capacity in East Asia," in Brodsgaard and Young (eds.), *State Capacity in East Asia: Japan, Taiwan, China, and Vietnam*, Oxford: Oxford University Press, 2000, pp. 1–16.

Brook, Timothy and B. Michael Frolic (eds.), *Civil Society in China*, Armonk, NY: M. E. Sharpe, 1997.

Burns, John (ed.), *The Chinese Communist Party's Nomenklatura System*, Armonk, NY: M. E. Sharpe, 1989.

Burns, John P., "Reforming China's Bureaucracy, 1979–82," *Asian Survey*, xxiii: 6 (June 1983), pp. 692–722.

Business Times, Singapore, October 30, 1998.

Byrd, William A. and Lin Qingsong (eds.), *China's Rural Industry: Structure, Development, and Reform*, Oxford: Oxford University Press, 1990.

Cable, Vincent, "The Diminished Nation-State: A Study in the Loss of Economic Power," *Daedalus*, special issue, "What Future for the State?" 124: 2 (Spring 1995), pp. 23–53.

Cai Dingjian, "Constitutional Supervision and Interpretation in the People's Republic of China," *Journal of Chinese Law*," 9: 2 (Fall 1995), pp. 219–45.

Calhoun, C. (ed.), *Habermas and the Public Sphere*, Cambridge, MA: The MIT Press, 1992.

Cao Jianming, "Jinrong anquan yu fazhi jianshe" (Financial Securities and Legal Construction), *People's Daily*, June 16, 1998.

The Center for Legal Information at Beijing Univeristy and Beijing Zhongtian Software Company (eds.), *Zhongguo falu fagui guizhang daquan* (Complete Collection of Laws, Regulations and Rules in China), Beijing: Beijing University Press, 1997.

Chen, Feng, "Order and Stability in Social Transition: Neoconservative Political Thought in Post-1989 China," *The China Quarterly* 151 (September 1997), pp. 593–613.

Chen, Feng, "Subsistence Crisis, Managerial Corruption and Labor Protests in China," *The China Journal*, 44 (July 2000), pp. 41–63.

Chen, Hongyi, *The Institutional Transition of China's Township and Village Enterprises: Market Liberalization, Contractual Form Innovation and Privatization*, Aldershot: Ashgate, 2000.

Chen, Kang, Arye L. Millman and Qingyang Gu, "From the Helping Hand to the Grabbing Hand: Fiscal Federalism and Corruption in China," *EAI Working Paper* No. 67, East Asian Institute, National University of Singapore, February 2001.

Chen Shaoming, "Minzu zhuyi: fuxing zhidao?" (Nationalism: A Way of Revival?), *Dong Fang* (The Orient), 2 (1996), pp. 74–6.

Chen Yuan, "Woguo jingji de shenceng wenti he xuanze: guanyu woguo jingji fazhan geju he yunxing jizhi de ruogan wenti" (Deep Problems of Our Economy and Choice: On Some Problems on the Situation of Our Economic Development and Operating Mechanism), internal government circulation, March 1991.

Chen Zhongdong (ed.), *Shehui tuanti zuzhi daquan* (Almanac of Social Organizations in China), three volumes, Beijing: Zhuanli wenxian chubanshe, 1998.

Cheng Baisong and Zhang Bing, "Nongmin fudan xianzhuang, chengyin ji duice" (The Current Situation of Peasant Burdens, its Origins, and Policy Choice), *Nongye jingji wenti* (Agricultural Economy Studies), no. 3 (1993), pp. 4–11.

Cheng Fengjun, "Lun dongya chenggong de zonghe yaosu: dongya jingji minzu zhuyi" (A Comprehensive Factor of East Asian Miracle: East Asian Economic Nationalism), *Zhongguo shehui kexue jikan* (Chinese Social Sciences Quarterly), 15 (Summer 1996), pp. 88–99.

Cheng Ming, "Dongya moshi de meili" (The Glamour of the East Asian Model), *Zhanlue yu guanli* (Strategy and Management), 2 (1994), pp. 18–27.

Cheng Rulong (ed.), *Dangdai Zhongguo de caizheng* (China Today: Finance, volumes 1 and 2), Beijing: Zhongguo shehui kexue chubanshe, 1988.

Cheng, Tiejun and Mark Selden, "The Construction of Spatial Hierarchies: China's Hukou and Danwei System," in Timothy Cheek and Tony Saich (eds.), *New Perspectives on State Socialism in China*, Armonk, NY: M. E. Sharpe, 1977, pp. 23–50.

China Daily, August 25, 1994.

China Daily, February 28, 1998.

China Daily, October 26, 1998.

China Daily, July 22, 1999.

China Daily, July 22, 1999.

China Daily, March 6, 2000.

China Daily, August 8, 2000.

China Daily, August 10, 2000.

China Daily, May 16, 2001.

China Economic News (HK), no. 39, October 11, 1999.

China Economic News (HK), no. 38, October 4, 1999.

China Economic News (HK), no. 33, August 30, 1999.

China Industrial and Commercial Times, "The 6-Measure of Promoting SOE Reform," Beijing, March 2, 1997.

China News Service, August 22, 2000.

"China Telecom IPO faces crucial test," *South China Morning Post*, April 9, 2001.

Chong Pengrong, *Shinian jingji gaige: licheng, xianzhuang, wenti, chulu* (Ten Years of Economic Reforms: Process, Current Situation, Problems and Prospects), Zhengzhou: Henan renmin chubanshe, 1990.

Crane, George T., *The Political Economy of China's Special Economic Zones*, Armonk: M. E. Sharpe, 1990.

Cui Zhiyuan, *Di'erci sixiang jiefang yu zhidu chuangxin* (The Second Thought Liberation and Institutional Innovation), Hong Kong: Oxford University Press, 1997.

Cui Zhiyuan, "Mao Zedong 'wenge' lilun de deshi yu 'xiandaixing' de chongjian" (Mao Zedong's Idea of Cultural Revolution and The Restructuring of Chinese Modernity), *Xianggang shehui kexue xuebao* (Hong Kong Journal of Social Sciences), 7 (Spring 1996), pp. 49–74.

Cui Zhiyuan, "Angang xianfa yu hou fute zhuyi" (The Angang Constitution and Post-Fordism), *Dushu* 3 (1996), pp. 11–21.

Cui Zhiyuan, "Zhongguo shijian dui xingudian zhuyi jingjixue de tiaozhan" (China's Practice and Its Challenges to Neo-Classical Economics), *Xianggang shehui kexue xuebao* (Hong Kong Journal of Social Sciences), Special Issue (July 1995), pp. 1–33.

Cui Zhiyuan, "Zhidu chuangxin yu di'erci sixiang jiefang" (Institutional Innovation and A Second Liberation of Thoughts), *Ershiyi shiji* (Twenty-First Century), 24 (1994), pp. 5–15.

Daedalus, 124: 2 (Spring 1995), special issue "What Future for the State?"

Dahl, Robert, *Democracy and Its Critics*, New Haven: Yale University Press, 1989.

Dahlgren, P., *Television and the Public Sphere: Citizenship, Democracy and the Media*, London: Sage, 1995.

Dauvergne, Peter (ed.), *Weak and Strong States in Asia-Pacific Societies*, Sydney: Allen & Unwin, 1988.

Davis, Deborah S., Richard Kraus, Barry Naughton, and Elizabeth J. Perry (eds.), *Urban Spaces in Contemporary China: the Potential for Autonomy and Community in post-Mao China*, Washington, DC and New York, Woodrow Wilson Center Press and Cambridge University Press, 1995.

Day, Lincoln H., and Ma Xia (eds.), *Migration and Urbanization in China*, Armonk, NY: M. E. Sharpe, 1994.

De Barry, Wm. Theodore, "The 'Constitutional Tradition' in China," *Journal of Chinese Law*, 9: 1 (Spring 1995), pp. 7–34.

Deng Xiaoping, "Women ba gaige dangzuo yizhong geming" (We Regard the Reform as A Revolution, October 10, 1984), in Deng Xiaoping, *Deng Xiaoping wenxuan* (Selected Works of Deng Xiaoping), vol. 3, Beijing: Renmin chubanshe, 1993, pp. 81–2.

Deng Xiaoping, "Zai Wuchang, shenzhen, Zhuhai, Shanghai de di de tanhua yaodian" (Main points of the talks made in Wuchang, Shenzhen, Zhuhai, and Shanghai, January 18 – February 21, 1992), in Deng Xiaoping, *Deng Xiaoping wenxuan*, vol. 3, pp. 370–83.

Deng Xiaoping, "Zenyang pingjia yige guojia de zhengzhi tizhi" (How A Country's Political System Should Be Evaluated, March 27, 1987), in Deng Xiaoping, *Deng Xiaoping wenxuan*, vol. 3, pp. 213–4.

Deng Xiaoping, "Zhengzhi shang fazhan minzhu, jingji shang shixing gaige" (To Develop Democracy in Politics, and to Implement Reform in Economics, April 15, 1985), in Deng Xiaoping, *Deng Xiaoping wenxuan*, vol. 3, pp. 115–18.

Deng Xiaoping, "Gaige shi Zhongguo de di'erci geming" (The Reform Is China's Second Revolution," March 28, 1985), in Deng Xiaoping, *Deng Xiaoping wenxuan*, vol. 3, pp. 113–14.

Deng Xiaoping, "Guanyu zhengzhi tizhi gaige wenti" (On the Problems of Reforming the Political System," September–November 1986), in Deng Xiaoping, *Deng Xiaoping wenxuan*, vol. 3, pp. 176–80.

Deng Xiaoping, "On the Reform of the System of Party and State Leadership," in Deng Xiaoping, *Selected Works of Deng Xiaoping (1975–1982)*, Beijing: Foreign Languages Press, 1984, pp. 302–25.

Deng Xiaoping, "Emancipate the Mind; Seek Truth from Facts and Unite as One in Looking to the Future," December 13, 1978, in Deng Xiaoping, *Selected Works of Deng Xiaoping (1975–1982)*, Beijing: Foreign Languages Press, 1984, pp. 151–65.

Deng Yingtao, Miao zhuang, and Cui Zhiyuan, "Nanjie cun jingyan de sikao" (Reflection on the Experience of Nanjie Village), *Zhanlue yu guanli* (Strategy and Management), 3 (1996), pp. 14–24.

Deng Zhenglai and Jing Yuejing, "Jian'gou Zhongguo de shimin shehui" (Building Civil Society in China), in Luo Gang and Ni Wenjian (eds.), *Jiushi niandai sixiang wenxuan* (Selected Papers of Thoughts in the 1990), Nanning: Guangxi renmin chubanshe, 2000, vol. 2, pp. 3–22.

The Department of Thought and Theory of *China's Youth*, "Sulian jubian zhihou Zhongguo de xianshi yingdui yu zhanlue xuanze" (China's Practical Countermeasures and Strategic Choice after Dramatic Changes in the Soviet Union), internal government circulation, September 9, 1991.

The Development Research Center of the State Council and the Editorial Office of *Peasants Daily*, "Maodun, yindao he lishi de qiji – guanyu 196 feng nongmin laixin de chubu fenxi" (Contradictions, Proper Guidance, and Historical Opportunities – A Primary Analysis of the 196 Letters from Peasants), *Peasants Daily*, December 8, 1998.

Ding Jianming and Li Jianxin, "Dongnanya jinrong weiji de qishi" (Lessons of the Southeast Asian Financial Crisis), *People's Daily*, January 5, 1998.

Ding, X. L., "The Illicit Asset Stripping of Chinese State Firms," *The China Journal*, 43 (January 2000), pp. 1–28.

Ding, Yijiang, "The Conceptual Evolution of Democracy in Intellectual Circles' Rethinking of State and Society," in Zhao Suisheng (ed.), *China and Democracy*, New York: Routledge, 2000, pp. 111–40.

Dirlik, Arif, "The Ideological Foundations of the New Life Movement: A Study in Counterrevolution," *Journal of Asian Study*, 34: 4 (August 1975), pp. 945–80.

Durkheim, Emile, *The Division of Labor in Society*, New York: Free Press, 1969.

Dittmer, Lowell and Samuel S. Kim (eds.), *China's Quest for National Identity*, Ithaca, NY: Cornell University Press, 1993.

Eckholm, Erik, "China Party Says Unrest Is Spreading in Country: Frank Official Report Calls Relations with the Masses 'Tense'," *International Herald Tribune*, June 2–3, 2001.

Economy, Elizabeth and Michel Oksenberg (eds.), *China Joins the World: Progress and Prospects*, New York: Council On Foreign Relations Press, 1999.

Editorial Office of the Law Year Book of China (ed.), *Zhongguo falu nianjian* (The Law Year Book of China), Beijing: Zhongguo falu nianjian chubanshe, 1985–98.

Editorial Office of *The Outlook Weekly* (ed.), *Guowuyuan jigou gaige gailan* (A General Survey of Institutional Reforms of the State Council), Beijing: Xinhua chubanshe, 1998.

Epstein, Edward J., "Law and Legitimation in Post-Mao China," in Pitman B. Potter (ed.), *Domestic Law Reforms in Post-Mao China*, Armonk, NY: M. E. Sharpe, 1994, pp. 19–55.

Evans, Peter, "The Eclipse of the State? Reflection on Stateness in an Era of Globalization," *World Politics*, 50 (October 1997), pp. 62–82.

Evans, Peter, *Embedded Autonomy: States and Industrial Transformation*, Princeton: Princeton University Press, 1995.

Evans, Peter B., D. Rueschmeyer, and T. Skocpol (eds.), *Bringing the State Back In*, Cambridge: Cambridge University Press, 1985.

The Finance Study Team of the State Planning Commission, *Jinrong tizhi gaige yu hongguan jingji guanli* (Financial System Reform and Macro-Economic Management), Beijing: Jingji kexue chubanshe, 1988.

Findlay, Christopher, Andrew Watson, and Harry X. Wu (eds.), *Rural Enterprises in China*, New York: St. Martin's Press, 1994.

Friedman, Milton, *Capitalism and Freedom*, Chicago: University of Chicago Press, 1982.

Fukuyama, Francis, *Trust*, New York: Free Press, 1995.

Fukuyama, Francis, "Confucianism and Democracy", *Journal of Democracy*, 6: 2 (1995), pp. 20–33.

Fukuyama, Francis, *The End of History and the Last Man*, New York: The Free Press, 1992.

Gan Yang, "Wenhua zhongguo yu xiangtu zhongguo" (Cultural China and Rural China), in Gan, *Jiangcuo jiucuo* (Leave the Mistake Uncorrected and Make the Best of It), Hong Kong: Oxford University Press, 2000.

Gilpin, Robert, *The Challenge of Global Capitalism: The World Economy in the 21stCentury*, Princeton, NJ: Princeton University Press, 2000.

Gilpin, Robert, *The Political Economy of International Relations*, Princeton, NJ: Princeton University Press, 1987.

Goldman, Merle, *Sowing the Seeds of Democracy in China: Political Reform in the Deng Xiaoping Era*, Cambridge, MA: Harvard University Press, 1994.

Grossman, L. K., *The Electronic Republic: Reshaping Democracy in the Information Age*, New York: Viking, 1995.

Grewlich, K. W., and F. H. Pederson (eds.), *Power and Participation in an Information Society*, Brussels: Europe Commission, 1994.

Grindle, Merilee S., and John W. Thomas, *Public Choices and Policy Change: The Political Economy of Reform in Developing Countries*, Baltimore: Johns Hopkins University Press, 1991.

Groves, Theodore, Yongmiao Hong, John McMillan and Barry Naughton, "Autonomy and Incentives in Chinese State Enterprises," *Quarterly Journal of Economics*, 109: 1 (1994), pp. 183–209.

Gu Yuanyang, "Dangdai shijie jingji quanqiuhua: shijie jingji fazhan zong qushi" (Economic Globalization in Contemporary World: Grand Trend of World Economy), in The Department of Educational Administration (ed.), *Wuge dangdai jianggao xuanbian* (Five Selected Contemporary Lectures), Beijing: Zhonggong zhongyang dangxiao chubanshe, 2000, pp. 17–45.

Gu, Edward Xin, "Employment Service and Unemployment Insurance," in John Wong and Zheng Yongnian (eds.), *The Nanxun Legacy and China's Development in the Post-Deng Era*, Singapore and London: Singapore University Press and World Scientific, 2001, pp. 143–69.

Gu, Edward Xin, "Plural Institutionalism and the Emergence of Intellectual Public Spaces in China: A Case Study of Four Intellectual Groups," in Suisheng Zhao (ed.), *China and Democracy: Reconsidering the Prospects for a Democratic China*, New York: Routledge, 2000, pp. 141–72.

Gu, Edward Xin, "The Political Economy of Public Housing Reform," in Wang Gungwu and Zheng Yongnian (eds.), *Reform, Legitimacy, and Dilemmas*, Singapore and London: Singapore University Press and World Scientific, 2000, pp. 195–230.

Gu, Edward Xin, "From Permanent Employment to Massive Lay-Offs: The Political Economy of 'Transitional Unemployment' in Urban China (1993–98)," *Economy and Society*, 28: 2 (May 1999), pp. 281–99.

Gu, Edward Xin, "Cultural Intellectuals and the Politics of Cultural Public Space in Communist China (1979–1989): A Case Study of Three Intellectual Groups," *The Journal of Asian Studies*, 58: 2 (May 1999), pp. 389–431.

Guan Chajia, "Jingji quanqiuhua huhuan jinrong anquan" (Economic Globalization Calls for Financial Security), *People's Daily*, overseas edition, October 22, 1998.

Guo Dingping, "Woguo shimin shehui de fazhan yu zhengzhi zhuanxing" (Development of Civil Society and Political Transition in China), *Shehui kexue* (Social Sciences), 12 (1994), pp. 52–5.

Habermas, Jürgen, *The Structural Transformation of the Public Sphere*, Cambridge: Polity Press, 1989.

Hall, David L, and Roger T. Ames, *The Democracy of the Dead: Dewey, Confucius, and the Hope for Democracy in China*, Chicago: Open Court, 1999.

Harris, Stuart and Gary Klintworth (eds.), *China as a Great Power, Myths, Realities and Challenges in the Asia-Pacific Region*, New York: St. Martin's Press, 1995.

Hass, Ernst B., *Beyond the Nation-State: Functionalism and International Organization*, Stanford, CA: Stanford University Press, 1964.

Hayey, F. A., *The Road to Serfdom*, The University of Chicago Press, 1994.

Hayes, Carlton J. H., *The Historical Evolution of Modern Nationalism*, New York: Macmillan, 1948.

He Qinglian, *Xiandaihua de xianjing: dangdai Zhongguo de jingji shehui wenti* (The Perils of Chinese Modernization: Economic and Social Problems in Contemporary China), Beijing: Jinri Zhongguo chubanshe, 1998.

He Shengming, *Zhongguo caizheng gaige ershi nian* (Twenty Years of Fiscal Reform in China), Zhengzhou: Zhonggu chubanshe, 1998.

Held, David, Anthony McGrew, David Goldblatt and Jonathan Perraton, *Global Transformations: Politics, Economics and Culture*, Stanford, CA: Stanford University Press, 1999.

Held, David, *Democracy and the Global Order: From the Modern State to Cosmopolitan Governance*, Cambridge: Polity Press, 1995.

Held, David, "Democracy, the Nation-State, and the Global System," in David Held (ed.), *Political Theory Today*, Cambridge; Polity Press, 1991, pp. 197–235.

Hill, Kevin A., and John E. Hughes, *Cyberpolitics: Citizen Activism in the Age of the Internet*, Lanham: Rowman & Littlefield, 1998.

Hirschman, Albert O., *Rival Views of Market Society and Other Recent Essays*, Cambridge, MA: Harvard University Press, 1992.

Hirschman, Albert O., *Shifting Involvements: Private Interest and Public Action*, Princeton, NJ: Princeton University Press, 1982.

Hirschman, Albert O., *The Passions and the Interests: Political Arguments for Capitalism before its Triumph*, Princeton, NJ: Princeton University Press, 1977.

Hirst, P., and G. Thompson, *Globalization in Question: The International Economy and the Possibilities of Governance*, Cambridge: Polity Press, 1996.

Hobsbawn, Eric J., *The Age of Capital 1848–1875*, London: Weidenfeld and Nicolson, 1975.

Holmes, David (ed.), *Virtual Politics: Identity and Community in Cyberspace*, London: Sage, 1997.

Holmes, Stephen, and Cass Sunstein, *The Cost of Rights: Why Liberty Depends on Taxation*, New York: Norton, 1999.

Horsman, Mathew and Andrew Marshall, *After the Nation-State*, New York: HarperCollins, 1994.

Hu Angang (ed.), *Zhongguo tiaozhan fubai* (China: Fighting Against Corruption), Hanzhou: Zhejiang renmin chubanshe, 2001.

Hu Angang, "Kuaru xin shiji de zuida tiaozhan: woguo jinru gaoshiye jieduan" (The Biggest Challenge in Entering a New Century: China Enters a Period of High Unemployment) in Hu Angang (ed.), *Zhongguo zouxiang* (Prospects of China), Hangzhou: Zhejiang renmin chubanshe, 2000, pp. 49–77.

Hu Angang, "High Unemployment in China: Estimates and Policies," a paper presented at International Conference "Center-Periphery Relations in China: Integration, Disintegration or Reshaping of An Empire?", The French Center for Contemporary China and the Chinese University of Hong Kong, Hong Kong, March 25, 2000.

Hu Angang, "Kuaru xin shiji de zuida tiaozhan: woguo jinru gaoshiye jieduan" (The Biggest Challenge in Entering a New Century: China Enters a Period of High Unemployment), unpublished manuscript, Beijing: Chinese Academy of Science, 1999.

Hu Wei, "Zhongguo fazhan de 'bijiao youshi' hezai? – chaoyue chun jingji guandian de fenxi" (Where Does China's Comparative Advantage Locate for Its Development? – An Analysis beyond a Pure Economic Point of View), *Zhanlue yu guanli* (Strategy and Management), 5 (1995), pp. 69–78.

Huang Yanxin, "Nongmin fudan guozhong de zhidu xing genyuan yu duice" (The Institutional Origins of Peasant Burdens and Policy Choices), *Zhongguo nongcun jingji* (Agricultural Economy in China), 5 (1994), pp. 38–42.

Hunt, Michael H., "Chinese National Identity and the Strong State: The Late Qing-Republic Crisis," in Lowell Dittmer and Samuel Kim (eds.), *China's Quest for National Identity*, Ithaca, NY: Cornell University Press, 1993, pp. 62–79.

Huntington, Samuel, *The Clash of Civilizations and the Remaking of World Order*, New York: Simon and Schuster, 1996.

Huntington, Samuel S., *The Third Wave: Democratization in the Late Twentieth Century*, Norman: University of Oklahoma Press, 1991.

Huntington, Samuel, "Will More Countries Become Democratic?" *Political Science Quarterly*, 99 (Summer 1984), pp. 193–218.

Jacobson, Harold K., and Michel Oksenberg, *China's Participation in the IMF, the World Bank, and GATT: Toward a Global Economic Order*, Ann Arbor: University of Michigan Press, 1990.

Ji Weidong, "Xianzheng de fuquan" (Return Power to Constitutional Arrangement), in Luo Gang and Ni Wenjian (eds.), *Jiushi niandai sixiang wenxuan* (Selected Papers of Thoughts in the 1990), Nanning: Guangxi renmin chubanshe, 2000, vol. 2, pp. 386–400.

Ji Weidong, "Zhongguo xianfa gaige de tujing yu caichanquan wenti" (The Path of China's Constitutional Reforms and the Problem of Property Rights), *Dangdai Zhongguo yanjiu* (Modern China Studies), 3 (1999), pp. 26–53.

Jiang Nanyang, "Lun siying qiyezhu de zhengzhi canyu" (Political Participation by the Owners of Private Businesses), in Zhang Houyi and Ming Zhili (eds.), *Zhongguo siying qiye fazhan baogao 1978–1998* (A Report of the Development of Private Enterprises in China, 1978–1998), Beijing: Shehui kexue wenxuan chubanshe, 1999, pp. 103–17.

Jiang Ping, "Chinese Legal Reform: Achievements, Problems and Prospects," *Journal of Chinese Law*, 9: 1 (Spring 1995), pp. 67–76.

Jiang Shixue, "Lamei, dongya fazhan moshi de bijiao yu qishi" (A Comparison of the Development Models in Latin America and East Asia and Its Implications), *Zhanlue yu guanli* (Strategy and Management), 5 (1995), pp. 58–68.

Jiang Zemin, "Jiang Zemin zai qingzhu Zhongguo gongchandang chengli bashi zhounian dahui shang de jianghau" (Jiang Zemin's Speech at the Conference Celebrating the Eightieth Anniversary of the Chinese Communist Party, July 1, 2001), *People's Daily*, July 2, 2001.

Jiang Zemin, "Jiang Zemin Stresses It Is Necessary to Rule the Country Both by Law and by Virtue," Zhongguo xinwen she (China News Service), January 10, 2001.

Jiang Zemin, "Jiang Zemin tongzhi zai quanguo dangxiao huiyi shang de jianghua" (Comrade Jiang Zemin's Speech at the National Conference for Party Schools," June 9, 2000), *People's Daily*, July 7, 2000.

Jiang Zemin, "Jinmi jiehe xinde lishi tiaojian jiaqiang dang de jianshe, shizhong dailing quanguo renmin cujin shenchanli de fazhan" (Jiang Zemin emphasizes strengthening party building and steadfastly leading the people to improve productivity in view of new conditions) *People's Daily*, February 26, 2000.

Jiang Zemin, "Lingdao ganbu yiding yao jiang zhengzhi" (Leading Cadres Must Talk Politics), *Lilun Tansuo* (Theoretical Exploration), special edition, 1996, pp. 2–3.

Jin, Hehui, Yingyi Qian and Barry R. Weigast, "Regional Decentralization and Fiscal Incentives: Federalism, Chinese Style," *Stanford University Working Paper*, SWP-99–013, 1999.

Jingji riboa (Economic Daily), January 26, 1999.

Johnson, Chalmers A., *Peasant Nationalism and Communist Power: The Emergence of Revolutionary China, 1937–1945*, Stanford, CA: Stanford University Press, 1962.

Kasza, Gregory J., *The Conscription Society: Administered Mass Organization*, New Haven: Yale University Press, 1995.

Kennedy, Paul, *The Rise and Fall of the Great Powers: Economic Change and Military Conflict from 1500 to 2000*, New York: Random House, 1987.

Keohane, Robert, and Joseph Nye, *Power and Interdependence: World Politics in Transition*, New York: Longman, 2000.

Keohane, Robert, and Joseph S. Nye, "Globalization: What's New? What's Not? (And So What?)" *Foreign Affairs*, 118 (Spring 2000), pp. 104–19.

Khalilzad, Zalmay M., Abram N. Shulsky, Daniel L. Byman et al., *The United States and a Rising China: Strategic and Military Implications*, Santa Monica, CA: Rand, 1999.

Kohli, Atul, "Democracy and Development," in John P. Lewis and Valeriana Kallab (eds.), *Development Strategies Reconsidered*, New Brunswick: Transaction, 1986, pp. 153–82.

Kohn, Hans, *The Age of Nationalism: The First Era of Global History*, New York: Harper, 1962.

Kohn, Hans, *The Idea of Nationalism*, New York: Collier, 1944.

Krasner, Stephen, *Sovereignty: Organized Hypocrisy*, Princeton, NJ: Princeton University Press, 1999.

Krasner, Stephen, "Economic Interdependence and Independent Statehood," in R. H. Jackson and A James (eds.), *States in a Changing World*, Oxford: Oxford University Press, 1993, pp. 301–21.

Lai, Harry Hongyi, "Behind China's World Trade Organization Agreement with the USA," *Third World Quarterly*, 22: 2 (2001), pp. 237–55.

Lardy, Nicholas, *Integrating China into Global Economy*, Washington, DC: Brookings Institution Press, 2002.

Lardy, Nicholas, "China and the Asian Contagion," *Foreign Affairs* (July/August), 1998.

Lardy, Nicholas, *China's Unfinished Economic Revolution*, Washington, DC: Brookings Institution Press, 1998.

Lardy, Nicholas R., *China in the World Economy*, Washington, DC: Institute for International Economics, 1994.

Lardy, Nicholas R., *Foreign Trade and Economic Reform in China, 1978–1990*, Cambridge: Cambridge University Press, 1992.

Lardy, Nicholas R., *China's Entry Into the World Economy: Implications for Northeast Asia and the United States*, Lanham, MD: University Press of America, 1987.

Lardy, Nicholas and Kenneth Lieberthal (eds.), *Chen Yun's Strategy for China's Development*, Armonk, NY: M. E. Sharpe, 1983.

Lau Siu-kai, et al. (eds.), *Shichang, jieji yu zhengzhi* (Market, Class and Politics), Hong Kong: Hong Kong Institute of Asian-Pacific Studies, The Chinese University of Hong Kong, 2000.

Lee, Ching Kwan, "Pathways of Labor Insurgency," in Elizabeth J. Perry and Mark Selden (eds.), *Chinese Society: Change, Conflict and Resistance*, New York: Routledge, 2000, pp. 41–61.

Lee, Ching Kwan, "From Organized Dependence to Disorganized Despotism: Changing Labor Regimes in Chinese Factories," *The China Quarterly*, 157 (March 1999), pp. 44–71.

Lee, Ching Kwan, "The Labor Politics of Market Socialism-Collective Inaction and Class Experience Among State Workers in Guangzhou," *Modern China*, 24: 1 (1998), pp. 3–33.

Lee, Hong Yong, *From Revolutionary Cadres to Party Technocrats in Socialist China*, Berkeley, CA: University of California Press, 1991.

Lee Siew Hua, "China will be 'more democratic over time' ", *The Straits Times*, Singapore, January 30, 1997, p. 1.

Levenson, Joseph L., *Liang Ch'i Ch'ao and the Mind of Modern China*, Berkeley, CA: University of California Press, 1970.

Li, Cheng, *China's Leaders: The New Generation*, Lanham, MD: Rowman & Littlefield Publishers, Inc., 2001.

Li, Cheng, and Lynn White, "The Fifteenth Central Committee of the Chinese Communist Party: Full-Fledged Technocratic Leadership with Partial Control by Jiang Zemin," *Asian Survey*, 38: 3 (March 1998), pp. 231–64.

Li, Cheng, "Surplus Rural Laborers and Internal Migration in China: Current Status and Future Prospects," *Asian Survey*, xxxvi: 11 (November 1996), pp. 1122–45.

Li, Clara, "Culture as Vital as Law, says Jiang aide," *South China Morning Post*, February 13, 2001.

Li Ming, "City Beefs up Anti-Graft Drive," *China Daily*, April 22, 2000.

Li Peng, "Government Work Report" presented at the National People's Congress in March 1997, in *Zhongguo gongshang shibao* (The China Commercial and Industrial Times), March 2, 1997.

Li Qiang, "Guanyu siyingjingji de ruogan ziliao" (Some Data on the Private Economy), *Zhenli de zhuiqiu* (The Seeking of Truth), 5 (2001), pp. 17–27.

Li Shenzhi, "Quanqiuhua shidai zhongguoren de shiming" (Chinese Mission in an Age of Globalization), *Dong Fang* (The Orient) 5 (1994), pp. 13–18.

Li Shenzhi, "Cong quanqiuhua shidian kan Zhongguo de xiandaihua wenti" (Understanding the Problems of China's Modernization from the Perspective of Globalization), *Zhan lue yu guanli* (Strategy and Management), 1 (1994), pp. 5–6.

Li Xiangang, "Guanyu nongcun feishui zhidu gaige de diaocha yu sikao" (An Investigation of the Reform of the Rural Tax-for-Fee System and Some Thoughts), *Nongcun diaocha* (Rural Investigation), 7 (1995), pp. 6–10.

Li, Wei, "The Impact of Economic Reform on the Performance of Chinese State Enterprises 1980–1989," *Journal of Political Economy*, 105: 5 (1997), pp. 1080–106.

Liao Jinjing, "Nongmin fudan guozhong de diaocha yu sikao" (An Investigation to Peasant Burdens and Some Thoughts), *Zhongguo nongcun jingji* (Agricultural Economy in China), 6 (1993), pp. 54–6.

Liao, Kuang-sheng, *Antiforeignism and Modernization in China, 1860–1980: Linkage Between Domestic Politics and Foreign Policy*, New York: St. Martin's Press, 1984.

Lieberthal, Kenneth, and Michel Oksenberg, *Policy Making in China: Leaders, Structures, and Processes*, Princeton, NJ: Princeton University Press, 1988.

Lin Yanzhi, "Gongchandang yao lingdao he jiayu xin zichan jieji" (The CCP Must Lead and Control the New Bourgeoisie), *Zhenli de zhuiqiu* (The Seeking of Truth), 5 (2001), pp. 2–11.

Lin Yifu, Cai Fang and Li Zhou, "Ziyuan jiegou shengji: ganchao zhanlue de wuqu – dui 'bijiao youshi zhanlue'piping de jidian huiying" (The Upgrading of Resource Structure: Misunderstanding of the Catching-Up and Surpassing Strategy – Some Responses to Criticism on the 'Comparative Advantage

Strategy'), *Zhanlue yu guanli* (Strategy and Management), 1 (1996), pp. 35–45.

Lin Yifu, Cai Fang and Li Zhou, *Zhongguo de qiji: fazhan zhanlue he jingji gaige* (China's Miracle: Development Strategy and Economic Reform), Shanghai: Sanlian shudian, 1994.

Lin Zhiyuan, "Shangye yinhang yao yingjie jinrong quanqiuhua de tiaozhan" (Commercial Banks Should Meet the Challenge of Financial Globalization), *Financial News*, May 15, 1999.

Lindblom, Charles E., *Politics and Markets: The World's Political-Economic Systems*, New York: Basic Books, 1977.

Lipset, Seymour. M., *Political Man: The Social Base of Politics*, New York: Doubleday & Company, Inc., 1963.

Lipset, Seymour. M., "Some Social Requisites of Democracy: Economic Development and Political Legitimacy," *American Political Science Review*, 53 (1959), pp. 69–105.

Liu Jun and Li Lin (eds.), *Xin quanwei zhuyi: dui gaige lilun gangling de lunzheng* (Neo-Authoritarianism: A Debate on the Theories of China's Reform), Beijing: Jingji xueyuan chubanshe, 1989.

Liu Junning, "Feng neng jin, yu neng jin, guowang buneng jin: zhengzhi lilun shiye zhong de caichanquan yu renlei wenming" (Wind Can Enter, Rain Can Enter, but Not King: Property Rights and Human Civilization from the Perspective of Political Theory), in Luo Gang and Ni Wenjian (eds.), *Jiushi niandai sixiang wenxuan* (Selected Papers of Thoughts in the 1990), Nanning: Guangxi renmin chubanshe, 2000, vol. 2, pp. 33–59.

Liu Junning, "Ziyou zhuyi yu gongzheng: dui ruogan jienan de huida" (Liberalism and Justice: Responses to Some Major Criticisms), *Dangdai Zhongguo yanjiu* (Modern China Studies), 4 (2000), pp. 50–67.

Liu Junning (ed.), *Ziyouzhuyi de xiansheng: Beida chuantong yu jindai Zhongguo* (The Herald of Liberalism: The Tradition of Beijing University and Modern China), Beijing: Zhongguo renshi chubanshe, 1998.

Liu Junning, "Chanquan baohu yu youxian zhengfu" (Property Rights Protection and Limited Government), in Dong Xuyu and Shi Binhai (eds.), *Zhengzhi Zhongguo: Mianxiang xintizhi xuanzede shidai* (Political China: An Age Facing New Institutional Choices), Beijing: Jinri Zhongguo chubanshe, 1998, pp. 40–8.

Liu Liqun, "Chukou daoxiang xing jingji fazhan moshi bu shihe Zhongguo guoqing" (An Export-Led Model of Economic Development Is not Suitable for China's National Conditions), *Zhanlue yu guanli* (Strategy and Management), 2 (1994), p. 44.

Liu Xinwu, "Queli renlei gongxiang wenmin guannian" (To Establish the Concept of Shared Human Civilization), an interview by Qiu Huadong, *Dong Fang* (The Orient), 6 (1996), pp. 21–5.

Liu Zhiqiang, "Progress in China's Banking Sector Reform," *EAI Background Brief* No. 62, East Asian Institute, National University of Singapore, May 9, 2000.

Lo, Vai Io, "Labor Law for Foreign Investment Enterprises in China," in Wang Gungwu and Zheng Yongnian (eds.), *Reform, Legitimacy and Dilemmas: China's Politics and Society*, Singapore and London: Singapore University Press and World Scientific, 2000, pp. 167–95.

Lu, Ding, "China's Institution Development for a Market Economy since Deng Xiaoping's 1992 *Nanxun*," in John Wong and Zheng Yongnian (eds.), *The Nanxun Legacy and China's Development*, London and Singapore: World Scientific & Singapore University Press, 2001, pp. 51–76.

Lu Pinyue, "Zhongguo lishi jincheng yu shimin shehui jian'gou" (China's Historical Progress and the Development of Civil Society), *Zhongguo shehui kexue jikan* (Chinese Social Sciences Quarterly), 8 (1994), pp. 173–8.

Lu Xueyi, "Zhongguo nongcun zhuangkuang ji cunzai wenti de genyuan" (China's Rural Situation, Problems and their Origins), in Ru Xin, Lu Xueyi and Shan Tianlun (eds.), *Shehui lanpishu 2001* (Social Bluebook), Beijing: Shehui kexue wenxian chubanshe, 2001, pp. 159–66.

Lu Xueyi and Jing Tiankuai (eds.), *Zhuanxing zhong de Zhongguo shehui* (Chinese Society in Transition), Ha'erbin: Helongjiang renmin chubanshe, 1994.

Lü, Xiaobo, "The Politics of Peasant Burdens in Reform China," *Journal of Peasant Studies*, vol. 25, no. 1 (1997), pp. 113–38.

Lü, Xiaobo, and Elizabeth J. Perry (eds.), *Danwei: The Changing Chinese Workplace in Historical and Comparative Perspective*, Armonk, NY: M. E. Sharpe, 1997.

Lubman, Stanley, *Bird in a Cage: Legal Reform in China After Mao*, Stanford, CA: Stanford University Press, 1999.

Luo Gan, "Guanyu guowuyuan jigou gaige fang'an de jidian shuoming" (Some Explanations to the Plan of Organizational Reform of the State Council), *Wen Hui Bao* (Hong Kong), March 7, 1998, A7.

Luo Rongqu, "Zouxiang xiandaihua de Zhongguo daolu" (Chinese Way to Modernization), *Zhongguo shehui kexue jikan* (Chinese Social Sciences Quarterly), 17 (Winter 1996), pp. 43–53.

Ma Hong and Sun Shangqing (eds.), *Zhongguo jingji xingshi yu zhanwang* (China's Economic Situation and Prospects, 1991–1992), Beijing: Zhongguo fazhan chubanshe, 1992.

Mallee, Hein, "China's Household Registration System under Reform," in Alan Hunter and Kim-kwong Chan (eds.), *Protestantism in Contemporary China*, Cambridge: Cambridge University Press, 1993, pp. 10–16.

Mann, Michael, "Has globalization ended the rise and rise of the nation-state?" in T. V. Paul and John A. Hall (eds.), *International Order and the Future of World Politics*, Cambridge University Press, 1999, pp. 237–61.

Mann, Michael, *The Source of Social Power*, vol. 1: *A History of Power from the Beginning to AD 1760*, Cambridge: Cambridge University Press, 1986.

Mao Zedong, "The Role of the Chinese Communist Party in the National War," in Mao Zedong, *Selected Works of Mao Zedong*, vol. 2, Beijing: Foreign Languages Press, 1975, pp. 209–10.

Mao Zedong, "The Chinese Revolution and the Chinese Communist Party," in Mao Zedong, *Selected Works of Mao Zedong*, vol. 2, Beijing: Foreign Languages Press, 1967, pp. 311–14.

Marshall, T. H., *Class, Citizenship and Social Development*, New York: Doubleday, 1964.

Marx, Karl, and F. Engels, "Manifesto of the Communist Party," in Robert C. Tucker (ed.), *The Marx–Engels Reader*, New York: W. W. Norton & Company, Inc., 1978, pp. 469–500.

McAdam, Doug, John D. McCarthy, Mayer N. Zald (eds.), *Comparative Perspectives on Social Movements: Political Opportunities, Mobilizing Structures, and Cultural Framings*, New York: Cambridge University Press, 1996.

McAdam, Doug, *Political Process and the Development of Black Insurgence, 1930–1970*, Chicago: University of Chicago Press, 1982.

Meier, Gerald M., "Policy Lessons and Policy Formation," in Gerald M. Meier (ed.), *Politics and Policy Making in Developing Countries: Perspectives on the New Political Economy*, San Francisco, CA: ICS Press, 1991, pp. 3–12.

Meyer, John W., John Boli, George M. Thomas, and Franciso O. Ramirez, "World Society and the Nation-State," in Frank J. Lechner and John Boli (eds.), *The Globalization Reader*, Oxford: Blackwell Publishers, 2000, pp. 84–92.

Migdal, Joel S., Atul Kohli and Vivinne Shue (eds.), *State Power and Social Forces: Domination and Transformation in the Third World*, New York: Cambridge University Press, 1994.

Migdal, Joel S., *Strong Societies and Weak States: State-Society Relations and State Capabilities in the Third World*, Princeton, NJ: Princeton University Press, 1988.

Ming Pao, Hong Kong, December 15, 1998.

Ming Pao, Hong Kong, January 8, 1998.

Mirror Post Editorial Department (ed.), *Jiang Zemin yunchou weimo* (Jiang Zemin Devises Strategies within a Command Tent), Hong Kong: The Mirror Post Cultural Enterprises Co., Ltd, 1999.

Mo, Y. J., "The Current Status and Future Prospects of China's Mobile Telecommunication," paper presented at the Conference on China's WTO Accession and Its Impact on Northeast Asia, Seoul, Korea, June 28–29, 2000.

Moore, Barrington, Jr., *Social Origins of Dictatorship and Democracy: Lord and Peasant in the Making of the Modern World*, Boston, MA.: Beacon Press, 1966.

Moore, G. Thomas, *China in the World Market: Chinese Industry and International Sources of Reform in the Post-Mao Era*, Cambridge: Cambridge University Press, 2002.

Myers, Charles A., *Industrialism and Industrial Man*, Cambridge, MA.: Harvard University Press, 1960.

Nathan, Andrew J., *China's Transition*, New York: Columbia University Press, 1997.

Nathan, Andrew J., *China's Crisis: Dilemmas of Reform and Prospects for Democracy*, New York: Columbia University Press, 1990.

Nathan, Andrew, *Chinese Democracy*, New York: Knopf, 1985.

Naughton, Barry, *Growing Out of the Plan: Chinese Economic Reform 1978–1993*, New York: Cambridge University Press, 1996.

The OECD Public Management Service, *Globalization: What Challenges and Opportunities for Government?* Paris: OECD, 1996.

The Office of the Documentary Research of the Central Committee of the CCP (ed.), *Xinshiqi dang de jianshe wenjian xuanbian* (Selected Documents of Party Building in the New Era), Beijing: Renmin chubanshe, 1991.

Ohmae, Kenichi, *The Borderless World*, London: Collins, 1990.

Ohmae, Kenichi, *The End of the Nation State*, New York: HarperCollins, 1995.

Oi, Jean, *Rural China Takes Off*, Berkeley, CA: University of California Press, 1999.

Olson, Mancur, *Power and Prosperity: Outgrowing Communist and Capitalist Dictatorship*, New York: Basic Books, 2000.

Olson, Mancur, and Satu Kahkonen (eds.), *A Not-So-Dismal Science: A Broader View of Economics and Societies*, New York: Oxford University Press, 2000.

Olson, Mancur, *The Rise and Decline of Nations*, New Haven: Yale University Press, 1982.

Pang Zhongying, "Guoji jinrong tixi yunniang gaige" (International Financial System Considers Reform," *People's Daily*, April 9, 1998.

Park, Albert, Scott Rozelle, Christine Wong, and Changqing Ren, "Distributional Consequences of Reforming Local Public Finance in China," *The China Quarterly*, 147 (1996), pp. 751–79.

Peking Review, no. 52, December 29, 1978.

People's Daily, November 9, 2002.

People's Daily, February 1, 2001.

People's Daily, January 11, 2001.

People's Daily, September 15, 2000.

People's Daily, August 9, 2000.

People's Daily, April 10, 1989.

People's Daily (overseas edition), March 10, 1994.

Perkins, F. C., "Productivity Performance and Priorities for the Reform of China's State-Owned Enterprises," *The Journal of Developmental Studies*, 32: 3 (1996), pp. 414–44.

Perry, Elizabeth, "Labor's Battle for Political Space: the Role of Worker Associations in Contemporary China," in Deborah S. Davis, Richard Kraus, Barry Naughton, and Elizabeth J. Perry (eds.), *Urban Spaces in Contemporary China: the Potential for Autonomy and Community in Post-Mao China*, Washington, DC and New York, Woodrow Wilson Center Press and Cambridge University Press, 1995, pp. 302–25.

Perry, Elizabeth, "Shanghai's Strike Wave of 1957," *The China Quarterly*, 137 (March 1994), pp. 1–27.

Perry, Elizabeth J., and Mark Selden (eds.), *Chinese Society: Change, Conflict and Resistance*, New York: Routledge, 2000.

Perry, Elizabeth, and Li Xun, *Proletarian Power: Shanghai in the Cultural Revolution*, Boulder: Westview, 1997.

Petracca, Mark P., and Mong Xiong, "The Concept of Chinese Neo-Authoritarianism: An Exploration and Democratic Critique," *Asian Survey* xxx: 11 (November 1990), 1099–117.

Poggi, G., *The Development of the Modern State*, Stanford, CA: Stanford University Press, 1978.

Pomfret, John, "Why 'Beijing Spring' Cooled: Dissidents Overstepped," *International Herald Tribune*, January 4, 1999, pp. 1 and 7.

Pomfret, John, "Jiang Orders Military to Go Out of Business: in effort to end rampant smuggling, army must close commercial empire," *International Herald Tribune*, July 23, 1998.

Potter, David, David Goldblatt, Margaret Kiloh, and Paul Lewis (eds.), *Democratization*, Cambridge: Polity Press, 1997.

Potter, Pitman B., "The Administrative Litigation Law of the PRC: Judicial Review and Bureaucratic Reform," in Potter (ed.), *Domestic Law Reforms in Post-Mao China*, Armonk, NY: M. E. Sharpe, 1994, pp. 270–304.

Putman, Robert D., *Making Democracy Work: Civic Traditions in Modern Italy*, Princeton, NJ: Princeton University Press, 1993.

Qian, Yingyi and Barry R. Weigast, "Federalism as a Commitment to Market Incentives," *Journal of Economic Perspective*, 11 (1997), pp. 83–92.

Qian, Yingyi and Barry R. Weigast, "China's Transition to Market: Market-Preserving Federalism, Chinese Style," *Journal of Policy Reform*, 1 (1996), pp. 149–85.

Qin Hui, "Ziyou zhuyi yu minzu zhuyi de jiehedian zai nali" (Where Is the Meeting Point of Liberalism and Nationalism), *Dong Fang* (The Orient), 3 (1996), p. 45.

Qin Shaoxiang and Jia Ting, *Shehui xin qunti tanmi: Zhongguo siying qiyezhu jieceng* (A Study of A New Social Group: China's Private Enterprise Class), Beijing: Zhongguo fazhan chubanshe, 1993.

Qiu Zeqi and Zheng Yongnian, "Xia-Gang and Its Sociological Implications of Reducing Labor Redundancy in China's SOEs," in Wang Gungwu and John Wong (eds.), *China's Political Economy*, London and Singapore: World Scientific and Singapore University Press, 1998, pp. 211–26.

The Research Group of the Department of Organization, the CCP Central Committee (ed.), *2000–2001 Zhongguo diaocha baogao: xin xingshi xia renmin neibu maodun yanjiu* (China Investigation Report, 2000–2001: Studies of Contradictions Within the People under New Conditions), Beijing: Zhongyang bianyi chubanshe, 2001.

The Research Team of the Suzhou University, "Dangqian nongcun luan shoufei xianxiang chengyin fenxi ji duice" (An Analysis of the Origins of Illegal Levies in Rural Areas and Policy Choices), *Zhongguo nongcun jingji* (Agricultural Economy in China), 3 (1997).

Rheingold, Howard, *The Virtual Community: Homesteading on the Electronic Frontier*, New York: Harper & Row, 1994.

Rodrik, Dani, *Has Globalization Gone Too Far?* Washington, DC: Institute for International Economics, 1997.

Rosenau, James N., *Turbulence in World Politic: A Theory of Change and Continuity*, Princeton, NJ: Princeton University Press, 1990.

Rosow, Stephen, "Commerce, Power and Justice: Montesquieu on International Politics," *Review of Politics*, 46: 3 (1984), pp. 346–67.

Ru Xin, Lu Xueyi and Shan Tianlun (eds.), *Shehui lanpishu: Zhongguo shehui xingshi fenxi yu yuce* (Social Bluebook: Analysis and Forecast of Social Situation in China), Beijing: Shehui kexue wenxian chubanshe, 1993, 1994, 1995, 1996, 1997, 1998, 1999, 2000, 2001.

Rueschemeyer, Dietrich, Evelyne H. Stephens, and John D. Stephens, *Capitalist Development and Democracy*, Chicago: Chicago University Press, 1992.

Ruigrok, W., and R. van Tulder, The Logic of International Restructuring, London: Routledge, 1995.

Schiffrin, Harold Z., *Sun Yat-sen and the Origins of the Chinese Revolution*, Berkeley, CA: University of California Press, 1968.

Schuler, D., *New Community Networks: Wired for a Change*, New York: ACM Press, 1996.

Schurmann, Franz, *Ideology and Organization in Communist China*, Berkeley, CA: University of California Press, 1968.

Schwartz, Benjamin I., "Themes in Intellectual History: May Fourth and After," in John K. Fairbank (ed.), *The Cambridge History of China*, vol. 12. Cambridge: Cambridge University Press, 1983, pp. 406–50.

Scott, James, *Weapons of the Weak: Everyday Forms of Peasant Resistance*, New Haven: Yale University Press, 1985.

Shambaugh, David (ed.), *The Modern Chinese State*, New York: Cambridge University Press, 2000.

Shen Ruji, *Zhongguo bu dang "Bu Xiansheng"* (China Does Not Want to Be "Mr. No"), Beijing: Jinri Zhongguo chubanshe, 1998.

Shi Zhong, "Bu ying ba bijiao youshi de luoji tuixiang jiduan" (The Logic of Comparative Advantages Should not Be Pushed to Extremes), *Zhanlue yu guanli* (Strategy and Management), 3 (1995), pp. 11–15.

Shieh, Milton J. T., *The Kuomintang: Selected Historical Documents, 1894–1969*, New York: St. John's University Press, 1970.

Shinn, James (ed.), *Weaving the Net: Conditional Engagement with China*, New York: Council On Foreign Relations Press, 1996.

Shirk, Susan, *The Political Logic of Economic Reform in China*, Berkeley, CA: University of California Press, 1993.

Shue, Vivienne, *The Reach of the State: Sketches of the Chinese Body Politic*, Stanford, CA: Stanford University Press, 1988.

Shue, Vivienne, "State Power and Social Organization in China," in Joel S. Migdal, Atul Kohli, and Vivienne Shue (eds.), *State Power and Social Forces: Domination and Transformation in the Third World*, Cambridge: Cambridge University Press, 1994, pp. 65–88.

Skinner, Q., *The Foundations of Modern Political Thought*, vol. 2, Cambridge: Cambridge University Press, 1978.

Smith, Adam, *Wealth of Nations*, Oxford University Press, 1976.

Smith, Anthony D., *Nations and Nationalism in a Global Era*, Cambridge: Polity Press, 1995.

Smith, Anthony D., *Theories of Nationalism*, London: Duckworth, 1971.

South China Morning Post, July 12, 2000.

South China Morning Post, April 29, 1999.

South China Morning Post, October 9, 1998.

South China Morning Post, March 12, 1998.

South China Morning Post, August 3, 1998.

South China Morning Post, August 30, 1997.

The State Council, *Hulianwang xinxi fuwu guanli banfa* (Methods for Management of Internet Information), The Xinhua News Agency, 1 October 2000.

The State Council, *Zhongyang zhengfu zuzhi jigou* (The Organizational Structure of the Central Government), Beijing: Zhongguo fazhan chubanshe, 1995.

The State Statistical Bureau, *Zhongguo jiage ji chengzhen jumin jiating shouzhi diaocha* (Annual Prices and Family Incomes and Expenditures in Chinese Cities, 1998), Beijing: Zhongguo tongji chubanshe, 1998.

The State Statistical Bureau, *Zhongguo jinrong nianjian* (The Finance Yearbook of China), Beijing: Zhongguo tongji chubanshe, 1997.

The State Statistical Bureau, *Zhongguo laodong nianjian* (China Labor Statistical Yearbook, 1996), Beijing: Zhongguo nianjian chubanshe, 1996.

The State Tax Bureau, *Zhongguo shuizhi gaige shinian (1978–1988)* (China's Ten Years of Taxation Reform), Dalian: Dongbei caijing daxue chubanshe, 1988.

The State Statistical Bureau, *Zhongguo siying jingji nianjian* (The Yearbook of Private Businesses in China, various issues), Beijing: Zhongguo tongji chubanshe, various years.

The State Statistical Bureau, *Zhongguo tongji nianjian* (China Statistical Yearbook, various issues), Beijing: Zhongguo tongji chubanshe, various years.

The State Statistical Bureau, *Zhongguo tongji zhaiyao* (The Statistical Survey of China 1996), Beijing: Zhongguo tongji chubanshe, 1997.

The Straits Times, Singapore, July 31, 1999.

Strange, Susan, *The Retreat of the State: The Diffusion of Power in the World Economy*, Cambridge: Cambridge University Press, 1996.

Strange, Susan "The Defective State," *Daedalus*, special issue "What Future for the State?" 124: 2 (Spring 1995), pp. 55–73.

The Study Group on the Proportion of Financial Revenue in the National Income, "Jizhong caili rugai wenti de lilun pouxi" (Some Theoretical Analysis on Resource Concentration), *Caimao jingji* (Finance and Trade Economics), 4 (April 1991), pp. 23–32.

Su Shangxiao and Han Wenwei, *Zhonghua renmin gongheguo zhongyang zhengfu jigou* (Central Government Organizations of the People's Republic of China), Beijing: Jingji kexue chubanshe, 1993.

Su Xiaokang, Yuan Zhiming and Wang Luxiang, *Heshang* (River Elegy), Beijing: xiandai chubanshe, 1988.

Suleiman, Erza, *Politics, Power, and Bureaucracy in France: The Administrative Elite*, Princeton, NJ: Princeton University Press, 1974.

Sun Yat-sen, *San min zhu yi* (Three People's Principles), Taipei: China Publishing Co., 1974.

Sun Yat-sen, *Sun Zhongshan quanji* (Collected Works of Sun Zhongshan), vols. 8 and 9, Beijing: Zhonghua shuju, 1986.

Sun, Yan, *The Chinese Reassessment of Socialism, 1976–1992*, Princeton, NJ: Princeton University Press, 1995.

Swaine, Michael D., *China: Domestic Change and Foreign Policy*, Santa Monica, CA: Rand, 1995.

Tanner, Murray Scot, *The Politics of Lawmaking in Post-Mao China: Institutions, Processes, and Democratic Prospects*, New York: Oxford University Press, 1998.

Tarrow, Sidney, "States and Opportunities: The Political Structuring of Social Movement," in Doug McAdam, John D. McCarthy, Mayer N. Zald (eds.), *Comparative Perspectives on Social Movements: Political Opportunities, Mobilizing Structures, and Cultural Framings*, New York: Cambridge University Press, 1996.

Tarrow, Sidney, *Power in Movement: Social Movements, Collective Action and Politics*, New York: Cambridge University Press, 1994.

Teng, Ssu-yu and John King Fairbank, *China's Response to the West: A Documentary Survey, 1839–1923*, Cambridge, MA: Harvard University Press, 1979.

Tian, Xiaowen, "The Rise of Non-State Owned Enterprises in China," *Communist Economies and Economic Transformation*, 9: 2 (1997), pp. 219–31.

Tilly, Charles, *Coercion, Capital, and European States, A. D. 990–1990*, Cambridge, MA: Basil Blackwell, 1990.

Tilly, Charles, "Social Movements and National Politics," in Charles Bright and Susan Harding (eds.), *Statemaking and Social Movements*, Ann Arbor: University of Michigan Press, 1984, pp. 297–317.

Tilly, Charles, *From Mobilization to Revolution*, Reading, MA: Addison-Wesley Publishing Co., 1978.

Tilly, Charles (ed.), *The Formation of National States in Western Europe*, Princeton, NJ: Princeton University Press, 1975.

Tsagarousianou, R., D. Tambini and C. Bryan (eds.), *Cyberdemocracy: Technology, Cities, and Civic Networks*, London: Routledge, 1998.

Tsang Shu-ki and Cheng Yuk-shing, "China's Tax Reforms of 1994: Breakthrough or Compromise," *Asian Survey*, 34: 9 (September 1994), pp. 769–88.

Tsou, Tang, *The Cultural Revolution and Post-Mao Reforms: A Historical Perspective*, Chicago: University of Chicago Press, 1986.

Tyau, Min-Shien (ed.), *Two Years of Nationalist China*, Shanghai: Kelly and Walsh, 1930.

Unger, Jonathan (ed.), *Chinese Nationalism*, Armonk, NY: M. E. Sharpe, 1996.

Vincent, Andrew, *Theories of the State*, Oxford: Basil Blackwell, 1987.

Vogel, Ezra F. (ed.), *Living with China: U. S.–China Relations in the Twenty-First Century*, New York: W. W. Norton & Company, 1997.

Wade, Robert, "Globalization and Its Limits: Reports of the Death of the National Economy Are Greatly Exaggerated," in Suzanne Berger and Ronald Dore (eds.), *National Diversity and Global Capitalism*, Ithaca, NY: Cornell University Press, 1996, pp. 60–88.

Wade, Robert, *Governing the Market: Economic Theory and the Role of Government in East Asian Industrialization*, Princeton, NJ: Princeton University Press, 1990.

Walder, Andrew (ed.), *Zouping in Transition: The Process of Reform in Rural North China*, Cambridge, MA: Harvard University Press, 1998.

Walder, Andrew, "Workers, Managers and the State: The Reform Era and the Political Crisis of 1989," *The China Quarterly*, 127 (September 1991), pp. 467–92.

Walder, Andrew, *Communist Neo-Traditionalism*, Berkeley, CA: University of California Press, 1986.

Wallerstein, Immanuel, *The Capitalist World-Economy*, Cambridge: Cambridge University Press, 1979.

Wan Yan Shu, "Some Elements that Influence Our National Security," *Yazhou Zhoukan* (Asiaweek), Hong Kong, January 14, 1996.

Wang Chunguang, "1997–1998 nian: Zhongguo shehui wending zhuangkuang de diaocha" (A Survey on Social Stability in 1997–1998), in Ru Xin, Lu Xueyi and Shan Tianlun (eds.), *Shehui lanpishu 1998* (Social Bluebook), Beijing: Shehui kexue wenxian chubanshe, 1998, pp. 121–32.

Wang Dingding, "Zhongguo guoyou zichan guanli tizhi gaige de kunjing" (The Dilemma of Reforming the Management of China's State-Owned Assets), *Ershiyi shiji* (The Twenty-First Century), Hong Kong, 6 (1995), pp. 15–21.

Wang, Gungwu, *Joining the Modern World: Inside and Outside China*, Singapore and London: Singapore University Press and World Scientific, 2000.

Wang, Gungwu, *Nationalism and Confucianism*, Singapore: Unipress, 1996.

Wang, Gungwu, *The Revival of Chinese Nationalism*, Leiden, International Institute for Asian Studies, 1996.

Wang, Gungwu, *The Chinese Way: China's Position in International Relations*, Oslo, Scandinavian University Press, 1995.

Wang, Gungwu, *The Chineseness of China: Selected Essays*, Hong Kong: Oxford University Press, 1991.

Wang, Gungwu and Zheng Yongnian (eds.), *Reform, Legitimacy and Dilemmas: China's Politics and Society*, Singapore and London: Singapore University Press and World Scientific, 2000.

Wang, Hongying, "The Asian Financial Crisis as Impetus for Financial Reforms in China," *EAI Working Paper* No. 27, East Asian Institute, National University of Singapore, June 18, 1999.

Wang Huning, "Zhongguo gaige nanti de fei jingji sikao" (Non-Economic Causes of Difficulties in China's Reform), in *Shijie jingji daobao* (World Economic Herald), August 29, 1988.

Wang Shaofei, "Caizheng zhuangkuang guanxi shehuizhuyi jingji gaige qiantu" (The Vital Importance of Fiscal Status to the Fate of Socialist Economic Reform), *Caimao jingji* (Finance and Trade Economics), 4 (1990), pp. 23–8.

Wang, Shaoguang, "Kaifang xing, fenpei xing chongtu he shehui baozhang: Zhongguo jiaru WTO de shehui he zhengzhi yiyi" (Openness, Distributive Conflict and Social Assurance: The Social and Political Implications of China's WTO Membership), Working paper, The Department of Government and Public Administration, The Chinese University of Hong Kong, 2002.

Wang, Shaoguang, "The Social and Political Implications of China's WTO Membership," *Journal of Contemporary China*, 9: 25 (2000), pp. 373–405.

Wang Shaoguang, "Quanli de daijia yu gaige de lujing yilai" (The Cost of Liberty and the Path-Dependence of the Reform), Zhanlue yu guanli (Strategy and Management), 5 (2000), pp. 112–15.

Wang, Shaoguang and Hu Angang, *The Political Economy of Uneven Development: The Case of China*, Armonk, NY: M.E Sharpe, 1999.

Wang, Shaoguang, "The Rise of the Regions: Fiscal Reform and the Decline of Central State Capacity in China," in Andrew Walder (ed.), *The Waning of the Communist State*, Berkeley, CA: University of California Press, 1995, pp. 87–113.

Wang Shaoguang and Hu Angang, *Zhongguo guojia nengli baogao* (A Study of China State Capacity), Shengyang: Liaoning renmin chubanshe, 1993.

Wang Shaoguang, *Jianli yi ge qiang you li de minzhu guojia* (Building a Strong Democratic State: On Regime Type and State Capacity), Papers of the Center for Modern China, 4 (February 1991).

Wang Ying, "Xin jiti zhuyi yu Zhongguo tese de shichang jingji" (New Collectivism and A Market Economy with Chinese Charteristics), *Ershiyi shiji* (Twenty-First Century), 25 (1994), pp. 11–14.

Wang Ying, *Shehui zhongjian ceng: gaige yu Zhongguo de shetuan zuzhi* (Intermediate Social Strata: the Reform and Social Groups in China), Beijing: Zhongguo fazhan chubanshe, 1993.

Weber, Max, *The Theory of Social and Economic Organization*, edited by Talcott Parsons, New York: Free Press, 1964.

Wei Yi, "Zhongguo xin dezhi lunxi: gaige qian Zhongguo daode hua zhengzhi de lishi fenxi" (An Analysis of New Theory of Rule by Virtue in China: A Historical Reflection of Chinese Moralized Politics in Pre-Reform China), *Zhanlue yu guanli* (Strategy and Management), 2 (2001), pp. 25–38.

Weiss, Linda, *The Myth of the Powerless State: Governing the Economy in a Global Era*, Cambridge: Polity, 1998.

Weizman, Martin L. and Chenggang Xu, *Chinese Township Village Enterprises as Vaguely Defined Cooperatives*, London: Development Economics Research program, 1992.

White, Gordon, Jude Howell, and Shang Xiaoyuan, *In Search of Civil Society: Market Reform and Social Change in Contemporary China*, Oxford: Oxford University Press, 1996.

Whitney, Joseph B. R., *China: Area, Administration, and Nation Building*, Chicago, Department of Geography, University of Chicago, 1970.

Williamson, John (ed.), *Latin American Adjustment: How Much Has Happened?* Washington, DC: Institute for International Economics, 1990.

Wong, John and Yongnian Zheng (eds.), *The Nanxun Legacy and China's Development*, Singapore and London: Singapore University Press and World Scientific, 2001.

Wong, John and Sarah Chan, "China's Rapidly Changing Export Structure," *EAI Background Brief* No. 85, East Asian Institute, National University of Singapore, April 9, 2001.

Wong, John and Liu Zhiqiang, "China's Progress in Banking Reform and Financial Liberalization," *EAI Working Paper* No. 52, East Asian Institute, National University of Singapore, August 23, 2000.

Wong, John and William T. Liu, *The Mystery of China's Falun Gong: Its Rise and Its Sociological Implications*, Singapore and London: Singapore University Press and World Scientific, 1999.

Wong, John, "*Xiao-kang*: Deng Xiaoping's Socio-Economic Development Target for China," in Wang Gungwu and John Wong (eds.), *China's Political Economy*, Singapore and London: Singapore University Press and World Scientific, 1998, pp. 211–26.

Wong, John, Rong Ma and Mu Yang (eds), *China's Rural Entrepreneurs: Ten Case Studies*, Singapore, Times Academic Press, 1995.

Wong, John, "The *Xia Hai* Phenomenon in China," *Ritsumeikan Journal of International Relations and Area Studies*, 6 (March 1994), pp. 1–10.

Wong, Christine P. W. (ed.), *Financing Local Government in the People's Republic of China*, Hong Kong: Oxford University Press, 1997.

The World Bank, *China 2020: Sharing Rising Incomes*, Washington, DC: The World Bank, 1997.

The World Bank, *China: Reform of State-Owned Enterprises*, Washington, DC: The World Bank, 1996.

The World Bank, *China: Revenue Mobilization and Tax Policy*, Washington, DC: World Bank, 1990.

Wriston, Water B., *The Twilight of Sovereignty*, New York: Charles Scribners Sons, 1992.

Wu Guoguang, "The Return of Ideology? Struggling to Organize Politics During Socio-Economic Transitions," in John Wong and Yongnian Zheng (eds.), *The Nanxun Legacy and China's Post-Deng Development* (Singapore and London: Singapore University Press & World Scientific, 2001), pp. 221–46.

Wu Guoguang, *Zhao Ziyang yu zhengzhi gaige* (Political Reform under Zhao Ziyang), Hong Kong: The Institute of Pacific Century, 1997.

Wu Jie (ed.), *Zhongguo zhengfu yu jiegou gaige* (Chinese Government and Institutional Reforms), Beijing: Guojia xingzheng xueyuan chubanshe, 1998.

Wu Yuetao and Zhang Haitao, *Waizi nengfou tunbing Zhongguo – Zhongguo minzu chanye xiang he chu qu* (Can Foreign Capital Swallow up China: Whither China's National Industries), Beijing: Qiye guanli chubanshe, 1997.

Xiao Gongqin, "Cong 'Zhongguo minzhu dang' zudang shijian kan hou Deng shidai Zhongguo de zhengzhi zouxiang" (The 'China Democratic Party' Event and the Political Trends in Post-Deng China), *EAI Working Paper* (Chinese Series), No 37, East Asian Institute, National University of Singapore, January 21, 2002.

Xin Xiangyang, "Zhongguo zhengfu jigou gaige: sannian jincheng yu weilai zoushi" (The Reform of Government Organizations in China: Progress in the Past Three Years and Future Trends), in Ru Xin, Lu Xueyi and Shan Tianlun (eds.), *Shehui lanpishu 2001* (Social Bluebook), Beijing: Shehui kexue wenxian chubanshe, 2001, pp. 107–20.

The Xinhua New Agency, December 19, 2002.

The Xinhua News Agency, April 11, 1995.

The Xinhua News Agency, November 18, 2002.

The Xinhua News Agency, March 6, 2000.

The Xinhua News Agency, "Jiang Zemin tongzhi zai quanguo dangxiao gongzuo huiyi shang de jianghua" (June 9, 2000) (Comrade Jiang Zemin's Talk in National Party Schools Working Conference), *People's Daily*, July 17, 2000.

Xu Jilin, "Qimeng de mingyun: Ershi nianlai de Zhongguo sixiangjie"(The Fate of the Enlightenment: China's Intellectual Realm in the Past Twenty Years), *Ershiyi shiji* (The Twenty-First Century), Hong Kong, 50 (1998), pp. 4–13.

Xu Yi and Xiang Jinquan, *Diliuge wunian jihua shiqi de guojia caizheng (1981–1985)* (State Finance During the Sixth Five Year Plan), Beijing: Zhongguo caizheng jingji chubanshe, 1987.

Yang Aihua and Lu Sishan, *Zapo 'santie' hou de Zhongguo ren* (The Chinese After the Smashing of the 'Three Irons'), Beijing: Beijing ligong daxue chubanshe, 1992.

Yang Yiyong, "2000nian zhongguo jiuye xinshi jiqi zhengce xuanze," (Employment in 2000 and Policy Options), in Liu Guoguang (ed.), *Jinji lanpishu 2000* (Economic Bluebook 2000), Beijing: Shehui wenxian chubanshe, 2000.

Yin Baoyun, "Jiquan guanliaozhi de xiandaihua daolu: Hanguo fazhan jingyan tansuo" (The Centralist-Bureaucratic Model of Modernization: An Exploration of the Experiences of Development in South Korea), *Zhanlue yu guanli* (Strategy and Management), 2 (1994), pp. 35–42.

Yu Xiaoping, "Zai woguo shixing fenshuizhi de jiben gouxiang" (Basic Ideas On Implementing the Revenue-Division System in China), *Caimao jingji* (Finance and Trade Economics), 2 (1990), pp. 60–2.

Zhang Dejiang, "Yao mingque siying qiyezhu buneng rudang" (To Make Clear that Private Entrepreneurs Cannot Join the Party), *Zhenli de zhuiqiu* (The Seeking of Truth), 5 (2001).

Zhang Houyi and Ming Zhili (eds.), *Zhongguo siying qiye fazhan baogao 1978–1998* (A Report on the Development of Private Enterprises in China, 1978–1998), Beijing: Shehui kexue wenxuan chubanshe, 1999.

Zhang Qian and Ji Haiqing, "Fade jianzhi, jianshe you Zhongguo tese shehuizhuyi fazhi guojia" (Rule of Law cum Rule by Virtue: Building a Socialist State of Rule of Law with Chinese Characteristics), *Shanghai shehui kexueyuan jikan* (Quarterly Journal of the Shanghai Academy of Social Sciences), no. 2 (2001), pp. 189–92.

Zhang Weiying, *Qiye de qiyejia: qiyue lilun* (Entrepreneurs in Enterprises: Contract Theory), Shanghai: Sanlian shudian, 1995.

Zhang Yuanhong, "Lun Zhongguo nongye shuizhi gaige" (Reforming China's Agricultural Tax System), *Zhongguo nongcun jingji* (Agricultural Economy in China), 12 (1997), pp. 4–11.

Zhang Zhenlong (ed.), *Jundui shengchan jingying guanli* (Management of Military Production), Beijing, Jiefangjun chubanshe, 1989.

Zhao, Suisheng, "Chinese Nationalism and Its International Orientations," *Political Science Quarterly*, 115 (Spring 2000), pp. 1–33.

Zhao, Suisheng, "Chinese Intellectuals' Quest for National Greatness and Nationalistic Writing in the 1990s," *The China Quarterly*, 152 (December 1997), pp. 725–45.

Zhao Yang and Zhou Feizhou, "Nongmin fudan he caishui tizhi" (Peasants' Burdens and Fiscal System), *Hong Kong Journal of Social Sciences*, 17 (Autumn 2000), pp. 67–85.

Zheng, Shiping, *Party vs. State in Post-1949 China: The Institutional Dilemma*, Cambridge: Cambridge University Press, 1997.

Zheng, Yongnian, "Zhongguo xinyibo minzu zhuyi: genyuan, guocheng he qianjing" (A New Wave of Chinese Nationalism: Origins, Processes, and Prospects), in Lin Chia-lung and Zheng Yongnian (eds.), *Minzu zhuyi yu liang'an guanxi* (Nationalism and Cross-Strait Relations), Taipei: Xinziran zhuyi gufen chuban youxian gongsi, 2001), pp. 21–40.

Zheng, Yongnian, *Discovering Chinese Nationalism in China*, Cambridge: Cambridge University Press, 1999.

Zheng, Yongnian, "From Rule by Law to Rule of Law: A Realistic View of China's Legal Development," *China Perspective*, 25 (1999), pp. 31–43.

Zheng, Yongnian, "Political Incrementalism: Political Lessons from China's 20 Years of Reform," *Third World Quarterly*, 20: 6 (1999), pp. 1157–77.

Zheng, Yongnian, "Development and Democracy: Are They Compatible in China?" *Political Science Quarterly*, 109: 2 (Summer 1994), pp. 235–59.

Zheng, Yongnian and Zou Keyuan, *Toward More Effective Governance: China's Politics in 1998*, Singapore and London: Singapore University Press and World Scientific, 1999.

Zhonghua gongshang shibao (China Industrial and Commercial Daily) (Beijing), April 29, 1996.

Zhu Guanglei, *Dangdai Zhongguo shehui ge jieceng fenxi* (An Analysis of Social Strata in Contemporary China), Tianjin: Tianjin renmin chubanshe, 1998.

Zhu Min, "Dongya jinrong dongdang yinfa de sikao" (Thoughts Provoked by the East Asian Financial Upheabal), *People's Daily*, January 26, 1998.

Zou, K., and Y. Zheng, "China's Third Constitutional Amendment: A Leap Forward Towards Rule of Law in China," in A. J. de Roo and R. W. Jagtenberg (eds.), *Yearbook: Law & Legal Practice in East Asia 1999*, 4 (The Hague: Kluwer Law International, 2000), pp. 29–42.

Zweig, David, *Internationalizing China: Domestic Interests and Global Linkages*, Ithaca, NY: Cornell University Press, 2002.

Index

CAMBRIDGE ASIA-PACIFIC STUDIES

Other titles in the series: